The American
Job
Machine

The American Job Machine

Richard B. McKenzie

A CATO INSTITUTE BOOK
UNIVERSE BOOKS, NEW YORK

To Professor Dwight R. Lee

Published in the United States of America in 1988
by Universe Books
381 Park Avenue South, New York, NY 10016

© 1988 by Cato Institute

88 89 90 91 92 / 10 9 8 7 6 5 4 3 2 1

Printed in the United States of America

Library of Congress Cataloging-in-Publication Data

McKenzie, Richard B.
    The American job machine. / Richard B. McKenzie.
        p.   cm.
    Includes index.
    ISBN 0-87663-682-2
    1. Labor policy—United States.   2. Manpower policy—United
States.   I. Title.
HD8072.5M395 1988
331.11'0973—dc19   87-37605

BOOK DESIGN BY EILEEN SCHLESINGER

Contents

65186

Preface

The American Job Machine is an intellectual black box that causes most of us to marvel at its capacity to create "jobs." Not fully understanding what is in the "machine," most of us take for granted that the purpose of an economy is to create jobs. But is job creation, apart from any corresponding increase in output, the proper measure of economic success? If so, then forget all the complicated platforms to make America competitive, for there is a one-line statute that will create 60 million jobs overnight. Outlaw farm machinery.

The very absurdity of this suggests a radical notion: Contrary to what may be thought by considering the title of this book, we would better measure economic success by the *elimination* of jobs than by their creation. That sounds sacrilegious, but think a minute. Economic progress has two legs. One is eliminating jobs with new technologies, the other finding new tasks for workers.

In the past century we have taken farmers off the land and made them teachers, nurses, and store clerks, thereby raising our standard of living. Now, which is more difficult, the job elimination or the job creation? There have been painful periods in our history when job creation was the problem, but these were the exceptions. The real hurdle is the first one, finding new technologies and amassing the capital to apply them. What makes China a poorer country than the United States? Is it a shortage of tasks that need doing? Or is it a shortage of farm machinery?

But the whole process of replacing jobs with others is deeply unsettling to our country's leaders. Isn't that what is behind the lamentation that we are becoming a "service economy" or, worse, a "productionless society"— a nation of "short-order cooks and . . . messenger boys"? Isn't that what undergirds the plethora of protectionist proposals and "job bills" perennially introduced in Congress?

Unfortunately, the nation has begun to direct policy on the basis of "jobs." So powerful is the emotional appeal of "jobs" (and its undergirding political philosophy discussed under the rubric of "jobilism" in Chapter 11) that proponents of free trade cannot tell the truth about what international trade does to jobs. The free traders will say, in defending their stance, that foreign trade creates jobs. It does, in the sense that a thriving world economy provides many expanding employment opportunities. But in the narrow context of a specific swap of goods—these jet engines for those sweaters—free trade does the reverse. It eliminates jobs. There would be no point for it otherwise. If we cannot replace 1,000 knitters with 500 aerospace workers, then why go to the trouble of shipping goods across the ocean?

The typical reader might have picked up this book with the intent of gaining some understanding of the job-creation process in America. The book will deal with that topic, but in discussing the full complexity of the American job machine, I will try to be even-handed. I would be less than candid if I did not admit at the start that the book is also concerned with the unrecognized advantages of job destruction. If you care to understand why, read on! The future of the economy rests on the country's willingness to endure the pain of job destructions, as well as find ways to facilitate job creation. Both job creation and destruction go hand-in-hand. That is a central message of the book.

This book was, partially, at least, born out of frustration. In 1985, I was appointed to Secretary of Labor William Brock's Task Force on Economic Adjustment and Worker Dislocation. The task force was organized to head-off a legislative drive in Congress to pass restrictions on plant closings. Because I had, prior to my appointment, written extensively *against* plant-closing bills, I assumed that the "task" of the task force would be to find market solutions to current labor problems. Although I am not a political partisan, I thought surely I could agree with the general direction of any program that would emerge from the expected year-long study, especially since the task force was organized by the "conservative" Reagan administration (which talks a great deal about the value of market solutions to social problems).

I was shocked to find that the intent of many members was to find additional government solutions to labor-market problems. I was also greatly disturbed with how widely-accepted economic myths were treated as fact in task-force discussions and with how uncritical people who testified before the task force were of current government policies. I was equally dumbfounded with how readily conventional economic arguments concerning the role of contracts, property rights, and prices and wages were readily ignored and, if raised, just as readily dismissed.

In the end, after 14 months of attending meetings practically once every month, I was no longer surprised that the task force recommended additional government agencies, programs, and expenditures to solve both the dislocated-worker and plant-closing problems and that Senator Howard Metzenbaum (D–Ohio), a political antagonist of the Reagan administration, could recommend the enactment of the entire task-force agenda—and then some. I was greatly disappointed that I not only was unable to sign the report but that I felt compelled to be openly critical of the task force's proposed reforms and the process by which the task-force report was developed. I am certain that few members could appreciate the difficulty I felt in taking issue with what they had accomplished.[1]

Nevertheless, my experience on that task force was valuable. I learned much, especially about how *not* to be effective in such policy deliberations. I also learned much about fundamental issues at stake in the modern labor-policy debate. The purpose of this book is to address those fundamental issues in ways I hope can be effective.

The book is an attempt to articulate concerns and positions that I was not able to fully address in the task-force meetings. If this book accomplishes nothing else, it might help explain to many of the task-force members—all of whom are highly competent and dedicated Americans—why we so often disagreed. It may help them, and others who accept their positions and disagree vehemently with mine, why I was rigid in my opposition. I hope, too, that it will provide the empirical and factual foundation for a fundamental redirection of the nation's labor policy.[2]

Beyond dealing with the frustrations of my work on the task force in the best, most constructive way I know how (by writing about them), this book is intended to explore what I believe is a current mythology about the workings of the American Job Machine. Its focus is on perceptions of *problems* and alternative *policies*. However, the book is also about *principles* because of my firmly-held conviction that government policies that are supposedly intended to deal with economic and social problems cannot be considered in isolation. They must be consistent with broad guiding principles that constrain the market *and* political process. Otherwise, the economy can be constantly battered by the ebbs and flows of political whim in Washington. Markets—in particular, labor markets—are dependent upon constraints on government, but that only means that government must be checked by rules—or principles—for the conduct of its policy.

Much of this book is concerned with the facts of the American job machine. But, all of the discussions about facts—descriptions of how well or poorly the "machine" works—have a fundamental objective: to get at the more important issue of the types of principles that should be devised for guiding government policies in dealing with market problems. In the main, the philosophical positions developed in the book lead to one overwhelming conclusion: Government has an important role in market economies. That essential role is not one of "creating jobs," but of insuring that people have the maximum opportunity to create their own jobs. Understanding the distinction between "creating jobs" and "creating opportunities" for job creation is a major task of this book.

1. The report of the task force, parts of which are considered in several chapters, is Task Force on Economic Adjustment, *Economic Adjustment and Worker Dislocation in a Competitive Society* (Washington: Office of the Secretary, U.S. Department of Labor, December 1987). My dissent to the report is *The Misguided Search for a National Labor Policy* (St. Louis: Center for the Study of American Business, Washington University, January 1987).

2. An alternative labor-policy agenda, consistent with the philosophical positions developed in this book, is found in Richard B. McKenzie, *U.S. Job Creation in a Competitive World Economy: A Positive Labor-Policy Agenda* (St. Louis: Center for the Study of American Business, Washington University, 1987).

Acknowledgments

This book is dependent upon the help of many people who, over the past two years, have graciously read, commented on, and published a series of labor-policy papers I have written. No acknowledgments list can be all-inclusive, but the following people have my special heartfelt thanks: William Baldwin, David Boaz, Richard Burr, Kenneth Chilton, Arthur Denzau, Clayton Hipp, Hugh Macaulay, Karen McKenzie, Harold Mulherin, Clark Nardinelli, Murray Weidenbaum, and Bruce Yandle. Murray Weidenbaum and Kenneth Chilton at the Center for the Study of American Business provided me important opportunities to participate in the labor-policy debate. I am very thankful to them for the considerable extra work they did on my behalf, without which this book may not have been possible.

The John M. Olin Foundation and the Earhart Foundation provided much-needed research funds. The financial help they gave greatly eased the research and writing tasks, and I am indebted to those organizations. The Cato Institute must be thanked for the help it provided in arranging the publication of the book.

I am especially grateful to Carolyn Foster for her careful reading of the entire manuscript and for the many editorial and substantive suggestions for improvement. Donna Tingle and Debbie Rosenthal were very helpful in easing the secretarial problems in seeing the manuscript to completion.

Several of the chapters have seen the light of publication in the form of articles. The Center for the Study of American Business originally distributed early versions of Chapters 2 (on the pace of economic change), 4 (displaced workers), and 7 (textile protectionism). The Cato Institute distributed Chapter 3, and the Joint Economic Committee in Congress published Chapter 5 (the "great U-turn"). *The Public Interest* published Chapter 6 (American competitiveness), and *Forbes* magazine carried a condensed version of Chapter 11 ("jobilism"). The U.S. Chamber of Commerce distributed the original version of Chapter 9 (minimum wages), while Chapter 10 (mandated benefits) formed the foundation of a paper presented at the Karl Eller Center for the Study of the Private Market Economy at the University of Arizona. Practically all of the previously published works have been substantially revised, updated, and expanded for inclusion in this volume. Nonetheless, the support these early publications represent were important to the development of the book.

Finally, I am very pleased to be able to dedicate this book to Professor Dwight Lee, who has been my colleague, coauthor, and friend for the past decade. To all of his academic colleagues, Dwight has one important, wonderful attribute: he helps us all keep our work in perspective—no mean task for most academics. More importantly, Dwight is the best of friends.

CHAPTER 1

Americans at Work

The American market economy has always been under development, and it will always continue to be in a fluid yet evolving state. Many industries have emerged, prospered, and expanded while others have contracted and even vanished. Many jobs have been eliminated while other jobs have been created. The economic adjustments people have had to make have caused problems, but the economic history of the nation has largely been a saga of people solving their own problems with an eye toward improvement of their own welfare.

Historically, the nation's economic troubles have been dominated by economic successes. On balance, over time, this has meant more jobs, more products, and more income. The day the country no longer has to face adjustment problems will probably be the day its people can no longer look forward to a better economic future.

In spite of the obvious improvements in economic well-being, many proponents of social reform can see only the dark side of economic adjustments in the market economy. They myopically focus their analytic attention on the "deindustrialization of America" as a source of "job destruction" and as a cause of the faltering dominance of American industries.

Proponents of reform fear that the American job machine is in a critical state of disrepair, unable to ensure that future Americans will find productive and satisfying work. Concerned scholars have joined the social chorus, repeating the refrain that the American market economy has lost its grip:

Measured in each of seven different ways—by unprecedented trade deficits in manufactured goods; by declining shares of world markets for exports; by lagging rates of productivity increases; by eroding profit margins; by declining real wages; by increasing price elasticities of imports; and by an eroding position in world high-technology markets—American industry confronts a severe problem of competitiveness, which it has never known before. Each measure has its limitations and can, perhaps, be explained away, but taken together they defy easy dismissal and portray a serious long-term problem.[1]

The reformists' varied analyses of the problems facing the American economy appear to have a political objective—that of declaring the market economy a failure with this expectation: policymakers will conclude that only greater government involvement in the economy can offer hope of continued progress.

The Search for a National Labor Policy

Several years ago these reformers sought to establish a "new national industrial policy" agenda that would adopt the twin objectives of promoting the progress of government-selected industrial "winners" and easing the pains of market-selected (and government-induced) industrial "losers." Now, many of these same reformers (supported in part by the U.S. Department of Labor in the Reagan administration) seek to promote the country's "competitiveness." In part, support comes through the creation of a "new national labor policy" that will use expanded governmental resources to ease the adjustment problems confronting workers and their communities and firms.

These proponents tell us that the number of "jobs" should be the benchmark measure of the international status and power of modern economies. America's economic success hinges critically on the extent to which the federal government takes dramatic action to create new jobs and to protect and improve existing jobs. Reformers propose the following:

- raising the minimum wage and tying it in percentage terms to average wage of production workers,
- providing workers with parental leave for childbirth and for child care,

- insuring that workers doing comparable work are paid comparable wages,
- seeking to secure jobs by discouraging imports and encouraging exports,
- making plant closings more expensive, and
- spending more taxpayer dollars to retrain workers and place these workers in the new jobs of the future.

The country's economic success, reformers say, also depends upon guiding state labor policies from Washington. Economic and social problems that are national in scope must be remedied by nothing less than national policies, or so we are told. In spite of a series of $200-billion deficits, reformists tell the country that the federal government must take actions such as the following:

- spend $1 billion on retraining,
- provide a whole new array of outplacement services for workers,
- create a new federal displaced-worker agency that has control over similar state displaced-worker agencies,
- impose plant closing restrictions, and
- insure that state labor policies are guided by "tripartite committees" (composed of selected representatives from businesses, unions, and government offices).

In general, this approach would insure that the country relies more on centralized federal controls and less on decentralized market incentives for determining how and where jobs are destroyed, how and where jobs are created.[2] At the same time, the firm would become the social agent of the state, supplanting many government-run welfare offices.[3] If the advocated policy agendas were nothing more than passing political fads without broad-based intellectual support, they could be ignored. But the political and intellectual support is broad, deep, and (very possibly) expanding, at least as measured by the number of cosigners on reform legislation introduced in 99th and 100th Congresses and by the string of books and monographs that have appeared in the 1980s offering much-needed empirical and conceptual support for the policy agendas. The reform proponents representing churches, universities, think tanks, unions, politicians, and even business organizations represent a formidable political coalition, especially since so many of the proponents are convinced that a deep sense of justice and fairness guides their efforts.

The Alternative Course

Many proponents behind the national labor-policy movement say, in so many words, that the country has no other effective choice but to adopt some variation of its agendas.[4] With a plethora of tables and charts and with much eloquent commentary about their concern for the welfare of others—especially America's working people and the poor—they challenge supporters of the market economy to refute their claims.

A major objective of this book is to accept the challenge of the reforms and to dispute the carefully-crafted empirical myths about failures in America's market economy. Several of the more important myths guiding contemporary labor-policy debates are considered in subsequent chapters, including:

- Myth 1. The pace of economic change is accelerating (Chapter 2).
- Myth 2. America is moving recklessly into a "service economy" as it destroys its manufacturing base (Chapter 3).
- Myth 3. The displaced-worker problem is large, so large as to justify expanded federal government efforts to rectify it (Chapter 4).
- Myth 4. The American economy has made a "Great U-Turn" on the road of economic progress due mainly to unbridled market forces (Chapter 5).
- Myth 5. American competitiveness is waning, evident in growing balance-of-merchandise-trade figures as well as other economic statistics, precisely because of its continued reliance on market principles; everyone understands that "there is no such thing as free trade except in textbooks" (Chapter 6).
- Myth 6. The massive loss of jobs in basic industries, such as textiles and apparel, is due almost exclusively to the forces of international competition (Chapter 7).
- Myth 7. Minimum-wage laws can be justified politically, if not morally, on the grounds that these laws help far more American workers than they hurt; they are also an effective anti-poverty device (Chapter 8).
- Myth 8. Government-funded retraining programs are necessary and productive components of any program that rebuilds the "American dream" of a brighter economic future for American workers (Chapter 9).

• Myth 9. Mandated fringe benefits can improve the welfare of the vast majority of American workers (Chapter 10).

The purpose of this book is also to argue that a policy course of greater government expenditures and labor-market controls is, for the most part, simply misguided. We shall suggest that the country does have other viable policy choices. Contemporary reformists fail to acknowledge that we live in a world of dramatic differences among workers—in their job skills and their preferences of working conditions, as well as many differences in production circumstances. Government mandates, subject to political manipulation, are simply too rigid to accommodate the country's rich diversity of people and circumstances.

A pluralistic society like the one in the United States needs a return to the acceptance of enforced property rights and to the rule of contracts that allow people to make mutually beneficial exchanges (Chapter 10). The policy choices that spring from recognizing the importance of rights and contracts include many reforms that, if enacted, could accomplish the commonly accepted national goals. Such goals include increasing job growth, accelerating the pace of economic adjustment, and decreasing unemployment hardship. However, favored policy options (mentioned from time to time throughout the book and summarized in the final chapter) seek in politically viable ways to accomplish these goals through greater reliance on markets and market-type incentives incorporated into government policies.

In all policy discussions, however, it is recognized that the enactment of specific policies, even good policies, will not end the debate. Other policies that reform the reforms can be expected from scholars and institutions representing all political persuasions. What is ultimately needed is a recognition that the policy process itself needs reforming. No economy can be expected to become and remain competitive for very long if government policies are in a constant state of flux. Ultimately, the policy process needs constraints, which will generally mean that there will be recognized areas of human existence that cannot be invaded by the whims of momentary politics. In this type of fundamental reform, the concept of rights will once again be elevated in public discourse.

The book ends with an exploration of two philosophical points. The first point deals with what is called "jobilism," an emerging ideology that causes many modern policymakers and commentators mistakenly to assess economic success and failure in terms of the number of jobs created and destroyed. The contemporary policy fetish with "jobs" will likely misguide public policy in much the same ways and for the same reasons that the mercantilist gold fetish misguided policy two hundred years ago (Chapter 11).

The final chapter compares and contrasts two visions of the social responsibility of businesses toward their workers. The first prescribes the content of "responsible" behavior. The second prescribes the legal framework within which businesses and workers are able to choose their own concept of "responsible" behavior toward each other. A limited number of specific policy recommendations that, if enacted, would be consistent with the second vision of responsible labor-management relations has been published elsewhere.[5]

Concluding Comments

Frequently, people who argue for market solutions to labor problems are automatically assumed to be defenders of the corporate class, meaning big business, and to be anti-labor. On the contrary, this book seeks to be "pro-labor" as well as "pro-business," acknowledging that labor, managers, and owners—in the final analysis—have compatible objectives. Granted, the book is founded on the author's conviction that, in general, free and open labor (and product) markets offer the country the best hope of revitalizing growth and expanding improved work opportunities for Americans. This conviction, in turn, is grounded in well-developed scholarly arguments and empirical studies contending that the government must insure that employee and employer rights of property and contract are *equally* enforced and protected at all levels by the government.

However, in this book, when arguments are made for "free markets," an uncorked or uncontrolled economy is never envisioned. The concept of "free markets" is tied inextricably to the concept of "competition," which can impose severe constraints on people's economic behavior. In this book, we argue for individual rather than government control precisely because it permits the creation of competitive drive and constraint.

Furthermore, because of the enormous quantity of information required to produce virtually all products and services (and to create new products and services) and because of the resulting complexity of production processes, decision-making in the economy must be decentralized. People must have *rights* that cannot be flagrantly violated by others (acting as individuals or agents of governments). A major share of the rights of individuals to act on their own or in concert with interested others must be captured in what are loosely called *property rights*—rights to one's own plant and equipment, but also rights to one's own labor, patents, information, and contracts.

The rights of labor must be no less protected and promoted by government than the rights of managers and owners because identifying people as "workers," "managers," and "owners" is largely arbitrary, at best. And such arbitrariness should be studiously avoided by any government that professes equal treatment for all and non-discriminatory justice.

Americans vary widely in their circumstances, in their needs and wants in terms of goods and services, and in their work experience. Contracts—which allow people to adapt exchanges to their own particular circumstances—are vital to the efficient use of the country's resources in producing goods and services. Restrictions on (labor) contracts standardized in Washington amount to constraints on what individuals, acting separately or collectively, can exchange. Contracts often, as a consequence, impose restrictions on mutually beneficial, income-generating trades—on workers as well as on their employers.[6]

This does not mean that government should do little or nothing to insure that people have adequate incomes. It only means that proposals to redistribute income through labor-market policies must be carefully examined and reexamined for their effectiveness in remedying observed market problems. This is because power assumed by government is power that can be exploited by interest groups with the worst motives as well as the best.

Nothing in the way of an unfettered economy is contemplated by this examination of labor-market problems and policies. In the final analysis, government has an important role to play, that of insuring as best it can a stable legal and economic environment in which people can seek to improve themselves. This generally means that government should avoid as much as possible the short-run political temptation of becoming a job-creation business. Instead, government should focus its limited resources on insuring that people have opportunities to create their own jobs to meet their own individual circumstances, as they, not some collective, view their circumstances.

Notes

1. Stephen S. Cohen and John Zysman, *Manufacturing Matters: The Myth of the Post-Industrial Economy* (New York: Basic Books, 1987), p. 61.

2. For example, see Task Force on Economic Adjustment and Worker Dislocation, *Economic Adjustment and Worker Dislocation in a Competitive Society* (Washington: Office of the Secretary, U.S. Department of Labor, December 1986), especially pp. 27–38.

3. This theme is developed in Robert Reich, *The Next American Frontier* (New York: Times Books, 1983).

4. Malcolm R. Lovell, Jr., chairman of the U.S. Department of Labor Task Force on Economic Adjustment and Worker Dislocation, in his efforts to refute the *Wall Street Journal*'s denunciation of the Task Force's recommendations (John Funt, "What Price Jobs?" editorial, *Wall Street Journal,* January 14, 1987, p. 22; and Lindley H. Clark, "How to Help Workers Who Really Need Help," *Wall Street Journal,* February 3, 1987, p. 35), notes, "*The Journal* criticizes the use of federal training programs to assist these displaced workers. But what do you recommend instead?" (See Malcolm R. Lovell, Jr., "Op-Ed Piece for the *Wall Street Journal*," a short paper distributed to the members of the task force—received by the author in early March 1987.)

5. See Richard B. McKenzie, *U.S. Job Creation in a Competitive World Economy: A Positive Agenda of Labor-Policy Reforms* (St. Louis: Center for the Study of American Business, Washington University, 1987).

6. This philosophical predisposition to policy is represented by the work of Milton and Rose Friedman, *Free to Choose* (New York: Harcourt Brace Jovanovich, 1980); F. A. Hayek, *Law, Legislation and Liberty,* Vols. I, II, and III (Chicago: University of Chicago Press, 1973, 1976, and 1979); and Richard B. McKenzie, *Bound to be Free* (Stanford, Calif.: Hoover Institution Press, 1982).

CHAPTER 2

The Pace of
Economic Change

Change is endemic to all economies, especially market economies.
Changes in consumer preferences, production technologies, worker
skills, market competitiveness, government policies, and resource
mobility inspire shifts in market forces that invariably fuel price and
output adjustments. Economic changes—and, just as importantly, the
public's perception of the magnitude and frequency of these
changes—also fuel public-policy debates. Currently, the area of federal
labor policy is the subject of debate.

This debate is replete with claims that the contemporary pace of
economic change, requiring worker adjustments, is accelerating.
Special public concern over the pace of change exists within and between the manufacturing and service sectors, giving rise to concern
that the United States is becoming a "productionless" society. This
chapter assesses the empirical validity of such claims.

The pace of change, or the perception thereof, is important for one
basic political reason: many policymakers believe that workers' difficulties in finding and retaining secure, well-paying jobs are directly
related to the speed of change in the economy. The faster the pace of
change, the greater the employment, unemployment, and reemployment problems for workers. And the faster the pace of change, the
louder the calls for government aid to workers and for restrictions on
businesses in order to maintain smooth and orderly labor markets.[1]

While the evidence developed in this chapter does not offer
definitive conclusions, careful examination of various economic data
series covering the period from the early 1950s to the recent past casts

considerable doubt on arguments that the pace of economic change is accelerating. Indeed, one might understandably conclude that the pace of employment change across industries actually has decelerated during the past decade or so. This deceleration may be partially responsible for the employment and reemployment problems faced by many American workers.

The Public-Policy Controversy

Public concern about the pace of change is understandable. As a consequence of continuously shifting market and political forces, economies restructure themselves. In the process, many firms emerge and expand while others contract and fail. Many workers are laid off and displaced; others are hired and called upon to work longer hours per week. Economic progress is the history of economic destruction dominated by economic success, and the U.S. economy has exhibited success in making this transition during much of the post–World War II era.

The inevitability of economic change is rarely disputed. However, the *pace* of economic change and the social problems caused by "excessive" change often motivate political activity designed to harness market forces—to slow the adjustments people and businesses are required to make. After all, according to this line of reasoning, the ability of people to adjust to their own economic fortune or misfortune depends on how many others are making similar adjustments at approximately the same time.

Similarly, according to this line of reasoning, the reemployment problems faced by displaced or terminated workers depend on how many other people with similar skills have also been displaced in their communities. With more people out of work, the competition for jobs is more fierce and more costly. As a consequence, workers must endure longer periods of unemployment, or so it is argued.[2]

Contemporary labor-policy discussions typically assume that the pace of economic change is speeding up, exceeding the ability of workers and communities to cope efficiently and coherently. For example, a researcher for the National Commission for Employment Policy has noted, "It is widely recognized that job terminations associated with plant closings, technological advances and changes in consumer demand have become more frequent in the past decade than in the years before the energy crisis of 1973–74."[3] In addition, the director of the New Jersey Department of Labor has written that "labor-market trends and projections for the U.S. economy indicate substantial structural change is occurring and will continue to occur at an accelerated rate for the foreseeable future."[4] Supposedly, conventional economic analysis of markets largely ignores the effects of the increasing pace of change on the ability of workers to adjust.[5]

Although the sources of economic adjustment in America are varied, the upward shift in the rate of change is generally attributed to some combination of the following factors:

- computerization of work,
- substitution of robots (and other more productive capital equipment) for people in the workplace,
- growing competitiveness in world markets, especially for manufactured goods,
- deregulation of previously regulated industries, and
- appreciation (as well as depreciation) of the dollar and resulting changes in the international merchandise trade flows.[6]

These economic forces have supposedly caused the demise (or "deindustrialization") of the "industrial society" and the emergence of the "service economy." In the process, these changes have resulted in destruction of difficult-to-replace, well-paying production jobs.[7]

In the past Congress has proposed a plethora of laws to soften the blow of work redistribution. As noted in Chapter 1, Congress has considered legislation that would extend employees' health insurance beyond their termination, make plant-closing decisions a subject of mandatory bargaining, target federal expenditures for "surplus" labor areas, require firms to cover their employees' relocation expenses, provide federal subsidies for retraining programs, offer tax credits to firms for their retraining expenditures, impose additional taxes on workers and their employers to develop "individual retraining accounts," require firms to provide their workers with advance notice of plant closings and permanent layoffs, and restrict plant closings by imposing severance-pay requirements and denying tax benefits for closing decisions.

Concerned about congressional interest in new social programs dealing with worker displacement, Secretary of Labor William Brock formed the Task Force on Economic Adjustment and Worker Dislocation in late 1985. At the first task-force meeting, Secretary Brock admonished members to recognize that the adjustment problems faced by many workers are "serious" because the pace of change is "accelerating."[8] This conclusion about the pace of the economy may have been inaccurate (a point that will be argued later in the chapter). Even if it were correct, the debate is not settled. Another critical question facing policymakers, over which there is room for disagreement, is whether unemployed workers face more severe reemployment difficulties today than in the past and thus warrant federal intervention to ease the increased burdens.

Certainly, computer and robot technology and biotechnology have spurred much recent economic change. However, other earlier minor and major technological advances—including sewing machines, hybrid seeds, supermarkets, trains, cars, and planes—have spurred much change. These past developments help put in perspective contemporary concerns. One of these concerns is that the "new microtechnology. . . is bringing change which is perhaps even more revolutionary than the industrial revolution."[9] For instance, in 1862, *Scientific American* maintained that "the rapid rise of the sewing machine business constitutes one of the wonders of this enterprising age. No industrial revolution can equal that which has been produced by it within the short space of sixteen years."[10] At that time, many people were probably just as concerned about the pace of change brought on by sewing machines as many are today about the pace of change spurred partially by developments in computers and robots.

Admittedly, in manufacturing there have been employment losses and gains in recent years. "Key" or "basic" U.S. industries—in particular, steel, automobiles, textiles, shoes, and apparel—have declined in employment, while electrical-equipment employment has expanded markedly. Consider the employment patterns for four of these industries. (See Figure 2.1) For example, between 1979 and 1985 steel employment was cut practically in half, while electrical equipment followed a highly cyclical upward trend.

But looking at individual industry employment can be misleading because employment losses in some sectors (for example, manufacturing) can be the direct consequence of employment gains in other sectors (for example, services). Scarcity of resources frequently dictates that when some industries expand, other industries contract because they are unable to secure at competitive prices the resources they need. Competition often means that some products and services will be driven out of the market by other better and more attractively priced products and services. In short, our interpretation of employment patterns in individual industries should not be isolated from developments in the rest of the economy.[11]

In addition, shifts in employment among industries and sectors of the economy (and concern for their positive and negative social con-

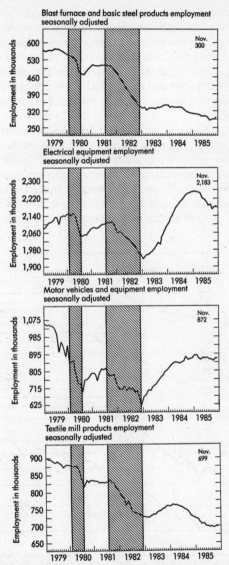

Fig. 2.1 Employment developments in selected U.S. manufacturing industries, 1979–1985. (*Source:* Thomas J. Plewes, "Briefing on Economic Adjustment and Worker Dislocation" [Washington: Bureau of Labor Statistics, December 17, 1985].)

sequences) are not new to modern economies, and, therefore, they do not necessarily warrant an expanded role for government. Employment in agriculture has been declining for centuries. Manufacturers of saddles and buggies, once prominent in American economic life, are inconsequential elements in modern life. Perhaps the only major difference between then and now is that our modern Congress is more inclined to respond to the demands for relief made by workers and business groups.

Accelerating change in and of itself does not necessarily warrant the government's applying policy brakes. Change implies new and expanding employment opportunities as well as job losses. Furthermore, any accelerating pace of change may not be accompanied by a decrease in the predictability of future employment. Indeed, an increase in the pace of change may be associated with a predictable increase in future employment opportunities. Contemporary workers also may be

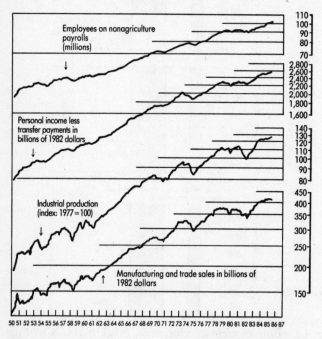

Fig. 2.2 Measures of economic activity in the U.S. macroeconomy, 1950–1986. (*Source: Business Conditions Digest*, May 1986.)

Table 2.1 Average Annual Rates of Change in Measures of National Production and Income, 1951–85 (percent)

	Real Gross National Product	Disposable Personal Income Per Capita	Industrial Production Index	Manufacturing and Trade Sales
1951–60	2.82	1.52	3.99	3.38
1960–70	4.51	3.48	6.09	4.72
1970–80	3.19	1.95	3.83	3.81
1980–85	2.42	1.61	2.93	2.82

Source: Business Conditions Digest, various issues.

better able to cope with change on their own, given increases in their wealth and income prospects as well as reductions in their net adjustment costs (for instance, transportation costs). Just because structural changes require greater skills is no reason to conclude that workers, who may be better educated and more mobile than workers who went before them, are less able to make the adjustments.

Nevertheless, the debate over the pace of change cannot be resolved by conceptual arguments alone. The evidence must be considered.

Questions of Evidence

To examine the issue of whether the pace of economic change is accelerating or decelerating, it is important to distinguish between transitory changes and more fundamental alterations in market forces.

American economic history is filled with abrupt changes in economic forces. Such historical episodes include three major shifts: the sharp rise and then precipitous drop in the worldwide demand for American manufactured goods at the turn of the 18th century, the dramatic industrialization of America between the Civil War and World War I, and the radical swings in national production levels during the Great Depression and the World War II production boom.[12] However, the real policy concern is the pace of relatively recent changes compared with our contemporary history.

Recent Macroeconomic History

More pertinent for our purposes are the macroeconomic changes during the post-World War II era. We need to determine whether or not

Table 2.2 Average Annual Rate of Change in Measures of
Employment and Productivity, 1951–85 (percent)

	Labor Force	Employment	Labor Force Participation Rate	Labor Productivity in Nonfarm Business Sector
1950–60	1.26	1.26	0.05	2.11
1960–70	1.87	1.95	0.17	2.57
1970–80	2.79	2.49	0.51	1.09
1980–85	1.59	1.58	0.31	1.09

Source: Calculated from data in the *Economic Report of the President, 1986.*

there has been a noticeable recent change in the direction or pace of
change.

The historical data on such factors as the number of employees on
nonagricultural payrolls, personal income (less transfers), the industrial
production index, and real manufacturing trade sales (plotted in Figure
2.2) provide a tentative answer. The log scales permit visual observations of any dramatic changes in the *rates of growth* in the data series.

While there is noticeable volatility in all of the graphs, reflecting the
seven recessions and recoveries during the period, there is no apparent
evidence of dramatic reversals in upward trends and only scant
evidence of changes in the rates of growth. All series are moving
upward. If the slopes of the curves reveal any evidence of change, it
is a decline in the rate of growth after 1970 in all of the series, as
evident in the slight flattening of the curves.

Indeed, as is evident in Table 2.1, the rise in the country's industrial
production has slowed considerably since the 1960s, rising at an
annual average rate during the first half of the 1980s of less than half
the rate of the 1960s. In a similar manner, real gross national product
(GNP), personal income, and manufacturing sales have also
decelerated.

A major reason for the curtailment in production increases has been
a slowing of the increase in the labor force and also in employment,
due in part to a reduction in growth of the labor-force participation
rate. (See Table 2.2) One of the reasons for the slower growth rate for
employment has been the decline in growth of the working-age
population. While labor productivity in the nonfarm business sector
increased at a faster pace during the 1960s than in any other decade
covered by Table 2.2, the average increase in labor productivity was

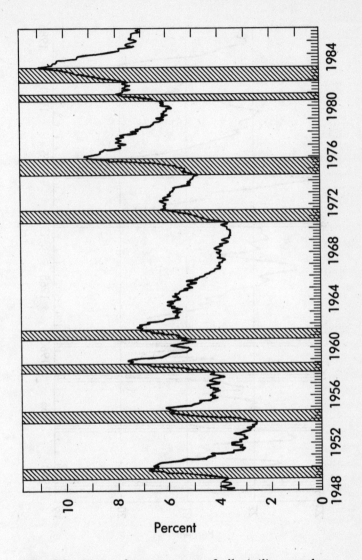

Fig. 2.3 Unemployment rate of all civilian workers, seasonally adjusted, 1948–1985. (*Source*: Thomas J. Plewes, "Briefing on Economic Adjustment and Worker Dislocation" [Washington: Bureau of Labor Statistics, December 17, 1985].)

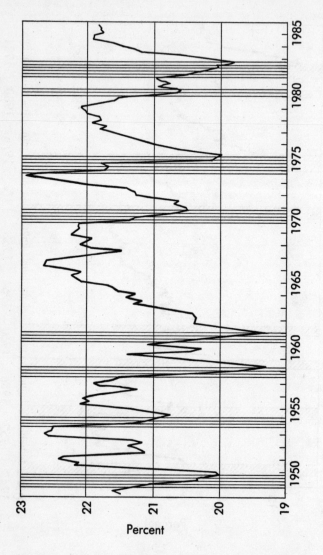

Fig. 2.4 U.S. manufacturing as a percentage of real gross national product, 1948–1985. (*Source:* John Tatom, "Domestic vs. International Explanations of Recent Developments in U.S. Manufacturing" [St. Louis: Federal Reserve Bank, draft, May 1986].)

the same annual rate in the first half of the 1980s as in the 1970s.

One net effect of the slowdown in industrial growth and the rise in the labor-force participation rate has been a general increase in the unemployment rate, shown in Figure 2.3. Even so, the unemployment rate has been peaking at higher rates during succeeding recessions since at least the early 1950s. In addition, the causes of the general upward trend in the unemployment rate are not at all clear at this point. An accelerating pace of change (if, in fact, such a change exists) could be one of the causative factors, but so could any number of other factors, including individual income, individual wealth, and government programs to subsidize unemployment. A decelerating pace of change, evident in productivity growth rates, could have had the same effect on unemployment rates as that observed in Figure 2.3.

Sector Shifts

Growth in production can mask dramatic shifts in production and employment among major sectors of the economy—for example, from manufacturing to services. As is evident in Figure 2.2, manufacturing production has continued to rise over recent decades. Furthermore, as Figure 2.4 shows, manufacturing output has varied markedly as a percent of GNP. However, oscillations of real manufacturing output have remained largely within its historic band of 20% to 24% of real GNP.

The unbroken, albeit erratic, connection between real GNP and manufacturing output is supported by growth-rate data. Figure 2.5 shows the growth rates of real manufacturing output and real GNP. Both data series demonstrate great variation, but there is no apparent (visual) evidence that the two series have established a dramatically different relationship in the last decade. Growth in real manufacturing output continues to vary more radically with the business cycle than real GNP varies. But the important point is that the relationship has not changed appreciably, a conclusion that is supported by more sophisticated econometric studies undertaken in recent years.[13] "The long-term 'problem' [of manufacturing]," writes St. Louis Federal Reserve Bank economist John Tatom (who has extensively studied via econometric models the fate of the manufacturing sector),

> is the strength of productivity improvement in the manufacturing sector generally. Faster productivity growth in this sector has contributed significantly to real income growth in the nation; it has also contributed to a significant decline in the relative price of manufac-

tured goods, reflecting their increased availability. While the share of manufacturing output has been maintained, its share of employment and total spending has declined. This long-standing pattern has continued from 1979 to 1985. Thus, there is no need to blame other popular villains [for example, the international trade imbalance] for manufacturing employment's failure to regain its previous peak.[14]

Much has been made of the rise of the "service economy," as if the relatively higher rate of growth in service employment is evidence of "accelerating" structural changes in the economy. Because the presumed expansion of the service economy is considered in detail in Chapter 3, we need only stress here that "service employment" is rapidly becoming a larger percentage of total employment. But that does not imply a dramatic recent redirection in the country's employment trends or that "goods" production and employment is drying up in the country. The relative shift toward "service" employment has been under way for decades. Goods-producing employment has grown (although slightly) from less than 20 million to approximately 25 million between the first half of the 1950s and the last half of the 1980s. The Bureau of Labor Statistics projects slight growth in goods-producing employment through 1995.[15] The absence of material change in aggregate employment patterns is further revealed in the breakdown of employment by sector in Figure 2.6. Even manufacturing employment is projected by the BLS to rise between 1984 and 1995. If there is evidence of any shift in employment by sector in Figure 2.6, it is slower growth in government employment, which began in the early 1980s.

Industry Shifts

The level of aggregation in the data, however, necessarily hides many contractions and expansions of employment in individual economic sectors and industries. (Reconsider Figure 2.1, which plots the employment fates of four basic industries — steel, motor vehicles, electrical equipment, and textiles — all of which have recently experienced wide swings in employment.) The difficult question to answer is whether recent or projected employment shifts across sectors and industries are greater or more severe than in earlier decades.

One way to attempt to measure the amount of change from sector to sector or industry to industry, over time, is through simple calculation of the correlation coefficient between employment levels of each

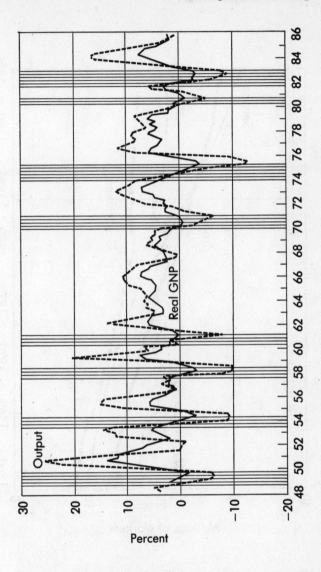

Fig. 2.5 Growth rates of manufacturing output and real gross national product, 1948–1985. (*Source:* John Tatom, "Domestic vs. International Explanations of Recent Developments in U.S. Manufacturing" [St. Louis: Federal Reserve Bank, draft, May 1986].)

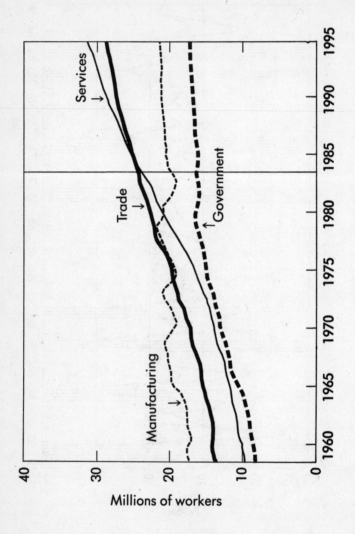

Fig. 2.6 Total U.S. employment in selected major economic sectors, 1959–1984, and projected, 1985–1995. (*Source:* Valerie A. Personick, "Industry Output and Employment to 1995," *Monthly Labor Review*, November 1985.)

sector or of each industry for selected years. If employment change among sectors and industries is accelerating, then more recent employment levels within a sector or industry would exhibit a progressively lower correlation with past employment levels. That is, more recent employment levels by sectors would be explained to a lesser extent by past employment levels.

In addition, as noted above, an important problem with change is its predictability. The predictability of change will affect the ability of workers to cope and adjust to change because their knowing what to expect affects their ability to plan for change. A low and/or falling correlation coefficient for employment patterns over time would suggest that employment patterns may be becoming progressively less predictable.

Table 2.3 contains the correlation coefficients for employment patterns—by actual count and percent distribution of the employment data—for 11 major sectors and 149 industries over selected intervals between 1959 and 1995. Contrary to the view that the pace of change is accelerating, the correlation coefficients are very high (close to 1.00 in most cases) and do not change markedly between 1959 and 1979—nor will they change until 1995, if BLS employment projections turn out to be reasonably accurate. There is only a slight, two-percentage-point decrease in the correlation coefficient for the percent distribution between the 1959–69 and 1969–79 periods. If there is any measurable change in the correlation coefficients for employment by the 149 industries, it is only a slight increase.

The reported coefficients are not without deficiencies in describing the extent of changes in the labor-force composition. Many changes in the labor force within industries and among occupations and regions of the country are not captured in the statistics. The projected employment patterns are based on past experience, and some high correlation between current and predicted employment patterns is expected.

However, the BLS employment-pattern projections are not simple extrapolations of current patterns; they involve assumptions about overall economic growth, sectorial-growth relationships, changes in productivity, and input-output tables. What is surprising about the coefficients is their magnitude and stability. As expected, the correlation coefficients for the five- and six-year intervals are generally higher than for the 10- and 11-year intervals. When the same analysis is undertaken for the 95 manufacturing industries and for the 15 service industries, subsets of the 149 industries covered in the above

Table 2.3 Correlation Coefficients of Employment Levels and Percent Distribution of Employment by Major Sector and Industry for Selected Intervals, 1959–95

| | Correlation Coefficients | | | | | | |
| | Ten- and 11-Year Intervals | | | | Five- and Six-Year Intervals | | |
	1959–69	1969–79	1979–90	1984–95	1979–84	1984–90	1990–95
Employment by major sectors							
by number	.9780	.9753	.9770	.9939	.9881	.9980	.9987
by percent	.9978	.9752	.9770	.9940	.9880	.9981	.9987
Employment by industry							
by number	.9831	.9856	.9865	.9929	.9951	.9974	.9987
by percent	.9831	.9856	.9865	.9929	.9951	.9974	.9987

Source: Computed from data reported in Valerie A. Personick, "Second Look at Industry Output and Employment Trends Through 1995," *Monthly Labor Review,* November 1985, pp. 28–41.

analysis, the same high and stable correlation coefficients are computed.

Basically, these findings mean that employment patterns across industries in any given year are highly related to employment patterns in previous years. While not conclusive (of course), these findings do, however, cast additional doubt on the thesis that the pace of economic change has greatly accelerated.

Other Evidence

The above findings are consistent with another study of the rising importance of service employment. Mack Ott, an economist with the St. Louis Federal Reserve Bank, has wondered whether there has been any dramatic shift in employment from goods production to service production. He observed a rather steady increase in share of all workers going into services from as far back as 1880. "An examination of the data from 1880 to 1930 reveals that the share of employment in services grew at an average annual rate of about 1.8%."[16] By applying the logistic growth rate to the years 1880–1985, he found that "the predicted 1985 services labor force share is 68.5%, while the actual labor share in service production for 1985 is 71.9%. Consequently, the shift of labor from commodities to service production has not only been proceeding for more than 180 years, it has also been fairly steady. Apparently, the shift from commodities to services has been proceeding fairly steadily for more than a century."[17]

Ott's basic findings on the movement of service employment share over time are captured in Figure 2.7. Since the 1940s, service employment as a percent of total employment has been above the long-term trend. Still, the employment share since the 1940s has followed a trend parellel to the long-term trend, based on earlier employment-share data.

Ott makes additional predictions of shares of employment in three broad categories of jobs: information provision, direct production, and noninformation services.[18] When 1900–1930 data is used to predict 1980 employment shares by the three categories of occupations, the predicted shares are reasonably close to the actual shares. Ott predicts an employment share of 55.9% for information services; the actual share is 53.0%. The predicted and actual share for direct production occupations are equally close: 37.4 predicted versus 34.1 actual.[19] No apparent acceleration in the pace of change is evident in the Ott study.

Concluding Comments

It is easy to observe dramatic, isolated changes in the economy and conclude that the current anecdotal experience is without precedent in economic history. Policymakers and commentators in practically every decade since World War II have been drawing similar conclusions and suggesting that current conditions warrant new and venturesome government policies.

Change across regions, industries, and occupations has been ever-present in the economy. However, the available evidence musters little, if any, support for the thesis that economic change across major sectors and industries is taking place at an accelerating pace and thereby leading to significant new problems in labor markets. Moreover, trying to restrain labor-market change may well prove counterproductive—providing little relief from the painful experience of unemployment while reducing employment opportunity.

Admittedly, our analysis of shifts in aggregate, sectorial, and industrial employment patterns may mask shifts in employment patterns across regions and occupations and between large and small plants. Those concerns, however, must be reserved for an expanded research effort (they do not appear of major importance in Mack Ott's study). In addition, even if dramatic changes were found in the data, such

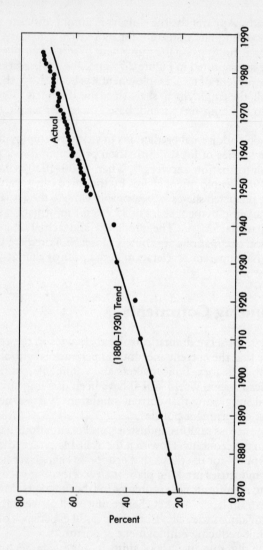

Fig. 2.7 Share of employment in the U.S. service sector, 1870–1985. (*Source:* Mack Ott, "The Growing Share of Services in the U.S. Economy—Degeneration or Evolution," *Review* [Federal Reserve Bank of St. Louis], June/July 1987, p. 15.)

observed shifts would necessitate rethinking the mix of public-policy responses. Much more would have to be known about the ability of workers to accommodate such shifts before any government programs designed to ease the burden and efficiency of adjustments could be devised.

Notes

1. For a discussion of the connection between structural shifts in the economy and the rising unemployment rate, see David M. Lilien, "Sector Shifts and Cyclical Unemployment" *Journal of Political Economy,* August 1982, pp. 777–793, and David M. Lilien, "A Sectoral Model of the Business Cycle," working paper (Los Angeles: University of Southern California, 1982).

2. Barry Bluestone, "Industrial Dislocation and Its Implication for Public Policy," *Displaced Workers: Implications for Educational and Training Institutions,* edited by Kevin Hollenbeck, Frank C. Pratzner, and Howard Rosen (Columbus, Ohio: National Center for Research in Vocational Education, 1984), pp. 45–68.

3. Wayne Vroman, "Innovative Developments in Unemployment Insurance," *Research Report* (Washington: National Commission for Employment Policy), February 1985, p. 34.

4. William A. Tracy, "Technology and the Labor Mismatch" (letter to the editor), *Wall Street Journal,* September 30, 1986, p. 33. Mr. Tracy continued, "The nature of work is changing because of technology in the work place. Increased worker displacement is occurring because of post-industrial evolution of the world economy. These factors, coupled with demographic changes in the labor force, suggest increased disequilibrium both in quantity and quality between the supply and demand for labor."

5. Concern about the failure of conventional economic analysis to consider the pace of change is raised by Barry Bluestone, "Industrial Dislocation . . .," pp. 45–46.

6. For example, William Tracy, director of the New Jersey Department of Labor, summarized several sources of labor-market adjustment: "The nature of work is changing because of application of technology in the work place. Increased worker displacement is occurring because of the post-industrial evolution of the world economy. These factors, coupled with demographic changes in the labor force, suggest increased disequilibrium both in quantity and quality between the supply and demand for labor" (Tracy, "Technology and the Labor Mismatch," p. 33).

7. The widespread belief that "production" jobs in the U.S. economy are evaporating is due to the focus on the declining number of production jobs in manufacturing and to the general view that little of value is produced in the service sector. There are "production and nonsupervisory" workers in the service economy, just as in the manufacturing sector. The total number of production and nonsupervisory workers has expanded steadily during the past

two decades. See Richard B. McKenzie, *The Good News About U.S. Production Jobs* (St. Louis: Center for the Study of American Business, Washington University, 1986).

8. Comments made by U.S. Secretary of Labor William Brock at the December 17, 1985, meeting of the Task Force on Economic Adjustment and Worker Dislocation.

9. AFL-CIO Committee on the Evolution of Work, *The Future of Work* (Washington: AFL-CIO, August 1983), as quoted in *Computers in the Workplace: Selected Issues,* no. 19 (Washington: National Commission for Employment Policy, March 1986), p. 23.

10. Ibid.

11. These points are developed at length in Richard B. McKenzie, *Free to Lose: The Bright Side of Economic Failure* (St. Louis: Center for the Study of American Business, Washington University, 1986).

12. For a short review of change in U.S. economic history, see Douglas C. North, Terry L. Anderson, and Peter J. Hill, *Growth and Welfare in the American Past: A New Economic History,* 3d ed. (Englewood Cliffs, N.J.: Prentice-Hall, 1983).

13. See Robert Lawrence, *Can America Compete?* (Washington: Brookings Institution, 1985); John A. Tatom, "Domestic vs. International Explanation of Recent Developments in U.S. Manufacturing," *Review* (St. Louis: Federal Reserve Bank of St. Louis), April 1986, pp. 5–18; and Council of Economic Advisors, *Economic Report of the President: 1986* (Washington: Executive Office of the President of the United States, February 1986), Chap. 5.

14. John A. Tatom, "Why Has Manufacturing Employment Declined?" *Federal Reserve Bank of St. Louis Review,* December 1986, p. 23.

15. As reported by Thomas J. Plewes, Bureau of Labor Statistics, "Briefing on Economic Adjustment and Worker Dislocation," a series of charts and tables prepared for presentation to the first meeting of the U.S. Department of Labor, Task Force on Economic Adjustment and Worker Dislocation (Washington, December 17, 1985).

16. Mack Ott, "The Growing Share of Services in the U.S. Economy—Degeneration or Evolution?" *Review* (St. Louis: Federal Reserve Bank of St. Louis), June/July 1987, p. 15.

17. Ibid.

18. According to Ott, "The first category encompasses the production of information by decisionmakers and all the supporting design, analysis, and record-keeping occupations and sales staff. The second comprises labor directly involved in production of goods and public utility services such as transport and electricity. The third consists of services other than information or utilities: private household services, police and fire services, and food and cleaning services" [Ibid., p. 16].

19. Ibid., p. 17.

CHAPTER 3

The Emergence of the "Service Economy"

The presumed rapid pace of structural change in the economy, studied in Chapter 2, is supposedly fully evident in the shift of jobs from goods to service production. And the emergence of the so-called service economy in the United States has given birth to public-policy worries that the country is being reduced to a nation of orderlies, fast-food workers, and busboys.

Much that has been written in the press, policy papers, and books has simply sought to describe structural changes in U.S. production and employment.[1] Drawing on the employment data depicted in Figure 3.1, some analysts have concluded that jobs in the U.S. service-producing sector have for some time risen at a healthy pace, while employment in the goods-producing sector, especially in manufacturing, has continued to languish or only creep slowly upward.[2] Such disparate employment-growth trends prompted a major U.S. newsmagazine in July 1985 to fill its cover with the banner, "Welcome to the Service Sector."[3]

However, much of the policy analysis, developed with political agendas in mind, has been artfully juxtaposed with heartfelt concern that market capitalism is operating like an unmanned bulldozer at full throttle. Wholesale economic destruction is said to be evident in many conditions: the accelerating pace of technological and structural change; the "deindustrialization of America"; the mounting financial and social problems of displaced and dislocated workers (particularly older workers) who have few transferable skills; the growing inability of American industry to compete in world markets; and the emer-

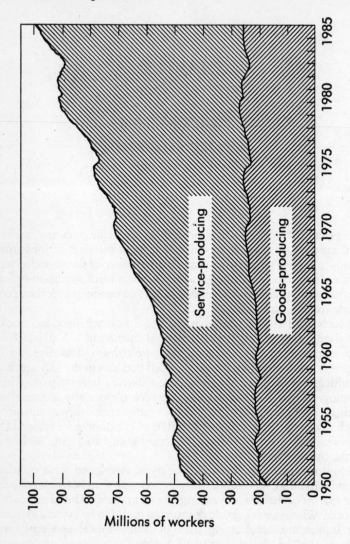

Fig. 3.1 Trends in U.S. service and goods producing employment 1950–1985. *Source:* Thomas J. Plewes, "Briefing on Economic Adjustment and Worker Dislocation" [Washington: Bureau of Labor Statistics, December 17, 1985].)

gence of a society represented by a "two-tiered," "bimodal," or "polarized" income distribution.[4]

We are told in explicit terms that "manufacturing matters." Why? Because the ultimate source of national wealth and good jobs lies in the "goods" sector and because of "direct linkages" between employment in the goods and service economies, manufacturing must be favored even at the expense of a growing presence of some service employment. "[A] substantial core of service employment is tightly tied to manufacturing. It is a complement and, not as the dominant view would have it, a substitute or successor for manufacturing. Lose manufacturing and you will lose — not develop — those high-wage services."[5]

In short, the dramatic expansion of the service economy observed in Figure 3.1 has been viewed as both cause and proof of fundamental failures in the U.S. market economy. Such widespread failures can be corrected, or so it is argued, only by the maintenance and/or creation of a wide variety of government-backed retraining and income-support programs, imposition of restrictions on the ability of firms to adjust to changing economic circumstances, and the creation of additional or higher U.S. barriers to imports.[6] The wandering bulldozer should, in other words, be given a government driver who will take orders from a number of federal and state agencies. Some of these agencies will be new agencies created to supplement governmental units already in place.

The expansion of the service economy has been perceived as a cause of economic malaise because wages in the service sector have been thought to be, on average, lower than wages in the goods economy. Also, without an industrial base, the United States will surely lose its status as the world's premier industrial power, only to be replaced by third-rate, third-world countries, or so we are told.

The expansion of the service economy has been looked upon as a symptom of economic malaise. Increases in service employment have appeared concurrently with emerging surpluses of labor in traditionally high-paying heavy industries and an upward long-run trend in the nation's unemployment rate. The expansion of the service economy presumably mirrors a decline in the international competitiveness of American firms. This decline has been interpreted and continues to be interpreted as an inability of American firms to "flex" their organizational structures and production levels to meet the accelerating changes in world market conditions. This presumed inability of U.S. goods-producing firms to compete in the world economy is supposedly measured by the country's growing deficit in its balance of merchandise trade and decline in industrial production.

Clearly, the U.S. economy is evolving naturally in response to a host of factors, not the least of which are changes in consumer preferences, opportunity costs, and production technologies. The national economy has always adjusted, and can be expected to continue to adjust. That has been a reemerging theme of this book. But no one should expect the adjustment process to be painless.

This chapter seeks to explain why concern over the emergence of the service economy in the United States is, for the most part, unwarranted and misplaced. Much too much has been read into data on trends in goods- and service-producing employment, for example, as shown in Figure 3.1. Many of the assumptions about the economic value (or lack thereof) of "services" are wrong. Many of the facts about the rise in the service economy are misunderstood, in part because of the arbitrary classifications of national production into "goods" and "services." One largely unexplored reason for the growth in the service economy, which will be given special attention in the last half of this chapter, is the fragmentation of firms into relatively smaller and more independent production units.

A major hypothesis is that much of the growth in the service economy, even in typically low-wage industries, has contributed to the growth in American income, even income created in goods–producing industries. Seen from this perspective, the presumed polarization of America (a subject touched on in this chapter and dealt with in detail in Chapter 5) is a social cause in a misguided and vain search for empirical and conceptual justification.

The Value of Services

The policy debate over what, if anything, should be done to thwart or encourage the perceived shift from an industrial to a service economy should be based on critical *facts* rather than popular *belief*, which is, perhaps, an outright *myth*. One such myth is frequently summarized in the claim that we may, with the emergence of the service economy, eventually end up doing each other's laundry. Adherents to this view come from virtually all economic-policy arenas. As financial advisor to industry and governments Felix Rohatyn has claimed, "We cannot become a nation of short-order cooks and saleswomen, Xerox-machine operators and messenger boys.... These jobs are a weak basis for the economy.... To let other countries make things while we concentrate on services is debilitating both in its substance and in its symbolism."[7]

Similarly, John F. McGillicuddy, chairman of Manufacturers Hanover Trust Co., worries, "All theories of post-industrial economies aside, we need to wonder whether we can really afford to become a nation of people solely engaged in selling Egg McMuffins and insurance to one another, treating each other's illnesses, or cutting each other's hedges or hair. Surely there must be a point of diminishing returns in all this. We may have reached it."[8] Or as the *Christian Science Monitor* editorialized, "Surely the American people are not willing to become merely a service economy. The American character is as much built around the sinews and muscle of the factory line as the white-collar office. American industry has been a major force for progressive social change."[9]

First, in order to understand the mythical dimensions of such claims, it should be understood that Figure 3.1 contains far less information on what has actually happened to "service" and "goods" employment than is assumed. Statisticians and policymakers have an understandable need to categorize "goods" and "services." After all, the world is complex, and the classification of employment and production outcomes is necessary to make policy discussions potentially intelligible. However, once categories have been devised, it is all too easy to converse *as if* the established categories are not arbitrary, or at least have more lasting economic meaning than is deserved.

The fact is that no matter how carefully definitions of "goods" and "services" are constructed, the actual division of production and employment levels into countable categories is largely arbitrary. The categories may be conventions to statisticians and policymakers, but the basis for the distinction among identified "goods" and "services" is frequently hard to discern (even when the criteria may be, for example, the extent to which the things produced are tangible, storable, or resalable).[10] As time passes and the composition of goods and services changes, the distinction is likely to become progressively more blurred and less meaningful. This is because so many different things are produced over time. Comparing the data on "goods" and "services" over long stretches of time amounts to comparing, literally, different things.

In more concrete terms, the point is that hamburgers are hamburgers to consumers, but they can be either a good or a service to data gatherers. According to official statisticians, a hamburger sold at a fast-food restaurant is part of a service, whereas hamburger sold at a grocery store is a good. Similarly, a computer is a manufactured good when sold to a household but is part of a service when leased by a time-sharing firm.

Interestingly because of the goods/services classification system, a truck driver is a manufacturing worker when he or she transfers intermediate products between plants in the same firm but is a service worker when, operating an independent business, he or she contracts with the same firm to make the very same deliveries. Finally, for example, a worker on an electronics assembly line is classified as a goods-producing (manufacturing) worker because he or she repeatedly attaches chip A to board B, whereas the worker sitting at a desk in an insurance claims office is classified as a service worker because he or she collates form A from pile B with form C in pile D. The "work" in the goods- and service-producing economies may, in other words, be very much the same.

Again, classifications are necessary to make sense out of the complex world. Having said that, however, we should recognize that arbitrariness of the goods/services classifications requires that considerable caution be exercised in drawing final conclusions from data contained in Figure 3.1. Many service workers are producing things that are no less "goods" than those produced by many goods workers. In other words, the official counts of goods and services can be only rough approximations of the "true" sizes of the goods and service economies. The emergence of the service economy may be as much an artifact of the classification system as it is a real phenomenon. If statisticians could separate the *true* service workers from the *true* goods workers in Figure 3.1, both employment patterns might slope upward significantly and, for all we know, follow much the same course, over time.

Second, the gradual development of goods—for example, washing machines and computers—leads to a reduction in the actual "material" content per unit produced. This means that the goods become, to an important degree, more a matter of intellect than substance. That is, intellect and creativity, the foundation of just about all services, is gradually substituted for substance. But, nothing that happens in the substitution process means that people are worse off; indeed, they are better off. Labor is still involved in the substitution process, only its form has changed, from "brawn" to "brains." Of course, this means that labor has to adjust, but it always has to adjust even in an expanding goods economy. Structural change in the economy did not begin with the current development in services. As long as different goods are produced, different types of labor will be needed, but, then again, the shift in the economy may be inspired by a willingness and demand by labor to shift its form.

Third, there seems to be a presumption among public-policy advocates that attention must be focused on the shift in production and employment from the goods to the service economy because goods are more valuable than services. Goods are real and tangible, whereas services are far less valuable because they are more ephemeral and cannot be as readily held, stored, and used at a later date. Such a position is hard to accept if it is assumed that the economic system is designed to satisfy wants and not to produce "real things." Furthermore, it is difficult to understand how many goods produced in the goods economy—for example, automobiles and cocktail napkins—are any more "real" (tangible or storable) than many services produced in the service economy—for example, house blueprints or computer programs.

Finally, there is the often unstated presumption that service workers do nothing more than "service" the real goods that are produced in manufacturing, construction, mining, and agriculture. In fact, it is hard to see, for example, how a service worker who moves a product from A to B (whether by truck, hand, or telephone line) is any less productive (in the sense that something valuable is accomplished) than a manufacturing worker who moves parts from one side of a plant (or desk) to the other or onto a truck. The fact of the matter is that textile mills are production units, but so are fast-food restaurants, accounting offices, and dry cleaners. Recognition of such elementary points should make policymakers wonder if the data in Figure 3.1 really suggest that the United States is "sacrificing its industrial base."

Third, it is hard to know exactly what causes the real concern over the development of the service market. Proponents seem to extol in flowery terms "basic industries" (by drawing attention to the plight of basic goods, steel and rubber), and to impugn in subtle ways "services" by always drawing attention to the more-or-less menial services such as laundry and fast-food meals. Perhaps services are viewed as less "important" to people's livelihood than goods, a point that must be disputed when consumers and firms have the freedom to choose what they want to buy. Perhaps by declaring certain industries "basic," reform proponents seek an emotional appeal for political policies. By treating their favored industries deferentially, they hope to ensure government subsidies and protection from competition.

There appears to be a presumption in public-policy discussion that the emergence of the service economy (captured in Figure 3.1) reflects the natural advancement of the economy from lower-order goods (that are goods) to higher-order services (that are often frivolous).[11] Perhaps these analysts view the emergence of the service economy as a movement up some imagined hierarchy of needs. In this hierarchy, the lower-order "physiological needs" are capable of being satisfied with physical, manufactured goods; the higher-order "self-actualization needs," capable of being satisfied with services that allow people to achieve "self-fulfillment," as, in the words of A. H. Maslow, "to become more and more what one is, to become everything that one is capable of becoming."[12] And reformists might worry that some people in the economy are becoming "self-actualized" with (frivolous?) services when others are being denied an adequate array of (basic?) physical goods.

Such an explanation of what is happening in the economy is not without merit. After all, it seems altogether reasonable to assume that as incomes increase, progressively less pressing needs will be satisfied. However, that does not mean that disproportionally more services that accommodate "self-actualization needs" will be purchased. The additional purchased services may be no more able (than goods) to "self-actuate" people. Many of the newly purchased services may, instead, meet other more pressing needs (physiological needs as well as psychological needs: to belong, to feel safe, or to have self-esteem and love) while (at the same time) they satisfy the less pressing needs of self-actualization. The additional services purchased with rising incomes may satisfy as many lower-order needs as higher-order needs. The purchase of laundry or accounting services is not always the sort of purchase that is self-actualizing; such purchases of services outside the home often permit people to become second-income earners (and at the same time, satisfy their lower-order needs).[13]

Fourth, the information on goods and service employment has been used to support false conclusions about the health of economic activity in the United States. When assessing the growing recorded split between service and goods employment, the following factual points developed with care in Chapter 2 need to be kept in mind:

• The rise of the service economy has not been accompanied by a contraction of the goods economy. U.S. gross national product (GNP) continues to record higher annual peaks. Although industrial production has not always moved steadily upward, the industrial-production index reached its all-time high in early 1988. The sale of manufactured goods has also continued to rise above previous peaks.

• Although manufacturing output has varied widely over the past several decades, the United States is far from "deindustrializing," even in a relative sense. After adjusting for the effects of inflation, the trend in manufacturing output as a percent of GNP has remained flat and between 20% and 24% for the past 40 years.[14] Indeed, the economy is *industrializing* in the sense that American industries are relying more and more heavily on capital for producing an expanding industrial output. It is deindustrializing *only* in the relative sense that industrial employment is falling as a percentage of the total employment, the achievement of an important goal of any economy: getting more industrial output with fewer workers, a mark of some distinction for a truly industrial society. As U.S. Department of Commerce economists Ronald Kutscher and Valerie Personick maintain,

> While some [20] manufacturing industries clearly have been in long-run decline, and the 1980–82 recessionary period may have accelerated their problems, our data indicate that the United States is not losing its industrial base. Most manufacturing industries, indeed most that would be considered "heavy" manufacturing, are at least expanding production, if not employment. Higher productivity has allowed domestic production of manufactured goods to increase without corresponding increases in employment.[15]

• Manufacturing production and employment have followed highly cyclical patterns over past decades. However, the trend in manufacturing employment has, for all practical purposes, been flat over the past two or three decades. Through 1995 the U.S. Bureau of Labor Statistics predicts some, albeit meager, increase in manufacturing employment.[16] In addition, there is, to date, no convincing evidence that the historical cyclical connection between the level of manufactured production and the overall level of economic activity has been broken to any statistically significant extent.[17]

• Change is endemic to economic life. However, frequently heard claims that the *pace* of economic change in the United States has accelerated has a highly dubious empirical foundation. Such claims have been made, citing statistics on the increase of service employment, but the growth in measured service employment has been under way for decades. An accelerating *pace* of change is not at all evident, even in Figure 3.1, or after more detailed analysis of changing employment patterns across all industries.[18]

• The widespread presumption that, in general, U.S. goods-producing firms are becoming less able to compete effectively in world markets should be doubted simply because of continuing growth in production of goods in the United States.[19] In a careful analysis, John Tatom, an economist with the Federal Reserve Bank of St. Louis, argues that the dramatic reversal of capital outflows from the United States and the increase in capital inflows to the United States in the early 1980s cannot be explained by conventional arguments that rely on high and increasing labor costs. On the contrary, Tatom argues that relatively recent changes in capital flows can best be explained by the growing competitiveness of U.S. firms as measured by, for example, decreases in per-unit labor costs of the United States.[20] One pro-competitive explanation for flow changes in foreign capital is that many U.S. firms offering investment opportunities (through the sale of stocks and bonds and real capital assets in this country) have outcompeted other domestic firms offering goods and services for the dollars of domestic and foreign residents. (More will be said about the competitiveness of the United States in Chapter 6.)

• The decline in the "production economy," as measured by the marked decrease in number of production workers in the manufacturing sector, fails to recognize that there are many "production and nonsupervisory workers" in the service economy. When production and nonsupervisory workers in manufacturing and the service-producing economy are combined, substantial growth in U.S. "production employment" can be observed. Indeed, between 1960 and the middle of 1985, the number of production and nonsupervisory workers in manufacturing and service-producing industries increased at an average annual rate of 2.8% and remained steady at approximately 75% of the labor force during the 1960–85 period.[21]

• Expansion of the service economy is due in part to the fact that goods-producing firms have begun to switch from internally supplied to externally supplied services. Goods-producing firms that have sought to "out-source" (or "contract-out" or "marketize") parts and entire product lines to outside suppliers (both domestic and foreign) can be expected to out-source many of their services for a large number of the same economic reasons.[22] A manufacturing firm, for example, may seek to out-source its accounting requirements simply because the outside cost is lower than the cost of the service delivered by the firm's internal accounting department. In other words, in its search for greater efficiency in production, the manufacturing firm may realize a comparative advantage in specializing in goods production, not service production. From this perspective, the growth of the service economy of businesses in the United States (even manufacturing firms) can be a sign of growing efficiency—and of competitiveness, the current national buzzword.

In short, much goods production is occurring in the economy under the service guise. Many of the jobs now being counted as a part of the service economy would have, in earlier times, shown up as jobs in the goods-producing economy, a point subsequently developed by considering the economics of the firm. As George Mason University economist Don Lavoie cautions, policy commentators should not forget that

> While it might damage some people's sense of patriotism to face the fact that America exports several agricultural products to Japan in exchange for manufacturing goods, surely this is a development with which mature adults can cope. It seems to me that our primary concern ought to be whether we *have* jobs and what the quality of life is that these jobs enable us to afford, not whether the goods we happen to be most efficient at producing might promote the symbolic image we have of ourselves.[23]

The Polarization of America

Has the relative expansion of services led to a "bimodal" income distribution? While this question is central to Chapter 5, a few major points developed there can be summarized here. In general, the answer to the above question to date is "Not very likely."

While average pay in the goods economy is higher than average pay in the service economy, many jobs in the service economy pay more than jobs in the goods economy.[24] The shift in employment from goods to services does not necessarily mean a reduction in the average pay of American workers. American incomes, on average, have not suffered as a consequence of the shift to services.

Furthermore, no credible argument leads us to expect that the country's income distribution is polarizing or that the country is losing, on balance, a large share of middle-income jobs. Proponents of the polarization argument seem to imagine that profit-greedy capitalists will walk away from highly productive workers who have kept their wages competitive (consistent with their productivity and alternative resource costs). The internal contradiction in the argument should be self-evident. By walking away from such employees, profit-greedy capitalists would be robbing themselves of profits. Proponents of the polarization argument also fail to see that firms often shift away from the use of labor, but the shifts are most often made in response to rising wages—and rising, not contracting, employment opportunities for workers.

In addition, proponents of the polarization arguments appear to believe that the service economy is emerging from the ashes of the industrial sector, that is, because displaced industrial workers have nowhere else to go. Clearly, many service firms do emerge at the site of shut-down industrial plants, and some displaced industrial workers seek service employment after they have been laid off from their goods-producing jobs, but such cases are far from typical. Many laid-off production *and* service workers end up reemployed in goods-producing jobs. Most service workers who relocate are attracted out of the industrial sector through important positive incentives: higher wages and fringe benefits, more interesting jobs, and better working conditions. Many workers have begun to seek service jobs because our massive public higher-education system trains few factory workers and makes the creation of service jobs (whether inside manufacturing firms or inside the service economy) so cheap that students cannot turn down the prospects of service employment. This is true even when the wages of service workers (for instance, schoolteachers) are depressed by the artificially inflated supply of service workers.

To the extent that growth in the service economy has been self-generating (that is, due to growing demands by consumers and firms for better and more cost-effective services), growth in the service economy can mean only higher-paying jobs for Americans—jobs that pay more than they would otherwise. There may be many low-income jobs created in the service economy, as Barry Bluestone and Bennett Harrison have maintained.[25] Yet what those two authors (and others) fail to see is that those service jobs are quite important to many low-income workers who, like other Americans, want improved employment opportunities.[26] In addition, *the growth in low-income jobs, even in disproportionate numbers, increases the demand for labor and puts upward pressure on worker wages—across much of the income spectrum.* Seen from this perspective, the relative growth in low-income jobs (to the extent that it has occurred) can only push up American income. The result might be an increase in the relative share of jobs at the low end of the income distribution, but that does not mean that workers across the relevant portions of income distribution are worse off because of the shift in job shares among income classes.

For the country as a whole, the available evidence on the polarization thesis is, at worst, mixed—and actually disputes the polarization thesis. According to a study conducted within the Bureau of Labor Statistics, if there is any general tendency in the loss of jobs across the income spectrum, the decline is in low-income jobs that are declining.[27] What appears to be happening in the employment patterns is a concurrent upward shift of employment toward higher-income categories and a slight downward shift of incomes within employment categories. The downward shift in incomes within job classifications can be partially explained by the arrival of the "baby-boom" generation to the work force and the relatively greater number of entrants in higher-income job classifications. The supply of "high-priced" labor has increased, imposing downward competitive pressure on wages in those higher-income classifications.[28]

To the extent that there has been a relative growth in low-wage jobs, reasonable explanation includes a variety of causes: growth in the rate of women participating in the labor force, expanding attraction of part-time employment, growth in nonreporting of income, the expansion of nonwage and nonsalary income, and increase in transfer payments that discourage high-income employment. The decline in the growth of higher-income jobs must be attributable, in part, to the increase in taxation, which discourages people from investing in human skills and capital assets that can create more income. Another cause of the decline is the growth in government regulations of all kinds, which, as expected, have imposed greater cost on businesses and reduced employment opportunities.

The Wealth of Nations

Much contemporary commentary on the rise of the service economy is, unfortunately, a throwback to *The Wealth of Nations,* in which the venerable Adam Smith mistakenly informed us that "the labour of manufacturing adds, generally, to the value of the materials which he works upon. . . . The labour of the menial servant, on the contrary, adds to the value of nothing."[29] The value of the menial labor cannot be recaptured in a later sale. Consequently, "a man [or country] grows rich by employing the multitude of manufacturers; he grows poor, by maintaining a multitude of menial servants.[30]

In the menial-worker group, Smith appears to have had in mind most (if not all) workers in the service economy. To Smith, government workers were clearly comparable to menial workers in most essential regards; however, "in the same class must be ranked, some of the gravest and most important, and some of the most frivolous professions: churchmen, lawyers, physicians, men of letters of all kinds; players, buffoons, musicians, opera-singers, and opera-dancers, etc."[31]

Like many modern commentators, Smith suggests that both "productive" workers (who generally seem to fit the description of goods workers) and "unproductive" workers (who generally seem to fit the description of service workers) must be maintained by the same "annual produce of land and labour of the country."[32] This implies a presumed limit to how many unproductive (service) workers can be maintained. Smith implicitly assumes that many of his listed service workers represent a net drain on the country's productive capacity; hence, the expansion of the service sector is part and parcel of a negative-sum game. This view, of course, contradicts the reality that services are as valuable to consumers as the goods they buy, asserts that services are often just as much goods as are "manufactured goods," and denies that services facilitate the production of both goods and services.

The Theory of the Firm and Growth in Service Employment

The central conclusion of previous sections is that the growth in the service economy thought to be accurately dramatized in Figure 3.1 may be explained, albeit partially, as an artifact of data gathering. Public-policy concern about the emergence of the "productionless" economy is, to that extent, exaggerated. This is not to say that the U.S. economy has not changed or that economic problems, one of which is persistent unemployment, do not exist. Of course not. (The prevalence of change was fully acknowledged in Chapter 2.) However, *measured* change may magnify (even grossly magnify) the extent of change in the composition of national output and accompanying employment requirements.

Nonetheless, there are many reasons for anticipating some rise in the "service economy," especially given the way the measurements are made. Several valid arguments have been widely recognized. For instance, the growing complexity and sophistication of goods *and* services has induced greater specialization in production and services. The growing complexity of accounting rules and laws and the development of the computer have, for example, given rise to independent accounting firms that handle a number of business clients. There are now payroll firms that do nothing other than compute, print, and distribute checks for manufacturing and service (even accounting) firms.

Improvements in communication, especially those relating to telephones and computers, may have disproportionally increased service employment because services may be more heavily dependent upon communications. Many services have traditionally been bound by time and place. Barber and cosmetology services are an obvious example of a class of services that requires the worker and the customer to be in approximately the same place at the same time. Improvements in communications may not materially affect the delivery of barber and cosmetology services (except to the extent that they facilitate the meetings). On the other hand, brokerage, accounting, travel, and a variety of other business and personal services have been greatly aided by enhancement of communications on a regional, national, or even international basis. (Brokerage services for the typical client can now be secured on a worldwide basis.)

Unions have traditionally dominated many key "basic industries" which have tended to be in the goods-producing sectors. Union wage and work-rule demands have caused capital to move from the union to the nonunion sectors, and services have historically been nonunion. The pace of growth in the services-producing economy (except in government) has not been extensively thwarted by union demands.

While explanations relating to communications, union influence, and government growth are important, there are other less obvious explanations that warrant more attention. These explanations relate to reductions in the cost of engaging in market transactions and developing legal biases against goods production.

Transaction Costs and the Theory of the Firm

The first explanation of why the size of the *measured,* as well as *real,* service economy can be expected to grow disproportionately to the goods economy again draws on the economic theory of why firms exist. The theory helps explain how growing international competition and decreasing cost of communications and transportation can lead to production fragmentation through out-sourcing.

The prototype of the ideally efficient firm is the much-maligned "hollow corporation." Such a firm, in a strict sense, "produces" nothing; it relies totally on outside sources for all parts and services and operates with minimum internal organization. By relying on outside sources for supplies, the "hollow firm" can at all times seek competitive bids on all parts and services and, through competitive forces, minimize its production costs. Unfortunately, reliance on external sources of supply can be costly, which explains why so few firms are, in fact, "hollow" (and why policymakers need not worry that hollow corporations will likely dominate many production processes).

Internally, firms are essentially nonmarket organizations that rely on structured commands (as opposed to negotiations) for getting things accomplished. Firms may exist for many reasons, but one of the more fundamental is reducing the costs incurred in consummating market transactions. Although often overlooked or ignored in conventional production theory, market exchanges are costly. Time, energy, and money are required to complete market exchanges and to insure that agreed-upon contracts are made with proficiency. Such costs, called "transaction costs," are especially high between contracting parties that are geographically distant because it takes considerable time to execute the contract. Consequently, production and service bureaus are maintained within firms to avoid the costs of negotiating exchanges on a continuing basis with external firms.

Firms (are said to) reduce transaction costs by substituting a hierarchical command structure for market transactions in order to increase profits of the firms. Many of the benefits of market competition may be lost in the process of forming firms, but, presumably, firms emerge and are able to survive by reducing, on balance, *net* production costs through reductions in transaction costs.

Management, of course, has an interest in minimizing the internal inefficiencies of its organizational structure. But in markets that are anything less than perfectly competitive, inefficiences are bound to arise. This is true for two reasons. First, there are costs in monitoring the internal organizational structure of a firm, in insuring that commands are obeyed and profits are maximized. Imprecision of monitoring will permit some inefficiencies (excessive costs or slack work).

Second, by creation of the firm, internal bureaus within firms (delivering parts and/or services) are, within limited bounds, established as sole-source suppliers of intermediate goods and/or services. In effect, these internal bureaus have a degree of monopoly power: they can be expected to exploit their monopoly power *to the extent that management fails to consider alternative outside sources of supply and to the extent that internal bureaus are hard to monitor.*

Among other considerations, attentiveness of management to external sources of supply will be dependent upon the competitiveness of final product markets of the firm, as well as the market's competitiveness in intermediate parts and services. The competitiveness of final and intermediate markets will, in turn, be dependent upon the extent of transaction costs. These costs can, in turn, be affected by communication and transportation costs—incurred by engaging internal and external sources of supply.

For many domestic firms, the widely heralded growth in the technology of producing goods and services (that has developed hand-in-hand with the internationalization of production) translates into growing competitiveness. Changes in both production technology and the internationalization of markets can impose greater price and quality pressures on management. As a consequence, management must search more diligently (that is, incur greater monitoring and search costs) for alternative, external sources of supply of intermediate goods and services. For both intermediate goods and services, increased attentiveness can be expected to lead to a relatively lower demand for internal sources of supply and a relatively greater demand for external sources.

In other words, the observed long-run relative decline in prices of goods produced in manufacturing (for example) could be expected to be a part of the competitive process that leads to greater out-sourcing (or threat of out-sourcing). The greater the fragmentation and internationalization of the economy, the greater the out-sourcing. The emergence of smaller intermediate manufacturing and service firms in the domestic and foreign economies can be anticipated. The (observed) increasing dominance of small firms in job creation in the United States should be expected in a period of growing international competitiveness.

Growth in intermediate manufacturing firms involved in the outsourcing process would still be measured as a part of the goods (manufacturing) economy. The goods economy would be expected to grow, but only to the extent that initially enhanced competitiveness and resulting out-sourcing spark decreases in the prices of final goods and increases in aggregate real income. Indeed, in the face of greater worldwide competition, measured employment in the *domestic* goods economy may actually decline (or grow at a slower rate) because of greater reliance on foreign sources of supply for intermediate and final goods.

The growing competitiveness of the goods sector, on the other hand, can be expected to lead to a disproportionate increase in the service economy. Out-sourcing of intermediate services may be no more dramatic than out-sourcing intermediate goods, but out-sourcing services results in a shift in production and employment from the goods economy to the service economy.[33]

There is no *a priori* reason for expecting the out-sourcing of services to be, necessarily, either more or less internationalized than goods. But we should not be surprised if a significantly greater share of the outsourcing of goods goes abroad, especially if the internationalization of production has been spurred by reductions in communication and transportation costs.

The line of analysis developed here suggests that reductions in the cost of communication could be expected to lead to increased reliance on out-sourcing of intermediate production, including services. Improvements in communication can expand the size of the market and increase the opportunities for specialization at all intermediate levels, but measured growth in the service economy would be disproportionately affected. The reduced transaction costs implied in the reduced cost and improved quality of communication would undercut the *raison d'être* of integrated firms.

This line of analysis has other implications. It suggests, for example, that deregulation of telephone service in the United States could be expected to lead to lower communication costs, improved ability of firms to engage in transactions with external goods- and service-producing units, greater out-sourcing of goods and services, and a relative expansion of the service economy.[34] Also, international events, like the break-up of OPEC (Organization of Petroleum Exporting Countries), which lower the cost of energy and transportation, could be expected to add to the disproportionate expansion of the service economy via reductions in the cost of transportation and communication—and greater reliance on out-sourcing.[35]

And it should not be forgotten that households are, among all else, producing units (in many substantive ways similar to firms), relying on resource inputs from household members (labor, for example) and from the market for intermediate goods and services (groceries and dry cleaning, for example). An increase in wages and employment opportunities for men and women (but for women especially, since women are the primary producers of many household goods and services) can result, and has resulted, in an increase in the relative price of home-produced goods and in a greater reliance on market-produced goods and services (a switch in home production that can also be viewed as a form of out-sourcing). As opposed to preparing meals from "scratch," household members can be expected, for example, to buy more meals out. They can also be expected to rely more heavily on services—dry cleaning and laundry, entertainment, and accounting services—that were once produced exclusively at home. The shift in production of goods and services from the home to the market will exaggerate the increase in employment, in income, and in possible reliance on services, especially since many of the market substitutes sought by households may be counted as services. This is because official statistics on employment, income, and services do not count what is done in the nation's homes.

Changes in the Institutional Environment

Growing reliance on out-sourcing can be stimulated by a host of factors, not all of which can possibly be considered here. Nonetheless, it is important to note that changes in governmental institutions can generally affect the extent of out-sourcing. Greater reliance on government, as measured by, say, government expenditures and taxes, can lead to greater uncertainty about the course of future economic events. With the changes in general market conditions, firms can be expected to cope with the possible instability by relying more heavily on out-sourcing and by using the external sources of supply as a means of expanding and contracting their labor force (and other resources). Greater reliance on out-sourcing in the face of growing uncertainty can be expected to be particularly evident in labor markets where the resource prices are not readily reduced—for instance, in the unionized sectors of the economy. As noted above, the out-sourcing process is likely to lead to a disproportionate growth in the service economy, simply because all out-sourcing of intermediate parts would stay within the measured goods economy.

In the contemporary legal environment in the United States, concentrated wealth within businesses carries a cost disadvantage that reduces the competitiveness of large firms. Concentrated wealth within firms represents a target that can be expropriated through lawsuits, not the least important of which are personal injury and wrongful death suits. Although hard data are scant, it is not unreasonable to deduce from observation of the legal process that in-court and out-of-court settlements for injuries and deaths have become more and more directly related to the size of the firm (measured roughly by profits and capital assets) under litigation, *ceteris paribus*. Given the mounting legal discrimination against large firms, we would anticipate a growing reliance on the fragmentation of production—for example, directly through breakup of firms or more indirectly through growing use of out-sourcing. The purpose of the greater out-sourcing would be to reduce the size of the legal target and, thereby, to cut production costs by cutting legal expenses and penalties.

Of course, none of these arguments means that the internal bureaus of firms will necessarily contract in absolute terms. The point is that disproportionate reliance on out-sourcing of services (and goods) can be anticipated. That is, external services can be expected to grow relative to internal services.

Obviously, there are good reasons to expect broad-based discrimination against goods production in the judicial system. By virtue of their intrinsic nature, goods are generally more easily defined than services and, thereby, more readily subjected to penalties by the legal system. (The prospect of penalties can give rise to more expenditures on legal defenses and less risky and higher-priced products.) The out-sourcing of intermediate goods encouraged by the legal system would, again, stay within the goods economy. The consequence of the intermediate goods out-sourcing would, on balance, likely be a marginal retardation in the growth of the goods economy, since the legal problems and out-sourcing would likely make production more costly. The measured service economy, on the other hand, might increase, in spite of the fact that the shift might also represent an increase in the costs of obtaining services.

What has caused firms producing goods to be discriminated against? As noted, because goods are readily defined, they represent relatively easier targets. In addition, the concept of "strict liability" (or liability without proof of fault or negligence) has been almost exclusively applied in the United States to goods and only rarely applied to services.[36] The legal discrimination against goods should have added disproportionally to the costs of producing goods and the fragmentation and relative contraction of the goods economy—and, therefore, to the relative expansion of the service economy.

Many other laws instituted in the 1960s and 1970s can be expected to discriminate against production of goods. The environmental movement, which led to stricter pollution controls (or restrictions on environmental resources largely used by goods producers), could have disproportionally increased the cost of goods production, retarding growth of the goods economy. Retarded growth in goods is especially likely since the pollution controls were more stringent for new entrants.[37]

Concluding Comments

The purpose of this chapter has been twofold. First, the commentary casts doubt on the reliability of reported data on the relative growth in the service economy. While it may be agreed that employment will, over time, become progressively concentrated in services, such an agreement may mean nothing more substantive than that people will gradually do different jobs, just as they have done different jobs, over time, within the goods-producing economy because of adjustments in market conditions. At all times, people will be engaged in *production* of things, whether labeled "goods" or "services," that satisfy wants. Granted, where robots are more effective, robots may gradually supplant workers, just as capital in other forms has historically supplanted people in order to enhance living standards. This trend in the replacement of people by capital will continue regardless of whether policymakers call the outputs goods or services.

Second, measured growth in the service economy is partly a reflection of real events—the production of more real services—but perceived growth is also a reflection of the ongoing, evolutionary (not revolutionary) changing structure of businesses. There are good reasons for expecting many political and legal, as well as economic, forces to alter organization structures of businesses, perhaps leading to the fragmentation of business and a relative expansion of the service economy. True reform in economic policy should, perhaps, start with identifying and eliminating governmental policies that discriminate in unwarranted ways against goods production.

How one views future policy toward the growth of services depends, in part, on the perception of the driving forces behind the data. If the growth in services is viewed as autonomous, uncontrolled by prices and society's drive to produce things that are wanted and needed, then greater government controls of the job-creation process may be warranted. However, if it is understood that the job-creation process is not a random walk, but is, in fact, the result of constraining market forces, further control may be unnecessary.

An implicit purpose of this chapter has been to suggest ways in which job creation in the goods and service economies is controlled, most often tolerably well, by market forces. From this perspective, solutions to observed labor-market problems may be found by removing institutional obstacles to the free flow of employment information within labor markets. Because the American job machine is nothing like the inner workings of a loom or typewriter, it does not depend on external sources of energy and controls. It is a self-generating process that derives its power, direction, and creativity from the parts—human beings, employers and employees alike—that make up the process.

Notes

1. See Ronald E. Kutscher and Jerome A. Mark, "The Service-Producing Sector: Some Common Perceptions Reviewed," *Monthly Labor Review,* April 1983, pp. 21–24; Michael Urquhart, "The Employment Shift to Services: Where Did It Come From?" *Monthly Labor Review,* April 1984, pp. 15–22; Ronald E. Kuitscher and Valerie A. Personick, "Deindustrialization and the Shift to Services," *Monthly Labor Review,* June 1986, pp. 3–13; and Patricia E. Beeson and Michael F. Bryan, "The Emerging Service Economy," *Economic Commentary,* June 15, 1986.

2. The service-producing sector includes transportation and public utilities, wholesale and retail trade, finance, insurance, real estate, business services, and government. The goods-producing sector includes mining,

construction, and manufacturing. For some purposes, agriculture is included in the goods-producing economy.

Goods-producing employment fell from 40.9% of the nonagriculture labor force in 1950 to 26.2% in November 1985. Manufacturing jobs fell from 33.7% of nonagriculture employment (equaling 82.3% of goods-producing employment) in 1950 to 20.6% of nonagriculture employment (equaling 78.9% of goods-producing employment) in November 1985. During the 1950–November 1985 period, service-producing employment rose from 59.1% to 73.8% of the nonagriculture labor force.

3. *National Journal,* July 27, 1985. However, it is worth noting that the magazine opened its discussion of the growth in the service-producing sector with commentary on the difficulty in defining what constitutes the "service sector" (Ibid., pp. 1724–25), suggesting that the magazine was not certain what it was welcoming.

4. See Larry Mishel. *The Polarization of America: The Loss of Good Jobs, Falling Incomes and Rising Inequality* (Washington: Industrial Union Department, AFL–CIO, 1986); and Barry Bluestone and Bennett Harrison, *The Great American Job Machine: The Proliferation of Low Wage Employment in the U.S. Economy* (Washington: Joint Economic Committee, U.S. Congress, December 1986).

5. Stephen S. Cohen and John Zysman, *Manufacturing Matters: The Myth of the Post-Industrial Economy* (New York: Basic Books, 1987), p. 3.

6. For a major set of proposals to solve the presumed training and retraining needs of American workers, see Task Force on Economic Adjustment and Worker Dislocation, *Adjustment Assistance in a Competitive Society* (Washington: Office of the Secretary, U.S. Department of Labor, December 1986). The Task Force recommends a new federal agency in the Department of Labor, alongside offspring state agencies that would spend an additional $500–600 million on retraining programs for displaced workers, those workers who have worked three or more years in their jobs before they are permanently displaced.

7. Felix G. Rohatyn as quoted in David M. Alpern, "Mr. Fixit for the Cities," *Newsweek,* May 4, 1981, p. 29.

8. John F. McGillicuddy, "The Corporate Pulpit," *The Corporate Board: The Journal of Corporate Governance,* July/August 1987, p. 1.

9. "Getting America Moving Again" (editorial), *Christian Science Monitor,* January 20, 1987.

10. Such statistical distinctions, of course, although important to researchers, will have no meaning to the people who seek to satisfy their wants and needs, including employment needs.

11. See Patricia E. Beeson and Michael E. Bryan, "The Emerging Service Economy," Federal Reserve Bank of Cleveland, *Economic Commentary,* June 15, 1986; and Colin Clark, *The Conditions of Economic Progress,* 3d ed. (London: Macmillan, 1951).

12. A. H. Maslow, *Motivation and Personality* (New York: Harper and Row, 1954), pp. 90–92.

13. Focus on a given hierarchy of needs developed by, say, Maslow may obscure the fact that the hierarchy was developed at a given time with given definitions of various needs and with given prices of ways to satisfy the needs. If prices of various ways had been different at the time of the survey, the ordering may have been substantially different. Put another way, movement up the hierarchy may reflect a change in relative prices of goods and services. Similarly, emergence of the service economy, in addition to reflecting higher incomes, may be explained by a decline in the relative prices of services (or an increase in the prices of alternative means of satisfying needs through purchased services). This point is more fully developed in Richard B. McKenzie and Gordon Tullock, *The New World of Economics,* 1st ed. (Homewood, Ill.: Richard D. Irwin, 1974), pp. 36–43.

14. Of course, real manufacturing output has never been a constant percentage of GNP. This is because manufacturing tends to be more affected by business cycles than other sectors of the economy. See Murray L. Weidenbaum, *Learning to Compete: The Feedback Effects of a Nonlinear Economy* (St. Louis: Center for the Study of American Business, Washington University, 1986), p. 27.

15. Kutscher and Personick, "Deindustrialization and the Shift to Services," p. 12.

16. Howard N. Fullerton, "The 1995 Labor Force: BLS' Latest Projections," *Monthly Labor Review,* November 1985, pp. 17–28; see also other related articles in this issue of the *Monthly Labor Review.*

Prior to 1987, BLS predicted a slight (0.4%) average annual increase in manufacturing employment through 1995. In late 1987, BLS released its new projections for various categories of employment to the year 2000. BLS now predicts a slight (0.3%) average annual rate of decline in manufacturing employment (Valerie A. Personick, "Projections 2000: Industry Output and Employment Through the End of the Century," *Monthly Labor Review,* September 1987, p. 32). Time restrictions on sending the book to the printers did not permit a full review of the change in the projected direction of manufacturing employment. The main concern is whether the new projection takes full account of the improvement in manufacturing employment (attributable to the depreciation of the dollar on international money markets and other factors) that had become fully evident in 1987. The central message of the text remains in place: manufacturing employment is not expected to change very much, either up or down, in terms of absolute numbers between the late 1980s and the year 2000. However, as a percentage of the labor force, manufacturing employment is expected to continue along its long-run downward trend.

17. The first and most complete empirical support for this point was developed by Robert Z. Lawrence, *Can America Compete?* (Washington: Brookings Institute, 1984). See also John E. Cremeans, "Three Measures of Structural Change," working paper (Washington: U.S. Department of Commerce, 1985); and Kutscher and Personick, "Deindustrialization and the Shift to Services." The continuing decline of manufacturing employment after

the recessions of the early 1980s may forbode a break in the tie that has bound manufacturing employment to the business cycle in the past. However, the history of the manufacturing sector, along with the two-year drop in the value of the dollar on international money markets, suggests that hasty conclusions are highly risky.

18. As noted in Chapter 2, if the pace of change had accelerated, then the correlation between the distributions of employment across all goods and service-producing industries would have fallen. That has not been found in the data. In fact, the correlation coefficient for 149 industrial classifications of employment between 1959 and 1969 was close to .98, which is approximately the same as the correlation coefficient between the employment patterns observed between 1969 and 1979 and the employment patterns recorded for 1979 and projected for 1990.

19. Also, it is important to remember that not all statements heard about the depressed state of several key manufacturing industries in the United States are true representations of the facts. Consider, for example, the U.S. textile and apparel industries. In real dollar terms in 1984, U.S. apparel production peaked and textile production was practically back to its peak of the late 1970s, in spite of what these industries in search of import protection called the "flood" of textile and apparel imports. Parts of the textile and apparel industries are in trouble, but the source of their trouble (as is true of other industries) is as much domestic as it is foreign. At fault are the substantial increase in textile and apparel productivity and the competitiveness of textile and apparel firms, many of which are foreign but many of which are also in the U.S. economy. (This point is developed in Chapter 7.)

20. John A. Tatom, "Domestic vs. International Explanations of Recent Development in U.S. Manufacturing," *Review* (St. Louis: Federal Reserve Bank of St. Louis, April 1986), pp. 5–18.

21. Richard B. McKenzie, *The Good News About U.S. Production Jobs* (St. Louis: Center for the Study of American Business, Washington University, 1986).

22. The expansion in the service economy is partially reflected in the decrease of the ratio between value added in manufacturing to manufacturing shipments. In 1970, that ratio was 47.3; by 1981 (the latest year for which data were available for this 1985 study), the ratio had fallen to 41.5 (or by 13%). See Richard B. McKenzie, *The Good News About U.S. Production Jobs,* p. 8.

23. Don Lavoie, *National Economic Planning: What is Left?* (Washington: Cato Institute, 1985), p. 179.

24. In fact, the average pay of all services was higher in 1985 than the average pay in textiles.

25. Bluestone and Harrison, *The Great American Job Machine.*

26. The value of low-wage employment to many workers is revealed in a survey of government-sponsored empirical studies of low-wage labor markets: Daniel J. Benjamin, Mark L. Mitchell, and John T. Warner, *Synthesis of Policy Implications from Studies of Low Wage Labor Markets* (Clemson, S.C.: Center for Policy Studies, Clemson University, February 1987).

27. Neal H. Rosenthal, "The Shrinking Middle Class: Myth or Reality," *Monthly Labor Review,* March 1985, pp. 3–10.

28. Patrick J. McMahon and John H. Tschetter, "The Declining Middle Class: A Further Analysis," *Monthly Labor Review,* September 1986, pp. 22–27.

29. Adam Smith, *An Inquiry into the Nature and Causes of the Wealth of Nations* (New York: Modern Library, 1937), p. 314.

30. Ibid.

31. Ibid., pp. 314–15.

32. Ibid.

33. In addition, many firms in the goods economy, finding their internal-service bureaus more competitive than external-service firms, can be expected to sell off, or spin off, their services to other firms — perhaps, from time to time, establishing their internal bureaus as independent businesses. Furthermore, employees in internal bureaus who are no longer able to secure rents from remaining internal parts of firms and yet are capable of being competitive with market rivals can be expected to move out to the service economy and offer their services back to the firms that once employed them.

34. The deregulation of the trucking, airlines, broadcast, and financial markets can also lead to greater fragmentation of markets.

35. Of course, relative improvements in the competitiveness of inter-mediate service producers, due to the various sources of reductions in trans-action costs, would likely be another source of relative expansion of the service economy.

36. For example, doctors and hospitals that provide services have been heavily sued. However, negligence must be proven. The point of the discussion is not that services have not been retarded by such suits but that their growth would have been even more retarded if the services had been subjected to the dictates of strict liability.

37. In addition, it may be worth mentioning that the Robinson–Patman Act, which forbade price discrimination in the sale of goods but not services, could have marginally reduced the efficiency of the goods economy and could have marginally increased the profitability of the service economy, resulting in a relative expansion of service production and employment. Many other examples of governmental discrimination against services could, of course, be cited.

CHAPTER 4

The Displaced-Worker Problem

Public-policy debates are frequently guided by official estimates of perceived social problems. This has been especially true of the continuing debate over the proper course for a redirected national labor policy dealing specifically with displaced workers and plant closings. This policy debate has been buttressed by two studies undertaken by the Bureau of Labor Statistics (BLS) and the General Accounting Office (GAO). These studies contain official counts for the incidence of worker dislocation and plant closings and define the prevalence and variety of termination benefits provided to workers.[1]

While most of us may consider numbers to be irrefutable, the BLS and GAO data are actually derived from parameters that necessarily constrain their usefulness. Unless appropriately understood, these numbers can misinform and mislead public decision-makers attempting to draw policy prescriptions from them.

The central purpose of this chapter is to contribute to the labor-policy discussion by critically analyzing the BLS and GAO numbers. More precisely, as has been true in all previous chapters, this chapter examines whether labor-market conditions actually support repeated claims, founded on the BLS and GAO studies, that the federal government should assume a new and expanded role in solving the adjustment problems of U.S. workers.

The Politics of Numbers

According to the AFL–CIO, the BLS and GAO studies "point anew to the need for federal legislation to require employers to show a degree of humane consideration for their workers." The AFL–CIO concluded that the evidence provided by these reports reinforces its own analysis that the U.S. House of Representatives made a "grievous mistake last November [1985] when it rejected a modest bill that would have required employers to give 90 days notice before closing a plant or laying off a large portion of the work force." The union's newsletter stressed that the "task force panel set up to explore 'the nature and magnitude of the problem' found that plant closings are not a dwindling problem, linked to a temporary recession, as some have argued." On the contrary, the "pace of worker dislocation has accelerated in recent years," affecting particularly minorities, women, higher-income, and older workers with years of tenure on their jobs.[2]

In subsequent deliberations concerning the future of the country's labor policy, Secretary Brock's Task Force on Economic Adjustment and Worker Dislocation, relying heavily on the BLS and GAO studies, concluded that the process of structural change in the United States

> has created a population of displaced workers, distinguished from other unemployed workers by the permanence of their job loss, as well as their substantial investment in the attachment to their former jobs. While displacement affects a broad spectrum of workers, it has tended to be concentrated in certain industries, occupations and geographic areas. As a result, mismatches between job need and job opportunity frequently occur, and some workers are more likely than others to experience difficulty in finding employment similar to that which they have lost.[3]

This conclusion was essential to the task force's recommendation that "new institutional mechanisms must be established as part of the nation's employment and training system to meet the needs of dislocated workers, including those workers covered by existing programs."[4] The "new institutional mechanisms" recommended included the creation of a federal Displaced Worker Unit along with similar state units. The task force also recommended a variety of additional or expanded federal retraining programs and "tripartite advisory committees" composed of representatives from unions, businesses, and government. (See Chapter 2.) The task force also recommended that additional payroll taxes be considered, if general revenues could not cover the cost of its proposed programs.[5]

After surveying the GAO findings on the amount of notice given to workers, the U.S. Office of Technology Assessment (OTA) also endorsed proposals that would require firms to provide workers with significant notice of plant closings. The OTA suggested that "there is broad consensus that advance notice is a humane thing to do, and that notice facilitates effective displaced worker programs."[6] Similarly, the Committee for Economic Development, composed of senior executives of many of America's largest corporations, has expressed support for new broad-based changes in the nation's labor policy, in part because of the total number of displaced workers and of plant closings reported by the BLS and GAO.[7] Their conclusion—that a redirected national labor policy is needed—appears to be founded on five basic propositions or suppositions:

1. The displaced-worker problem is large and national in scope.
2. Many displaced workers are unemployed for extended periods of time and receive limited termination benefits (for example, pre-notification of plant closings, severance pay, and outplacement services).
3. Legislated governmental remedies will improve worker welfare.
4. Given the magnitude of the displaced-worker problem, states and local communities cannot solve it working alone. Federal programs are needed.
5. Current resources available to the federal government are likewise inadequate.

To what extent these suppositions are correct remains the policy question.

The Nature and Scope of the Displaced-Worker Problem

The federal government does need a national labor policy, if for no other reason than that workers and employers alike need to know what to expect from their government. However, there remains considerable debate over just what that policy should be.[8]

The fundamental question is whether responsibility for adjusting to changing product and labor-market conditions should reside chiefly with individual workers and their local representatives in the work place or with their political representatives in Washington. Given the political dimensions of this policy issue, a key factor in determining the locus of responsibility for dealing with job displacement is the extent of the problem itself. This returns us squarely to the original problem: Precisely what are the Bureau of

Labor Statistics and the General Accounting Office telling us—or not telling us—about workers who have been "displaced" from their jobs?

The Definition of a Displaced Worker

Measuring the scope of the displaced-worker problem naturally requires a definition of a "displaced" worker. A displaced worker could be viewed as anyone who is unemployed, in which case the count would be several million each year. (For example, the count of unemployed workers exceeded 7 million in early 1987.) However, such a count of the unemployed includes teenagers who have newly entered the labor force (and have yet to be displaced from a job), workers who have been laid off and expect to return to their old jobs, and workers who are voluntarily changing jobs.[9]

Ordinary use of the term "displaced worker" is typically not meant to include everyone considered to be "unemployed." Conversational use of the term is usually applied to someone who is not a teenager and has more or less permanently lost a job. And for several years, the BLS has been counting those people (who represent a subset of the total number unemployed).

Without considering the total number of people who are employed and the length of time they have been employed, the displaced-worker problem would indeed appear severe. According to the first BLS survey, 13.9 million workers 20 years of age and older lost their jobs in the period from January 1979 to January 1984. In the latest BLS survery covering the period from January 1981 to January 1986, the count of displaced workers was down slightly to 13.1 million. (See Table 4.1.) Of the latter total, 10.8 million were "permanently" separated from their jobs, meaning they were not expected to be called back to work.[10] This figure certainly gives the impression that the displaced-worker problem is extensie. However, if this figure is recast in terms of the number of workers displaced in any given year, displaced workers represented less than 2% of the total annual labor force during the January 1981–January 1986 period.

The concept of a displaced worker generally connotes something more than a worker who has permanently lost his or her job. The above count of displaced workers includes many workers who may have been displaced from jobs that they may have held for only a short time, even as little as a few weeks. Typically, a "displaced worker" is viewed as someone who loses a job that has been important to his or her livelihood for some time. Job tenure represents an investment in the job and service to the company; therefore, it is generally presumed

Table 4.1 Estimates of the Number of Displaced Workers, 1981–86 (millions of workers)

Total number of workers who lost their jobs in the 1981–1986 period	13.1
Less: Workers who lost jobs for seasonal or other miscellaneous reasons	–2.3
Total number of workers "permanently" separated	10.8
Less: Workers with job tenure of one year or less	–4.1
Workers with job tenure between one and three years	–1.7
Total "displaced" workers — persons with more than three years tenure "permanently" separated from their jobs	5.1
Less: Workers with job tenure between three and ten years	–3.4
Total displaced workers with at least ten years job tenure	1.7

Labor Force and Employment Status in January 1986 of Workers "Displaced" in the 1981–86 Period

Total number of displaced workers	5.1
Employed	3.4
Unemployed	0.9
Not in the labor force	0.8

Note: "Total workers 'permanently' separated" refers to workers 20 years of age and older who lost their jobs between January 1981 and January 1986 because of plant closings or permanent layoffs. Displaced workers include those workers in this group who had three or more years of tenure in their jobs at the time of their termination.

Source: The calculations are based on William J. Gainer, *Dislocated Workers: Extent of Closures, Layoffs, and the Public and Private Response,* GAO/HDR-86-116BR (Washington: U.S. Government Accounting Office, July 1986), text and tables.

that serious economic consequences may result from loss of employment associated with significant job tenure.

What constitutes "significant economic consequences" associated with losing a job can be subjectively appraised only by the affected worker and cannot be assessed by official counts. Government officials make their assessments of the hardship of workers, but such assessments may have little relationship to the workers' own views of their hardships.

Counting the number of years workers have remained at a given job is only a rough method of defining significant economic consequences of job losses. Workers with long years of service may have invested little in their jobs. Others with few years of tenure may have made significant investments by developing skills and improving productivity. The public debate can be grossly biased by the abundance of easily measured data because they lack reliable data on actual worker welfare.

But even the available figures can present a clearer picture of the problem if we take into account the amount of job tenure. Of the 10.8 million permanent job losers between January 1981 and January 1986 (a fact mentioned earlier in this chapter), 4.1 million workers had one year or less job tenure.[11]. Another 1.7 million workers had from one to three years of seniority, leaving approximately 5.1 million job losers with three or more years on the job.[12]. This 5.1-million count of "displaced workers" is the one emphasized by the authors of the three BLS statistical reports and other researchers.[13]

Again, the number seems large, but the average number of displaced workers per annum represented less than 1% of the annual labor force during the period (or less than one-eighth the average unemployment rate). If the concept of the displaced worker is restricted even further, limiting it to, for example, permanent job losers with more than ten years of job tenure, the count of "displaced workers" falls to under 1.7 million for all five years, which amounts, on average, to less than 0.3% of the annual labor force.

If the definition of what constitutes a displaced worker is further limited to the older workers who are 55 to 65 years of age and have 10 of more years of service with a given firm, the displaced-worker group encompasses less than 0.1% of the average annual labor force for the period.[14] Public concern over the displaced-worker problem has often been aroused not by reports of young workers with relatively few years on their jobs, but by reports of older workers with few transferable skills losing their jobs after many years of service. Once they have lost their jobs, younger workers presumably have more time and opportunities to reorient their careers through education and to recoup their retraining investment.

Another factor overlooked in the popular reports on the displaced-worker problem is that many of these workers were not permanently unemployed. Some were out of work for only a matter of weeks. Of the total 5.1 million displaced workers (those with at least three years of job service), 67% had been reemployed by January 1986, when the survey was undertaken, and 16% had left the labor force, for example, to retire, work at home, or enter the underground economy. Many of the remaining displaced workers had not had sufficient time to search for a job. The continuing recovery of the economy from the recession of the early 1980s should further increase the reemployment of the displaced workers. In January 1984, when the survey was first taken, only 60% of the workers displaced in the January 1979–January 1984 peirod had been reemployed.[15]

This is not to say that there were no workers permanently displaced in the 1981–86 period who experienced hardship. Many experienced long-term unemployment and some even remained unemployed in early 1986. Unfortunately the data cannot tell us how many of these workers were older employees with significant tenure and no other major source of income or how long such an individual was out of work.

The Displaced-Worker Problem Through Time

The raw BLS data does indicate that the problem was "growing" from 1979 to 1985. (See Table 4.2.) There were 500,000 displaced workers with three or more years of job tenure in 1979 and 1.3 million in 1985.

Table 4.2 Number of Displaced Workers Compared to the Total Labor Force and to Total Job Losers, 1979–85

	1979	1980	1981	1982	1983	1984	1985
Number of displaced Workers[a] (thousands)	500	619	775	1,082	949	971	1,349
Percent of labor force	0.5%	0.6%	0.7%	1.0%	0.8%	0.9%	1.1%

[a]Includes workers 20 years of age and older who lost their jobs to plant closings or permanent layoffs and who had three or more years on the job they lost.

Source: The number of displaced workers for 1979 and 1980 drawn from Paul O. Flaim and Ellen Sehgal, Displaced Workers of 1979–83: How Well Have They Fared? (Washington: U.S. Bureau of Labor Statistics, Department of Labor, July 1985). The number of displaced workers for 1981–85 were obtained by telephone from Richard Devins, Bureau of Labor Statistics, U.S. Department of Labor (March 10, 1987). The data on the number of displaced workers by year needs to be interpreted with considerable care. The counts of displaced working for overlapping years in studies conducted in 1984 and 1986 are significantly different.

Although a small fraction of total employment, the official count of displaced workers was also expanding as a percentage of the labor force—from 0.5% in 1979 to 1.1% in 1985.

Does this mean that the displaced-worker problem is becoming more severe? It is difficult to answer this question from study of only the 1979-85 pattern of displacement counts. During the early 1980s, the economy was moving through a serious recession, with significant growth in job losers of all kinds. The recovery was still under way in January 1986. During the 1979-85 period, the official count of displaced workers fluctuated as a percentage of all job losers. More importantly, the reliability of the BLS data is disputed even by BLS researchers, who have found that the annual counts of displaced workers differed dramatically, by more than 20% up or down, when the surveys were repeated.[16]

Granted, there has been an upward trend in the unemployment rate and in the percentage of the unemployed who are job losers. However, it cannot be concluded from such trends that the displaced-worker problem is accelerating. Much more needs to be known to analyze this issue. We need to know changes in the composition of the labor force (age, sex, and race characteristics, for instance), income levels and distribution, prevalence of two-earner families, and changes in unemployment compensation and other unemployment relief, etc. Without this information it is mere speculation to suggest that the adjustment problems of American workers are becoming more severe.

In fact, the amount of time that a worker is unemployed can very well be inversely related to the hardship experienced. Workers with higher incomes and wealth can afford to search longer for more attractive jobs. Income expectations may encourage greater selectivity in the type of job and benefits they will accept. In families with two or more wage earners, the member who is unemployed may be able to "afford" a longer period of unemployment.[17]

Another reason for withholding judgment on the extent of the displaced-worker problem is the brief period of time covered by the data —1979-85. As a result of all the changing economic conditions in this period, we simply do not know whether the observed displacement pattern reflects transitory problems associated with public-policy changes and the business cycle or reflects an accelerating pace of fundamental structural changes.[18]

We do know that the composition of the nation's jobs is changing. As stressed in Chapter 3, the service industry, which has provided much of the nation's past job growth, is expected to continue providing many of the new jobs. Little or no job growth has occurred over the past two to three decades in manufacturing. Employment in specific manufacturing industries, such as steel, shoes, textiles, and apparel, continues to follow a downward trend. But many of these changes have been more "evolutionary" than "revolutionary."

As stated in Chapter 2, the notion of a speedup in the *pace of change* in employment and production patterns has been greatly exaggerated by proponents of an expanded federal role in labor markets.[19] Change, whether inspired by technology or international competition, has always been prevalent in the U.S. economy. As proponents of labor-policy reform stress, much current change in production and employment patterns in the country is a consequence of, for example, new computer and robotic technology. However, the economy has continually had to respond to earlier technological breakthroughs such as electricity, sewing machines, automobiles, drugs, and assembly-line techniques.

While the charge is often made that the pace of change is accelerating, little substantive, nonanecdotal evidence is available to support such claims. (See Chapter 2.) Manufacturing employment continues to move up and down with general economic conditions around a flat no-growth trend more or less the way it has for decades.[20] Service employment is on a steady upward trend.[21] The composition of the labor force is changing, but the changes projected through 1995 by the BLS do not offer evidence of any radical shifts in sectorial employment.[22]

The Role of Plant Closings in Worker Displacement

Plant closings have frequently been blamed for worker dislocation.[23] The BLS survey (evaluated above) found that nearly half of the displaced workers lost their jobs because their plant or company closed or moved.[24] In developing policy recommendations for the National Commission for Employment Policy, Wayne Vroman maintains that

> it is now widely recognized that job termination associated with plant closings, technological advances and changes in consumer demand have become more frequent in the past decade than in the years before the energy crisis of 1973–74. . . .
>
> In recent years, dislocation has become more widespread because the rate of job loss has increased, because many of the jobs that were eliminated were "good" jobs.[25]

The GAO Survey

The General Accounting Office has provided the first solid count of plant closings.[26] The official purpose of GAO's survey was to assess the distribution of plant closings by industries and regions and to determine the extent of the notice of plant closings and unemployment services provided by firms to their workers (for example, severance pay, extended health insurance, and job-search aid). Such information can presumably aid members of Congress and the administration in formulating improved policies to remedy the private and social consequences of plant closings.

The GAO survey covered a random stratified sample of 2,400 firms from a list of 28,000 firms that, according to the Small Business Administration, "appeared to have either closed or had a permanent layoff involving 20 percent of their workers (or 200 employees for establishments with 1,000 or more workers) during 1983 and 1984."[27] Through telephone calls, the GAO researchers determined that about 600 (or 25%) had actually experienced a closure or permanent layoff. Thus the GAO estimated that during each of the two years, about 8,800 establishments with 50 to 99 employees and 7,400 establishments with 100 or more employees experienced a closure or layoff, affecting 1.3 million workers annually.[28]

In addition, the GAO found in its original report that, while the manufacturing sector accounts for 35% of business establishments with 100 or more employees, manufacturing accounts for 60% of the closures and layoffs. This means that during the two years 13.2% of the nation's estimated 35,000 manufacturing establishments with 100 or more employees closed or had a permanent layoff.[29] The Northeast and Midwest experienced a relatively large number of closures and layoffs, partly because those regions have a disproportionate percentage of the country's manufacturing and nonmanufacturing establishments. It would, of course, be unusual if the distribution of plant closings were evenly distributed across the country.

The distribution of the closures across regions is shown in the accompanying map (Figure 4.1). For example, the GAO estimated that the Northeast (covering New England and Mid-Atlantic states) lost almost 1,900 establishments, or 24% of the total firms with 100 or more employees that closed in the 1983–84 period. However, because there are so many establishments in this region, the closing and layoff rate for establishments with 100 or more workers was only 9.3% for the New England states and only 6.9% for the Mid-Atlantic states.[30]

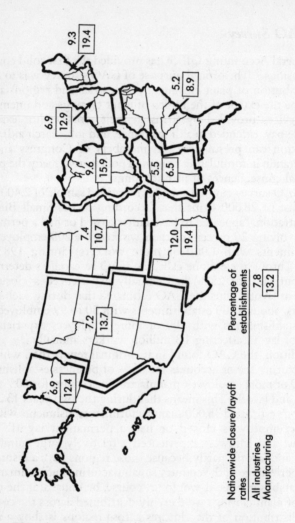

Fig. 4.1 Regional distribution of closures/ layoffs for firms with more than 100 employees, 1983 and 1984. (*Source: William J. Gainer, Dislocated Workers: Extent of Closures, Layoffs, and the Public and Private Response,* GAO/HDR-86-116BR [Washington: U.S. Government Accounting Office, July 1986.] p. 14.)

Finally, the GAO found that many firms provide their employees with little or no notice of pending plant closings or layoffs. One of the most damaging observations made by the GAO researchers in the preliminary version of their study is that "most establishments (66%) with 100 or more employees said they provided 14 days or fewer advance notice to their workers. About one-third of the establishments provided no advance warning to their employees."[31]

As Table 4.3 reports in detail, most workers also received few termination benefits.[32] For example, slightly more than half of the affected workers received severance pay. Only 43% of the affected workers received continued health insurance, and only 31% were assisted in their job search by their firms. Such data convince some

Table 4.3 Assistance Offered White-Collar and Blue-Collar Workers at Time of Plant Closing

Type of Assistance	Establishments Offering Assistance to Workers	
	White-Collar	Blue-Collar
Financial Assistance		
Severance pay	57	37
Continuation of health insurance	48	38
Continuation of life insurance	30	22
Early retirement	19	11
Pay in lieu of notice	14	9
Lump-sum payment	12	10
Supplementary unemployment benefits	10	11
Placement assistance		
Job search	35	26
Administrative support	29	21
Personal counseling	22	15
Company transfer option	23	11
Time off for job search	26	12
Career counseling	22	15
Relocation assistance	18	6
Testing/assessment of worker skills	6	4
Occupational training	3	4
Job club	2	2

Source: William J. Gainer, *Plant Closings: Information on Advance Notice and Assistance to Dislocated Workers,* GAO/HDR-87-86BR (Washington: U.S. Government Accounting Office, April 1987), pp. 8–11.

people (including many members of the Department of Labor Task Force on Economic Adjustment and Worker Dislocation) that workers are not treated well at plant-closing time. The task force noted in its report, "Many employers, particularly larger ones, appear to feel an obligation to provide assistance to displaced workers and may have the capability to do so. On the other hand, many employers appear to do little or nothing before, during or after a closing or permanent mass layoff."[33]

The Shortcomings of the GAO Study

Such data are being used to justify a more active federal role in ensuring that workers are provided with basic closing and layoff benefits.[34] Nonetheless, this case is far more fragile, both empirically and conceptually, than it might at first appear.

There are several empirical shortcomings of the GAO study. First of all, methodological biases are built into the survey. The survey concentrated on relatively *large* firms that appeared to have experienced a closing. Second, and more telling, regional closing rates are poor indicators of overall economic health. Regions with high closing rates in the GAO study could also be regions with high rates of plant openings and many expansions of old plants.[35] If regional economic distress is measured by rates of plant closings, then other regional economic variables—for example, income growth and employment rates—should be significantly and inversely related to regional plant-closing rates. On the other hand, regional unemployment rates should be directly related to plant-closing rates. In short, as plant-closing rates rise in a region, income and employment growth rates should fall and unemployment rates should rise.

However, no correlation is demonstrated when statistical analysis is applied to the data for regional plant-closing rates, unemployment rates, income-growth rates, and employment-growth rates for the 1983–84 period. (See Table 4.4 in the addendum to this chapter.) In other words, the GAO data on plant-closing rates do not show that higher closing rates result in higher regional unemployment rates or in reduced economic activity in the region.

The third weakness in the GAO survey is that it reports only the percentage of workers involved in a plant closing or permanent layoff who received a specified list of closing, unemployment, and reemployment benefits, even though plant-closing benefits can come in great variety. In addition, the GAO tabulation might suggest to the unwary reader that the employers who did not supply the specified benefits did something "wrong." The implication is that some explicit or implicit contractual agreement was violated.

Employers may have provided their workers with a variety of benefits that are not covered in the necessarily limited GAO tabulation. The value of these benefits may even have exceeded the value of the benefits listed in the GAO survey.

The determination of wrongdoing by employers hinges on whether firms actually violated their (explicit or implicit) labor contracts — for example, made misrepresentations about their closing policies. A firm that promises to provide closing and termination benefits can anticipate paying a relatively lower wage than firms that do not. If a firm reneges on such a promise, workers are denied benefits to which they are legally entitled and for which they sacrificed current income, a problem that few would deny deserves legal remedy.

On the other hand, a firm that offers no closing benefits can expect to pay higher wages in exchange for greater flexibility in closing plants and laying off workers. In effect, the workers are compensated for the closing and layoff risks they assume.

The GAO survey sheds no light on this critical issue. When the GAO official in charge of the study was asked if any of the surveyed businesses in the study had actually violated implicit or explicit contracts, he admitted that they had never investigated the matter.[36]

In addition, the GAO was actually playing political (literally deceptive) games with its final report. While the matter was left unacknowledged in the final report, the GAO in its preliminary report stressed that its survey sought to report the percentage of workers who were given "general" and "specific" notice of a pending plant closing.[37] The report of 66% of the surveyed firms providing 14 days or fewer advance notice to their workers refers solely to those firms giving "specific" notice, a fact that is nowhere evident in the final report. The GAO conveniently did not report that 80% of its surveyed firms gave "general" notice, 55% of which gave more than two weeks notice and 35% of which gave at least a month notice. The editors of *Regulation* magazine, which caught the GAO's slip of numbers, found that "When both general and specific notice are taken into account, the number of establishments giving notice rises to 88 percent, with almost 60 percent providing more than two weeks."[38]

Granted, there were 12% of the workers in the GAO survey who received neither "general" nor "specific" notice. However, it does mean that the workers did not have any advance warning that their plants were about to close. Employers often provide notice that may not be deemed "official" by workers or the GAO. From rumors and direct observation of work schedules, financial statements, and other outside financial services, employees typically have much advance information about their firms' pending official decisions.[39]

Finally, the GAO survey says nothing about how many firms provided the listed benefits at the time of the closing or, for that matter, how many of the workers actually needed, or even wanted, termination benefits. If all workers need job-research assistance (which is highly doubtful), then the percentage of workers who received help might be viewed as "low." On the other hand, if only a third of the workers need the various forms of assistance, then the percentage receiving them might be viewed as quite "high." Nor is there any information on the effectiveness of the outplacement services provided.

A presumption behind suggestions that workers "should have" specific termination benefits is that these benefits can be provided at more or less zero cost to the employees or that, if there is a cost, workers would still gladly pay for the benefits. For many worker groups, this simply may not be the case. If workers would gladly pay for the benefits, then employers could trade off these closing benefits for lower wages and would not resist providing them.[40]

Ignoring the current market mechanisms to provide termination benefits has led to a variety of proposals for government-mandated solutions to the presumed "market failure." Some would require workers to establish retraining accounts. Others would mandate that firms act more "responsibly" and "humanely" by providing specific termination benefits (notice of a given number of days and severance pay equal to a given number of weeks' wages, weighted by tenure with the firm). Unfortunately, these inflexible requirements would mean that employers would need to reduce other benefits not on the mandated list, including current wages and fringe benefits. These concerns will be explored in greater detail in Chapter 10.

Concluding Comments

Statistics are often instructive, but they can also be misleading. The data reported by the BLS and GAO are far less instructive on what to do about plant closings and worker displacement than has been commonly asserted. The BLS figures that purport to measure the number of displaced workers suffer from two basic flaws: (1) they are based on data from a brief time frame (1979–86) that includes a severe economic recession, and (2) the official designation of a displaced worker—a person with more than three years' tenure whose job has been eliminated—is often erroneously associated with the stereotype of an older worker with few marketable skills and little or no private means of coping with adjustment problems. The BLS study simply cannot be used to make the case that the displaced-worker problem is growing rapidly or that the hardships being experienced require federal intervention in labor markets.

The GAO data on plant closings likewise suffer from such problems as defining prenotification and limiting the survey to a predetermined list of closing benefits presumed to be effective in easing the burden of dislocation. When the closing rates for various regions are com-

Table 4.4 The Impact of Regional Plant Closing Rates on Regional Economies, 1983 and 1984

	Dependent Variables (percent)		
	Change in Total Employment	Unemployment Rate	Change in Personal Income
c	3.093	10.414	13.492
	(1.08)	(4.15)	(5.29)
	[0.32]	[0.01]	[0.01]
Frequency of all plant closings	0.037	–0.135	–0.536
	(0.10)	(–0.43)	(–1.69)
	[0.92]	[0.68]	[0.14]
R^2	0.002	0.026	0.290
c	0.002	11.499	11.335
	(1.26)	(5.77)	(4.63)
	[0.25]	[0.01]	[0.01]
Frequency of manufacturing plant closings	0.022	–0.160	–0.151
	(0.13)	(–1.12)	(–0.86)
	[0.90]	[0.30]	[0.42]
R^2	0.002	0.152	0.096

(T statistic)
[Significance level]
Source: Author's calculations based on plant-closing counts reported in William J. Gainer, *Dislocated Workers: Extent of Closures, Layoffs, and the Public and Private Response,* GAO/HDR-86-116BR (Washington: U.S. Government Accounting Office, July 1986), p. 14.

pared to other economic data implied to be related—unemployment rates and job-creation rates—no statistically significant relationship can be demonstrated. High rates of manufacturing-plant closings do not mean that a regional economy cannot be growing in other sectors.

These important limitations to the BLS and GAO studies need to be acknowledged if policymakers are to avoid the pleas of special interests that the federal government intervene in labor-management relations. The irony is that many of the advocates of more federal involvement have ignored the inevitable trade-off involved in providing specified termination benefits to workers. It is naive to continue to believe that there is a "free lunch" available to either employees or firms.

With the current emphasis on "competitiveness" of U.S. industry and the importance of labor and management cooperation to compete effectively in the international marketplace, it seems oddly out-of-step to legislate how these parties can interact. Businesses and workers need an improved capacity to cope with adjustment problems and to take advantage of new opportunities. Many policymakers and leaders who are supposedly most interested in the welfare of working men and women are advocating a labor policy agenda that would hamstring the ability of our relatively free labor markets to meet this challenge.

APPENDIX

A common presumption in policy studies of regional economic changes is that the frequency rates of plant closings are a useful measure of relative regional economic health. If that were the case, then regional economic variables—for example, income growth and employment rates—should be significantly and positively correlated with the regional plant-closing rate, and the regional unemployment rate would be significantly and negatively correlated with the regional plant-closing rate. That is to say, as plant-closing rates rise across regions, the income and employment growth rates should fall and the unemployment rate should rise.

However, as evident in Table 4.4, one-variable regression equations do not support such contentions. When regional unemployment rates, income growth rates, and employment growth rates for the 1983–84 period are used as the dependent variables and frequency of regional total plant closings and manufacturing plant closings (reported in

Figure 4.1 in the text) are used as dependent variables in separate equations, there is no statistically significant relationship that can be identified with any reasonable degree of confidence in any of the equations. In other words, a higher plant-closing rate is not statistically correlated with increases in regional unemployment rates or with decreases in regional employment or with income growth rates.

Notes

1. The initial BLS study on the number of displaced workers between 1979 and January 1984 was reported by Paul O. Flaim and Ellen Sehgal, *Displaced Workers of 1979–83: How Well Have They Fared?* (Washington: U.S. Bureau of Labor Statistics, Department of Labor, July 1985). This initial displaced-worker study was first updated to January 1985 by Richard M. Devins, "Displaced Workers: One Year Later," *Monthly Labor Review,* July 1986, pp. 40–43. This initial study was again updated to January 1986 (without the name of an author), "Reemployment Increases Among Displaced Workers," new release of the Bureau of Labor Statistics, U.S. Department of Labor, USDL 86–414 (October 14, 1986). The first GAO study on termination benefits was reported by William J. Gainer, *Dislocated Workers: Extent of Closures, Layoffs, and the Public and Private Response,* GAO/HDR-86-116BR (Washington: U.S. Government Accounting Office, July 1986). A similar study of termination benefits provided workers in plants closed during the last half of 1985, not covered in this report, can be found in Bureau of Labor Statistics, U.S. Department of Labor, "Analysis of Mass Layoff Data" (Washington: U.S. Department of Labor, January 1987). The final version of the GAO study of termination benefits was reported in William J. Gainer, *Plant Closings: Information on Advance Notice and Assistance to Dislocated Workers,* GAO/HDR-87-86BR (Washington: U.S. Government Printing Office, April 1987).

2. "Plant Closings Revisited," editorial, *AFL-CIO News,* May 10, 1986, p. 7.

3. Task Force on Economic Adjustment and Worker Dislocation, *Economic Adjustment and Worker Dislocation in a Competitive Society* (Washington: Office of the Secretary, U.S. Department of Labor, final report, December 31, 1986), p. 11.

4. Ibid., p. 4.

5. For a critique of the labor-policy recommendations offered by the task force, see Richard B. McKenzie, *A Misguided Search for a National Labor Policy* (St. Louis: Center for the Study of American Business, Washington University, January 1987).

6. Office of Technology Assessment, U.S. Congress, *Plant Closing: Advance Notice and Rapid Response* (Washington: U.S. Government Printing Office, September 1986), p. 4.

7. Research and Policy Committee, *Work and Change: Labor Market Adjust-*

ment Policies in a Competitive World (Washington: Committee for Economic Development, December 1986), pp. 23–25.

8. The labor-policy agenda outlined in Task Force on Economic Adjustment and Worker Dislocation, *Economic Adjustment and Worker Dislocation in a Competitive Society,* stands in sharp contrast to the labor-policy agenda by Richard B. McKenzie, *U.S. Employment Opportunities in a Competitive World Economy: Positive Approaches to a New Labor Policy Agenda* (St. Louis: Center for the Study of American Business, Washington University, July 1987).

9. The definition of an unemployed person has several interesting characteristics. It includes anyone who says he or she is looking for work but is not working. A teenager who professes to be looking for work, but is not employed, is defined as being unemployed. If that same teenager were not looking for work, he or she would not be classified as a part of the labor force (as being either employed or unemployed). However, a person who is not working and is not looking for work is also classified as being unemployed so long as he or she is within 30 days of reporting to a new job. (The same person is not counted as a part of the labor force if he or she is more than 30 days away from taking a new job.)

10. Bureau of Labor Statistics, "Reemployment Increases Among Displaced Workers" (see note 1), p. 1. The total number of displaced workers in the January 1979–January 1984 period was 6.5% higher, or 11.5 million. Paul O. Flaim and Ellen Sehgal, *Displaced Workers of 1979–83* (see note 1), p. 1.

11. The breakdown of the displaced-worker data is examined by Marvin H. Kosters, "Job Changes and Displaced Workers: An Examination of Employment Adjustment Experience," *Essays in Contemporary Economic Problems, 1986: The Impact of the Reagan Program,* edited by Phillip Cagan (Washington: American Enterprise Institute, 1986), pp. 275–305.

12. The count of "displaced workers" was exactly the same in the January 1979–January 1984 period: 5.1 million (Flaim and Sehgal, *Displaced Workers: 1979–83,* p. 1).

13. See Flaim and Sehgal, *Displaced Workers: 1979–83*; Devins, "Displaced Workers: One Year Later"; Bureau of Labor Statistics, "Reemployment Increases Among Displaced Workers." The 5.1-million count of displaced workers has also been stressed by the Task Force on Economic Adjustment and Worker Dislocation, *Economic Adjustment and Worker Dislocation in a Competitive Society*; Research and Policy Committee, *Work and Change: Labor Market Adjustment Policies in a Competitive Society*; Office of Technology Assessment, *Plant Closing: Advance Notice and Rapid Response*; Ronald E. Berenbeim, *Company Programs to Ease the Impact of Shutdowns* (New York: Conference Board, 1986).

14. The published data are broken down only in age categories of 20 to 54, 55 to 65, and above 65.

15. Flaim and Seghal, *Displaced Workers: 1979–83,* p. 6. Interpretation of these data for the BLS's "longitudinal survey" must be made with care and understanding of the survey's limitations and defects, the most important of which is that the exact same people are not interviewed from year to year. In

fact, a maximum of only 75% of the respondents in the 1985 survey were a part of the survey in 1984. Furthermore, the surveyors are required to question the people at given residences at the time of the interview, not the actual people questioned in previous years. Finally, "other sources of difficulty include respondent bias (answering identical questions differently when there is no change in status), interviewer error, transcription mistakes, processing problems, and noninterviews" (Devins, "Displaced Workers: One Year Later" (see note 1), p. 42.

16. For example, the 1984 survey found that the displaced-worker counts for 1981 was 833,000, and for both 1982 and 1983, 1,195,000. The 1986 survey counts for the same years were 775,000, 1,082,000, 949,000, respectively. The BLS simply cannot explain the wide variations in the reported data, other than the fact that the counts are dependent upon the accuracy (or lack thereof) of recall of the interviewees (reported by Richard Devins, Bureau of Labor Statistics, U.S. Department of Labor, by telephone, March 10, 1987).

17. For this reason older workers, who tend to have higher incomes and greater wealth, might be expected to remain unemployed for longer periods than younger workers. Because wealthier older workers can live without a weekly paycheck, a longer job search might for them make more economic sense.

18. Our study in Chapter 2 certainly casts doubt on any proposition that the pace of change is accelerating and is, therefore, contributing to the displaced-worker problem.

19. See Murray L. Weidenbaum with Richard Burr and Richard Cook, *Learning to Compete: Feedback Effects of the Non-Linear Economy* (St. Louis: Center for the Study of American Business, Washington University, 1986); and Richard B. McKenzie, *The Good News About U.S. Production Jobs* (St. Louis: Center for the Study of American Business, Washington University, 1986).

20. See Robert Z. Lawrence, *Can America Compete?* (Washington: Brookings Institution, 1984).

21. As studied in Chapter 3, the highly touted rise of the "service economy" may actually be more a product of the way data are collected rather than a fact of structural change.

22. The Bureau of Labor Statistics reports only modest shifts in the composition of the labor force before 1995. See Howard N. Fullerton, "The 1995 Labor Force: BLS's Latest Projections," Valarie A. Personick, "A Second Look at Industry Output and Employment Trends to 1995," and G. T. Silvesti and J. M. Lukasiewicz, "Occupational Employment Projections: The 1984–95 Outlook," *Monthly Labor Review,* November 1985, pp. 17–57.

23. For an extended discussion of plant-closing legislation, see Richard B. McKenzie, *Fugitive Industry: The Politics and Economics of Deindustrialization* (San Francisco: Pacific Institute, 1984), and Richard B. McKenzie, editor, *Plant Closings: Public or Private Choices?* 2d ed. (Washington: Cato Institute, 1985).

24. The remainder lost their jobs because of a lack of work (38.7%) or because their position or shift was abolished (12.4%) (Flaim and Sehgal, p. 7).

25. Wayne Vroman, "Innovative Developments in Unemployment Insur-

ance," *Research Report* (Washington: National Commission for Employment Policy, February 1985), p. 34.

26. Gainer, *Plant Closings: Information on Advance Notice and Assistance to Dislocated Workers.*

27. Ibid., pp. 1 and 2.

28. The GAO originally estimated that the total number of workers dislocated each year in all establishments, including those with 0 to 49 workers, was 2.3 million (Gainer, *Dislocated Workers,* pp. 10–11).

29. Ibid, p. 11.

30. Ibid., pp. 12–13.

31. Gainer, *Plant Closings: Information on Advance Notice and Assistance to Dislocated Workers,* p. 3. These estimates are dramatically higher than those originally reported in William J. Gainer, "GAO's Preliminary Analysis of U.S. Business Closures and Permanent Layoffs during 1983 and 1984," a paper presented at an Office of Technology Assessment/Government Accounting Office Workshop on Plant Closings (Washington, April 30–May 1, 1986), pp. 16 and 29.

32. Ibid., p. 18.

33. Task Force on Economic Adjustment and Worker Dislocation, *Economic Adjustment and Worker Dislocation in a Competitive Society,* p. 3.

34. Ibid., pp. 22–27.

35. Because resources are scarce, the expansion of some industries draws resources away from other industries, forcing permanent layoffs (and reduced operations) and plant closures. Many plants that are closed are simply not as efficient as many of the new plants or plants that expand. For the details of this line of argument, see Richard B. McKenzie, *Free to Lose: The Bright Side of Economic Failure* (St. Louis: Center for the Study of American Business, Washington University, 1986).

36. In response to questions posed by the author to William J. Gainer, associate director, Human Resources Division, U.S. General Accounting Office, who presented his research findings to the Private Response Subcommittee of the U.S. Department of Labor Task Force on Economic Adjustment and Worker Dislocation (Washington: U.S. Department of Labor, May 6, 1986).

37. A central problem in interpreting the results of surveys of the amount of notice given is that "notice" necessarily carries a very precise definition, although the GAO has not yet published the official definitions. All the GAO has said on the subject is that "a general notice is intended to provide workers and the community with some advanced warning but does not specify the exact date or the particular workers to be affected. A specific notice, on the other hand, informs individual workers that their employment will be terminated on a specific date" (Gainer, "GAO's Preliminary Analysis," p. 17). In other words, some unspecified (but necessarily precise) official action must be taken by the employer before "notice" is identifiable. Of course, many firms may have given their employees "notice" that did not fit the GAO's definitions.

38. "Pink Slips and Politics," *Regulation,* no. 1, 1987, p. 11

39. Obviously, which firms give notice and how much notice they give varies with who does the counting. Indeed, the GAO findings on plant-closing "announcements" sharply contrast with the findings of another recent plant-closing survey undertaken by the Conference Board, which used a different definition of "notice" (Ronald E. Berenbeim, *Company Programs to Ease the Impact of Shutdowns* [New York: Conference Board, 1986]. The author found that in 88% of the 224 plant closings covered in the survey, firms gave "some notice"; "over half of the shutdowns were announced more than three months in advance. And the 54 companies [almost one-quarter] that notified their employees more than six months in advance were significantly more likely to offer retraining and outplacement programs" (Ibid., p. 8). The Conference Board survey, however, was restricted to larger firms and relied more heavily on voluntary responses than did the GAO survey. However, editors of *Regulation* magazine found that by recomputing the GAO notice numbers approximately 88% of the firms covered in the GAO study received some form of notice ("Pink Slips and Politics," *Regulation,* no. 1, 1987, pp. 10–12).

40. This line of argument is more completely developed in Chapter 12 of this book.

CHAPTER 5

The "Great U-Turn" Reconsidered

The distribution of income in the United States has always been changing. Over the country's economic history, the median income has tended to creep along an upward trend. At the same time, intermittent cyclical, erratic, but modest swings in the median income have occurred as significant numbers of people have moved up and down the national income scale. Such distributional changes in income are altogether expected, over time, given people's persistent efforts to improve their individual welfares, the changes in technological and natural resources, and the inevitability of economic successes and failures in a dynamic economy.

Members of the media and policy think tanks and proponents of many labor-policy changes, which would rely more extensively on government guidance, fear that the American job machine has inadvertently slipped into reverse. They maintain that the nation's income distribution is being radically changed along with the nation's industrial structure. They charge that America is losing ground in its struggle to raise workers' incomes and that the "middle class" is in danger of extinction—unless Congress acts decisively.

Without hesitation, a reporter for a leading business periodical concludes, "The American standard of living is slipping."[1] An economist for the Urban Institute quipped, "The young middle class has experienced a dramatic decline in its ability to pursue the conventional American dream: a home, financial security, and education for their children."[2] Senator Lloyd Bentsen (D-Texas) worries that 'American workers will end up like the people in the biblical village who were condemned to be hewers of wood and drawers of waters."[3] Similarly, a labor attorney for the United Electrical, Radio and Machine Workers of America laments,

> Instead of a secure middle class we have an American working class whose wages are dropping, whose good jobs are disappearing and whose whole families have to work to make ends meet. Much of the vaunted middle class is looking at a future closer to the under-class nightmare than the American dream, but the unemployment figure on the nightly news remains the mark by which we measure the well-being of the people who actually do the work in this country, rather than those who simply devise new ways to profit from their investments.[4]

As noted in earlier chapters, the policy actions that reformers advocate include increasing by a substantial amount the legal minimum wage, subsidizing job training, fortifying collective-bargaining rights, and controlling plant closings, subsidizing both plant openings and worker buyouts of their firms.

The brewing public debate over the future direction of labor policy raises two questions: What are the facts on the alleged reversal of economic progress? And, would the recommended policies actually remedy perceived problems? This chapter analyzes the statistical foundations of growth-reversal fears and evaluates the policy solutions that have been proposed. Following chapters deal more specifically with policy recommendations to remedy the perceived reversal in the job machine.

Competing Policy Visions: A Matter of Modes

A country with a dynamic economy is unlikely to have a static distribution of income. Nonetheless, throughout people's economic adjustments to changing market and social conditions, the country's income distribution has tended to shift up and to remain approximately "bell-shaped." This means that the distribution of income in the United States has had a relatively large "middle class." Most people have had incomes close to the median level, which evenly divides the income distribution into halves. Only a relatively small percentage of the population has had incomes far below or far above the median.

The mere existence of income growth, especially for the "middle class," has presumably added stability to the polity and may have encouraged economic growth and the consolidation of the middle class. After all, past growth is a foundation of hope for future growth, and hope for a brighter future can encourage current investment and future income growth and, consequently, can reduce the need to redistribute the national income to improve the welfare of many in the low-income classes.

Furthermore, if most Americans are relatively close in income, their political and economic views cannot, presumably, be poles apart. Such disparity might induce wide and disruptive swings in government policies. In order to be elected and reelected, most politicians must cater to the interests of the relatively stable and prevailing middle class, or so it has been thought.

One of the more intriguing and seriously debated propositions in the emerging social politics of the 1980s is that the U.S. economy is in the process of making a "U-turn" on the road of economic progress.[5] According to proponents of this view, the current generation of Americans is, in effect, standing witness to a broad-based decline in its welfare. This decline is caused in part by the "deindustrializing" of the economy that, in turn, is leading to the destruction of the middle class and, possibly, the underpinnings of the democratic process as experienced over the past two centuries.

Partly as a consequence and partly as a cause of the reversal of economic growth, social analysts worry that the nation's income distribution is gradually losing its bell-shaped, single-mode appearance. Indeed, it is becoming "bimodal"—or, perhaps less technically, "polarized." That is, middle-skilled and middle-income jobs are eroding. The reformers contend that the new jobs that are taking their places in labor markets are all too often either low-skilled and low-income or high-skilled and high-income. Unless current trends are quickly reversed, the country's income distribution in the not-too-distant future will be distinguished not by a middle class but by its absence: by a "missing middle."[6]

The missing-middle thesis presents a substantial challenge to contemporary policymakers, for "what is at stake," states one business publication, "is the American dream of a decent job and comfortable existence."[7] The humanitarian concern is that large numbers of Americans have found their financial standing and sense of self-worth damaged by the loss of their middle-class status, while the economic concern is that incentives to save, invest, and work have been destroyed as the hope of self-improvement has evaporated.

The policy fear is that unless government becomes a far more active, expansive, and creative force—guiding structural change and the boundaries of domestic and international competition in the economy—the United States will continue its shift from long-term growth to long-term decay. The country's political stability might then unravel and people's economic and political interests diverge as their incomes decrease. With hope for economic improvement repressed by the reversal of growth, the only social issues worth contemplating might then be how to divide the "economic pie," rather than how to expand it. Economic decay can be self-perpetuating, given the prospects that resources might be progressively reallocated from expanding the nation's productive capacity to expanding its redistributive activities.

The "great U-turn" hypothesis, coupled with the missing-middle thesis, amounts to the proposition that in fundamental ways the American economy is becoming unglued at its core. Needless to say, the data, analytical techniques, and policy conclusions of the proponents of the missing-middle thesis need to be carefully examined. Before we accept the proponents' interventionist conclusions, we should at least know if there has been a "U-turn" in economic welfare—if the middle class is, indeed, beginning to disappear, and if many proposed interventionist policies are, in fact, warranted.

In short, we need to understand the extent and sources of our economic problems before solutions, especially ones that represent radical departures from past policies, are contemplated. Unfortunately, while the proponents of radical reform cite some impressive facts on economic decay, their selectiveness in choosing the facts to be studied leads them down the wrong analytical and policy roads.

The Economic Reversal

The upward trend of median family income has generally been persistent over long stretches of time. In 1947 median family income, measured in 1985 dollars, was approximately $14,900. By 1960, the median was nearly 38% greater, a little more than $20,400 in constant 1985 dollars. By 1980, the median had again increased in real terms by another 32%, or to $27,400.

However, as proponents of the U-turn hypothesis stress, isolated figures on the long-run trend hide the significant oscillation of the median family income around the trend, especially in the 1970s and 1980s. Indeed, as evident in Figure 5.1, median family income (top curve), once rising in real terms, has leveled off and, since the last half of the 1970s, appears to have reversed course. In 1985 median family income was just over $27,700, barely above the 1980 level and significantly below the 1973 constant-dollar peak of nearly $29,172.[8] What is particularly surprising is the fact that family income began to fall during a period in which the labor-force participation rate of family members was rising. This means that a growing number of family members may have been involved in earning the deteriorating family incomes.[9]

The statistical picture developed for the median-income family is more or less duplicated in data for the median income of year-round, full-time male workers. As shown in Figure 5.1, the median income of male workers in 1985 was recovering from the slump experienced during the twin recessions of the early 1980s—but was still 10% below its 1973 peak. On the other hand, by 1985, the median income of year-round, full-time female workers was 2% ($355) more than the preceding high in 1978. Although the median family-income level has been significantly lower in all years since 1973, the modest upward trend and the general stability in the median income of female workers

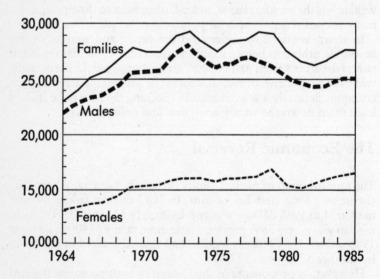

Fig. 5.1 Median income of families and year-round, full-time male and female workers (1985 dollars). (*Source: Economic Report of the President*, 1987.)

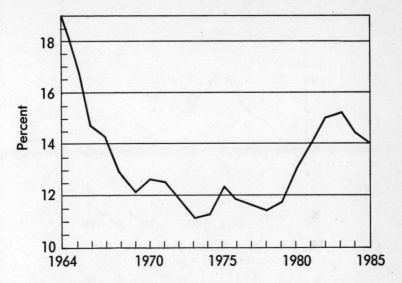

Fig. 5.2 Percentage of population below poverty income level. (*Source: Economic Report of the President*, 1987.)

has apparently moderated, to a limited degree, the irregular downward movement of the median family income.

In Figures 5.2, 5.3a, and 5.3b, which cover the poverty rate and hourly and weekly earnings of production (and nonsupervisory) workers, the general reversal in income trends is made even more dramatic (by intentional, careful selection of scales for the vertical axis). The poverty rate—defined as percentage of the population with incomes below the official "poverty level"—was 19%, the high point in 1964 (as shown in Figure 5.2) During the 1960s, the country appeared to be on the road to abolishing poverty, at least as measured by the poverty rate. By 1973, the poverty rate had descended to slightly more than 11%, only to move back up to a new high of more than 15% in 1983 and then back down slightly again in 1984 and in 1985. By 1985, the *number* of poor people was still over 33 million, 17% below the number of poor in 1960 but 44% above the low count of 23 million in 1973.

Obviously, a part of the explanation for the reversal in the median family income is the relative growth in the number of poor families over the past decade, which has pulled down the median. However, a more telling, albeit partial, explanation for the decline in the median

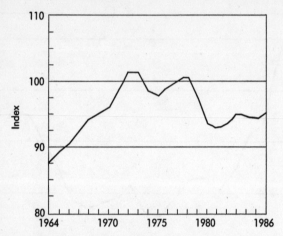

Fig. 5.3a   Index of hourly earnings for production workers (1977 = 100).

family income lies in the deterioration of workers' average real-
earning power. Figures 5.3a and 5.3b depict the changes in average
hourly and weekly earnings of production workers. The index of
hourly earnings graphed in Figure 5.3a peaked in 1972 at 101.2, and
was, therefore, 1.2% above the hourly-earnings index of the second
peak year, 1977, the base year. However, the income reversal was
clearly evident by 1986 when the index was down to 94.9, more than
5% below the 1977 hourly earnings base.[10]

Average real gross weekly earnings of production workers, which
combine the effects of both changes in hourly pay rates and hours
worked, rose during the 1960s only to peak at their all-time high in
1972 at slightly above $358 (in constant 1986 dollars). However, the
average weekly pay rate then generally decreased, with wide swings,
until 1986 when it was below $305, a drop of over 15% in average
purchasing power of income over the 13-year period.

Obviously, the distribution of money earnings has changed.
Standard monetary measures of economic progress do suggest that the
welfare of many people may have suffered. The most important
analytical question is "Why?" "Why the apparent reversal in economic
progress?" Unfortunately, the answers are many. Nevertheless, one of
the more prominent explanations offered by reform-minded analysts
is that the income distribution has undergone a radical restructuring,
shifting from a unimodal to a bimodal distribution.

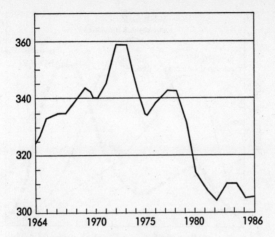

Fig. 5.3b Average weekly earnings of production workers (1986 dollars). (*Source: Economic Report of the President*, 1987.)

The "Missing-Middle" Thesis

The income distribution is normally expected to be "bell-shaped." This means, as explained at the beginning of this chapter, that most people can be expected to have incomes close to the mean, which will tend to be close to the median-income level, and that only a relatively small number of people can be expected to have incomes far removed from the mean and median levels. Indeed, the bell-shaped income distribution also means that there is only one mode-income level, the most frequently observed income level. This single mode has generally been thought to be reasonably close to the mean- and median-income levels.[11]

Such a "bell-shaped" income distribution is pictured by the dark line in Figure 5.4. While the shape of the curve can be spread out to a lesser or greater extent than the one drawn, there are important reasons for expecting the income distribution to have a bell shape.

Bell-shaped distributions, wherever they occur, often depend heavily upon randomness in the structure of events. And people's incomes are heavily dependent upon many random considerations, not the least of which is the distribution of genes within the population. Genes help determine the income distribution through their effects on

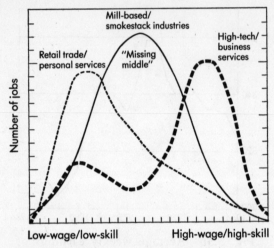

Fig. 5.4 The "old" and "new" wage and skill structures. (*Source:* Barry Bluestone, "Industrial Dislocation and Its Implications for Public Policy," *Displaced Workers: Implications for Educational and Training Institutions,* edited by Kevin Hollenbeck, et al. [Columbus, Ohio: National Center for Research in Vocational Education, 1984], p. 53.)

height, weight, strength, endurance, health, intelligence, etc.—that is, through human characteristics that affect individual productivity and earnings capacity. Incomes are also heavily dependent upon luck, which is, almost by definition, a random force in the economy.

However, the bell-shaped distribution of income can also be molded by purposeful economic forces. People plan their working careers, investments, and business ventures based in part on "expected values" of conceivable outcomes, and the mean outcome is often understandably viewed as the most likely and reasonable outcome. When people have exceptionally high incomes, other people move into their markets, seeking to duplicate the labor service and, in the process, drive down the pay rate. When the pay of many people is depressed, the wage rate can only be pulled up as the supply of the labor service is reduced.

The point is that a bell-shaped, unimodal distribution is generally expected and, in that restricted sense, may be viewed as part of the natural order of the economy. However, reformers argue that the natural order of things is breaking up; the economy is restructuring in radical ways through a process of "deindustrializing," brought on by wanton "capital flight," growing global "competitiveness," the emerging "service economy" and "information age," accelerating technological advances, and unchecked "corporate greed" (topics covered in preceding chapters). The perceived loss of manufacturing jobs (estimated at between 500,000 and 3 million, depending on the dates covered by the analysis) should be of concern (we are told) because "the majority of the newly created jobs are poor substitutes for the ones that are disappearing. A dramatic transformation in the structure of the entire national job distribution is responsible for a serious mismatch between the skills and income needs of displaced workers and the skill requirements and wage levels of the new jobs."[12]

In addition, within the growing employment sectors of the economy—for example, retail trade and personal services and high-tech and business services—the modes for the employment distribution are radically different from the modes in the collapsing mill-based smokestack industries, or so it has been argued. "In contrast to the auto industry," writes economist Barry Bluestone,

> the computer industry lacks a large, semiskilled, well-paid middle. Similarly, retail trade has developed a polarized distribution of jobs, with a well-paid bureaucracy comprised of managers, buyers, advertisers, and accountants at the top, and part-time, poorly paid sales clerks at the bottom. Again, no middle analogous to the blue-collar assembly worker in the auto industry or in the steel industry exists.[13]

According to Professor Bluestone, who has discussed the missing-middle thesis with a set of curves similar to Figure 5.4, the job structure of the retail trade/personal services looks like the dashed curve that is skewed to the left, while the job structure for the high-tech/business services has the more complicated bimodal appearance of the dashed curve with the higher peak in the right half of the graph. If the job market continues to restructure in the manner indicated, the two "humps" of the retail trade and high-tech industries will eventually dominate the national employment picture. Then, the middle-skilled/middle-paid workers, to secure a livelihood, will be caught in the "missing middle" with only unattractive employment opportunities, and perhaps the public coffers.

The evidence offered in support of the missing-middle thesis is not complete, of course, since the research topic is just a few years old. The more rudimentary evidence on the possible emergence of the missing middle comes from Bureau of Labor Statistics (BLS) reports on the number of jobs that are expected to be created in various occupations during the 1980s and 1990s. For example, *Atlantic Monthly* contributor Robert Kuttner relies on BLS estimates of the employment distribution by occupations between 1979 and 1990.[14] From the BLS projections, many low-income jobs will be created, including, for example, nurse's aides and orderlies (508,000), janitors (501,000), sales clerks (479,000), and secretaries (700,000).

However, such statistics do not necessarily support the missing-middle thesis. Because there already exist many nurse's aides, orderlies, sales clerks, and secretaries, the large numbers of new low-skilled jobs will not, according to the complete projections of the BLS, significantly alter, in percentages, the overall distribution of jobs before 1990.

Indeed, BLS projections even cast some doubt on the view that manufacturing employment will change very much in terms of the absolute number of jobs counted in 1990 or 1995. We noted in Chapter 2 that according to the BLS, manufacturing employment will expand at an average annual rate of 0.6% between 1984 and 1995 (not much, but something).[15] Yet even then, the lack of more growth in manufacturing jobs may be partially a matter of the way manufacturing employment is counted. Many service jobs that were once done for manufacturing firms by in-house departments, and, thereby, have in the past been counted as a part of "manufacturing employment," have been contracted-out to service-industry firms that can accomplish the service tasks more efficiently.[16]

While there is some evidence that the earnings distribution of department stores is unimodal and skewed toward the low-income jobs,[17] the distribution of earnings in one important high-tech industry, computers, appears to be reasonably "normal"—that is, bell-shaped. Even if individual industry studies do show cases of emerging "bimodalism" or shifts in the income distribution toward lower-income jobs, it does not follow that the *country's* job distribution is developing the same pattern or is even shifting to any appreciable extent. The individual changes could be offsetting, just as they may have been before the rising concern over the missing middle.

Neal Rosenthal, BLS researcher, has evaluated the missing-middle thesis with data on the employment status of full- and part-time wage and salary workers in 416 occupations in 1973 and 1982.[18] His study first involved ranking the occupations by earnings in 1982 and arranging them into thirds (top, middle, and bottom), with each third

Table 5.1 Employment Distribution by Occupational Structure (percent)

Earnings Group	Percent Distribution of Employment	
	1973	1982
Top third	26.3	29.0
Middle third	34.0	33.4
Bottom third	39.6	37.6

Source: Neal H. Rosenthal, "The Shrinking Middle Class: Myth or Reality?" *Monthly Labor Review,* March 1985, p. 4.

containing the same number of occupations. He then counted the number of workers in the occupations in each third and computed the distribution of employment by percentage. Finally, to assess the shift in occupational structure, he arrayed the employment by occupation in 1973 in the same order as in 1982 and determined the percentage distribution for 1973. The findings are reported below in Table 5.1.

Clearly, there was some deterioration in "middle-class" jobs, but not much, only 0.6 of a percentage point. Nevertheless, contrary to what would have been expected from the missing-middle thesis, employment in the bottom third fell by 2 percentage points, while employment in the top third rose by slightly more. If the data point to any restructuring of jobs, the movement is generally up, not down or to both ends of the employment spectrum.

Rosenthal recomputed the jobs distribution, but this time he also arrayed the occupations according to earnings in 1973, divided the ranking into thirds, counted the number of workers in each third, and compared the percentage distribution in 1973 with the percentage distribution obtained for 1982. The results reported in Table 5.2 once again indicate some shift in the percentage distribution over the ten-year period, but what is notable is that the bottom third falls significantly at the same time that the top two-thirds rises. These findings are hardly what one would expect from the perspective of the missing-middle thesis. Furthermore, when Rosenthal applies his analytical techniques to the expected employment patterns for 1995, he concludes:

> The projected data are consistent with the findings for the 1973–82 period. Namely, they show an increasing proportion of employment in higher-than-average earnings occupations and a declining

proportion in occupations with lower than average earnings, rather than a trend toward bipolarization.[19]

The Rosenthal results stand in slight contrast to the findings of Brookings Institution economist Robert Lawrence who found evidence of polarization in the 1969–83 period. Lawrence concluded that the observed structural shifts were largely a result of the baby-boom generation beginning to enter the labor forcre.[20] Patrick McMahon and John Tschetter, however, have been able to offer evidence that reconciles the Rosenthal–Lawrence studies.[21] These two economists, following Rosenthal, found that, grouped into thirds, there has been an upward shift in structure of employment. Nonetheless, there has also been a detectable downward shift among occupations within the broad occupational groups, and this downward shift in occupational composition may be explained partially by the baby-boom effect, once again leaving the missing-middle thesis in some doubt.

The Proliferation of Low-Wage Jobs

The proponents of the missing-middle thesis cannot be satisfied with scant evidence of slight downward shifts in the structure of jobs over time, even though such shifts were evident in the data. As noted at the start, change in the distribution of jobs has been endemic to the economy. Crucial to the missing-middle thesis is the proposition that there either is, or soon will be, a "serious mismatch" between the abilities of displaced workers and the skill requirements and wages in the new

Table 5.2 Employment Distribution by Occupational Earnings Structure in 1973 and 1982 (percent)

| | Percent Distribution of Employment | |
Occupational Group	1973	1982
Top third	27.7	29.0
Middle third	28.9	33.4
Bottom third	43.4	37.6

Source: Neal H. Rosenthal, "The Shrinking Middle Class: Myth or Reality?" *Monthly Labor Review,* March 1985, p. 4.

jobs, resulting in something that policymakers might view as an unreasonable depreciation of living standards.

Finally, it must be remembered that growing bimodalism, in and of itself, is not necessarily "bad," despite the fact that it may be considered "unnatural." Positive economic forces, which may give rise to bimodalism, could be more than offset by natural forces which may be guiding the economy toward a bell-shaped curve. At the same time that two, three, or half-a-dozen modes are developing in the distribution, the whole income distribution could be shifting upward. Indeed, bimodalism might be nothing more than a stage in the development of a more level distribution of people among jobs of different-skills requirements and of relative-income potential.

No matter how the jobs distribution is changing, the crucial policy questions are: "How fast are the structural changes occurring?", "Cannot people cope with the change on their own?", and "Are people in general actually better off or worse off?" As noted earlier in the book, at the same time the distribution of jobs is evolving, the ability of people to adjust may be changing just as rapidly or more so. In other

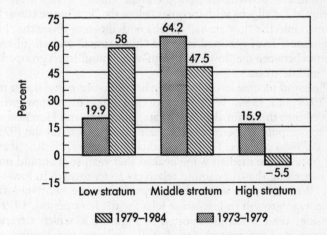

Fig. 5.5 Shares of new job growth in U.S. for all workers (percent). (*Source:* Barry Bluestone and Bennett Harrison, *The Great American Job Machine: The Proliferation of Low Wage Employment in the U.S. Economy* [Washington: Joint Economic Committee, U.S. Congress, December 1986], p.19.)

words, people may be better off in spite of emerging bimodalism.

Of course, proponents of the missing-middle thesis have not stopped gathering data that supports the missing-middle thesis. At the same time, they suggest that serious personal and social damage is being done. In late 1986, Professors Barry Bluestone and Bennett Harrison reported their comparative analysis of the relative numbers of "low-," "middle-," and "high-income jobs" created during the 1973–79 and 1979–84 periods.[22] The details of their study are worthy of close scrutiny; but for the purpose of this chapter, we need only stress their major findings, reproduced in Figure 5.5.

Using specially constructed data from the Current Population Survey, Bluestone and Harrison computed the growth of new "jobs" between 1973 and 1979 and between 1979 and 1984 according to three income strata. In order to divide total employment in 1973, 1979, and 1984 into thirds, they first established cutoff levels for "low" and "high" wage rates for 1973. They did this for 1973 by arbitrarily choosing the "low" income at 50% of the 1973 median wage and the "high" cutoff income at 200% of the 1973 median wage.[23] To compute the growth in new jobs, the three "strata" were then developed for all jobs with incomes below the "low"-wage cutoff level grouped into the "low strata," all jobs with incomes above the "high"-wage cutoff level grouped into the "high strata," and all jobs with incomes between the "low"- and "high"-wage cutoff levels grouped into the "middle strata."

The cutoff income levels were then held constant in real dollar terms for 1979 and 1984. With the working population appropriately divided into thirds for the three years, Bluestone and Harrison were able to compute the percentage increase in job growth for the 1973–79 and 1979–84 periods. They intentionally chose 1973 as the starting year because the median wage peaked that year, so it should not be too surprising that they found relatively faster growth in low-wage jobs. What may be somewhat surprising is the relatively faster percentage growth in low-wage jobs for the later period, 1979–84. Consider their findings reported in Figure 5.5, which covers the percentage of job growth for *all* (full- and part-time) workers for 1973–79 and 1979–84.

The dominance of middle-stratum job growth (64.2%) in the early period is clearly evident in the figure. In that period, the rest of the job growth was fairly evenly divided between the low and high strata (19.9% versus 15.9%, respectively). However, during the later period, a significant restructuring of job growth appears to develop. A majority of the jobs created (58%) were low-stratum. The *growth rate* of jobs in the middle declined, while the *absolute number* of high-end jobs dropped (by close to half a million).[24] Bluestone and Harrison conclude that the decrease in mean earnings (represented in, say, Figures 5.3a and 5.3b) is due to the proliferation of low-wage jobs and the net loss of high-wage jobs.

When they analyzed male employment patterns, the economists found that almost all the job growth was in the low-wage stratum; furthermore, "Only 3% of the two million net additional white male earners were found in employment outside the low stratum—in employment that paid more than $7,000 in 1984! It would be difficult to imagine a clearer indication of the tendency toward the proliferation of low-wage work."[25]

Contrary to what Bluestone and Harrison suggest, whether or not there has been a radical restructuring of the labor force along income lines, the causes of the development of a missing middle are not altogether clear, especially given conflicting evidence. What does appear to be reasonably clear is that since the late 1970s there has been a somewhat disproportionate, faster growth in the number of "low-wage jobs."

However, it should be stressed that the Bluestone–Harrison study does not play fair in its comparisons of employment levels by years. This is because the average unemployment rate in 1979 was 5.8% while the unemployment rate for 1984 was 7.4%. As *Newsweek* columnist Robert Samuelson notes, "As the recovery has continued and 'real' wages have slowly risen, the 'low' category [in the Bluestone–Harrison study] has contracted. An updating of the JEC [Bluestone–Harrison] study to 1985 puts 31.4% of workers in this group, the smallest proportion since 1973 except for the two years (1978, 1979)."[26] When Bluestone and Harrison extended their study to account for further recovery in general economic activity in 1985, the percentage of low-income jobs created in the 1979–85 period fell to 44%.[27]

In addition, although Bluestone and Harrison use the term "jobs" in their analysis, their data are really for "incomes." They rank people by incomes (which could be obtained during the year by holding more than one job at the same time, or in sequence during the year). It also means that someone who started to work in July in a given year, and may have, as a consequence, earned $7,000 that year, would have been counted as having a low-income job.[28]

Finally, it needs to be stressed that the absolute number of low-wage jobs in the economy is very large, amounting to approximately a third of the labor force; a dramatically faster growth in low-wage jobs will not, as a consequence, be reflected as dramatically in the percentage distribution of all jobs in the labor force. Consider Figure 5.6, which contains the distribution of real income for all jobs computed by the Bureau of Labor Statistics in a manner similar to the techniques employed by Bluestone and Harrison.[29] There are two impressive observations to be made from the graph: first, the total absence of an upward trend in the percentage of low-wage jobs; and, second, the fluctuation during the 1973–85 period of a very narrow band within which low-wage jobs, computed as a percentage of all jobs, occurred. In fact, low-wage jobs stayed between 31.4% and 33.0% — hardly what one would have expected from the Bluestone–Harrison findings.[30]

Causes and Competing Visions of Data

The disproportionate growth in low-wage jobs (even if limited) may help explain the U-turn in median and mean income, but it does not necessarily follow that the economy has gotten "worse," meaning in need of radical correction (especially with the type of reforms advo-

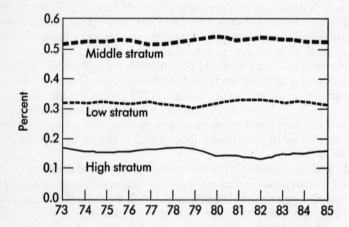

Fig. 5.6 Distribution of all jobs by low-, middle- and high-income strata, 1973–1985 (percent). (Note: Income earners divided into strata by 1973 real income levels.) (*Source:* Robert McIntire, Bureau of Labor Statistics, U.S. Department of Labor, December 30, 1986.)

cated by, say, Professors Bluestone and Harrison[31]). More needs to be known about the reasons for the growth in low-income jobs, as well as the decrease in high-income jobs.

Proponents of the U-turn and missing-middle thesis offer three levels of explanation for the statistical trends reported. At times, they seem to suggest that we do not need to know more than the facts: median income is falling and low-wage jobs are growing. Such facts, in and of themselves, presumably call for a policy response. At other times, the proponents appear to assert that the major *causes* of the U-turn and low-wage job growth include "the deindustrialization of America," or "the emergence of the service economy," or Reagan's economic policies, none of which are fully satisfying explanations.[32] The claim that the economy is "deindustrializing," or that the U-turn can be explained by ongoing restructuring forces is particularly appealing, especially since the employment declines in established industries—for example, steel and rubber—are readily apparent. Nonetheless, American Enterprise Institute economists Marvin Kosters and Murray Ross conclude that, when examined carefully, the slowdown in wage increases "is not attributable to any significant extent to factors such as changing industry employment shares."[33]

However, Bluestone and Harrison, in their work published by the Joint Economic Committee and elsewhere, at times push their deindustrialization theme further, attributing much of the nation's losses of high-income jobs and gains in low-income jobs to all or some combination of the following factors:

- the decline in union power,
- growth in international competition and the foreign invasion of American markets for goods,
- the exportation of American industrial jobs to non-"rustbelt" states (mainly, states in the South and West) and third-world countries, and
- the unwillingness of American governments, especially the federal government, to institute and/or expand a variety of industrial policies similar to those in full operation in other major industrial countries.

Clearly, Professors Bluestone and Harrison offer some explanation of the problem, but their explanations do not always point to economic decay. For example, unions have in the past been able to raise the wages of their members, imposing the added labor costs on the rest of the population, including many consumers who earn far less than union members. Unions have often been able to collect "monopoly rents," to use the jargon of economists. Over recent decades, the monopoly power of unions has slipped in many industries as consumers have sought to obtain cheaper, higher-quality products from firms that have shifted their capital to nonunion sectors of the economy. No longer able to capture the monopoly rents they once extracted when consumer purchases and capital were not so mobile, unions have been forced in several key industries, especially steel and automobiles, to give up some of their high-wage jobs through unemployment and through wage and fringe-benefit concessions or "give-backs."

However, there are other important explanations for the earnings U-turn and ongoing restructuring of jobs, several of which are evident in the Bluestone–Harrison analysis. For example, the emergence of low-wage jobs in the 1960s and 1970s can be partially attributed to the baby-boom generation.

Young workers can be expected to start their careers at the bottom of the wage ladder (When there is a "boom" in births, as there was in the post-World War II–1960 period, there will be a "boom" in new job entrants 18 to 25 years later.). The grown-up "baby-boomers" can be expected to cause a disproportionate growth in low-wage jobs.[34] This is true because the relatively greater supply of workers will,

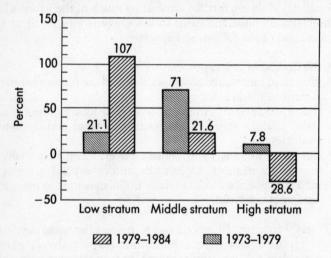

Fig. 5.7a Shares of new job growth in the U.S. for workers less than age 35 (percent).

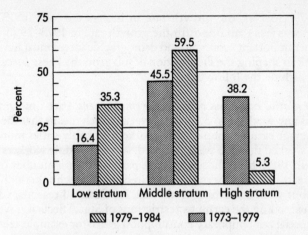

Fig. 5.7b Shares of new job growth in the U.S. for workers age 35 and older (percent). (*Source:* Barry Bluestone and Bennett Harrison, *The Great American Job Machine: The Proliferation of Low Wage Employment in the U.S. Economy* [Washington: Joint Economic Committee, U.S. Congress, December 1986], pp. 29 and 30.)

presumably, suppress average worker wages in two ways. The baby-boomers may compete wages down in those occupations representing their first jobs. In addition, the baby-boomers contributed to a reduction in the average age of the work force from 40.6 years in 1964 to 37.5 years in 1985,[35] and younger workers typically have less experience and, thereby, lower incomes.

When Bluestone and Harrison divide their population into the under-35 and 35-and-older age groups, the impact of the baby boom can be readily detected. (See Figures 5.7a and 5.7b.) The number of low-wage jobs among the under-35 group grew disproportionally to those among the 35-and-older group. For the under-35 group, low-wage jobs grew by 107% in the 1979–84 period, five times the same group's growth in 1973–79. A majority (59.5%) of the 35-and-older group's job growth was in the middle-job stratum.

Nevertheless, the baby-boom argument remains only a partial explanation of the disproportionate growth in low-wage jobs.[36] Even for the older group in the Bluestone–Harrison study, the growth rate of low-wage jobs in 1979–84 (35.3%) was more than twice the rate in

1973–79 (16.4%); the growth rate in high-wage jobs in 1979–84 (5.3%) was less than one-fifth the growth rate in 1973–79 (38.2%). Other important economic and demographic forces must have been at work in shaping the distribution of job growth. These forces very likely include the following.

The relative expansion of part-time employment. Part-time employment is any work up to 35 hours a week, which means that the mean and average earnings of part-time workers probably varies more with hours worked than the wage rate paid. Most part-time workers (two-thirds in 1982) have chosen to work part-time for a number of very good reasons. They are students; retired workers who do not have to work but want something to do and, for financial reasons, want to avoid exceeding the earnings restrictions of Social Security; workers with special but temporary consumption goals (for example, teenagers who want to buy a car or computer); or members of families with another high-income earner.[37] The growth in low-wage jobs can also reflect a relative growth in the attractiveness of low-wage jobs; that is to say, even though the jobs may be low-paid, the wages and fringe benefits, as well as the intrinsic value, of low-wage jobs may have increased. For example, the growth in market-provided household services through, for example, restaurants and laundries may not only include part-time employment opportunities, but may have also freed household workers to find part-time employment in the market economy.

It does not follow, in other words, that all, or even a major share, of the growth in part-time employment is "bad." A relative growth in part-time employment can give rise to an expansion of private employment opportunities and much private improvement, even though the *monetary measures* may suggest the contrary. And the growth may indirectly reflect purposeful collective decisions to increase the number of people who, for example, go to college or elect retirement. Still, the number of part-time, low-wage workers in their jobs for "economic reasons" appears to have increased only since the 1970s.[38] The causes of the increase is not at all clear.

The growing labor force participation rate of women and other demographic factors. As noted earlier, over the period under study, women have been entering the labor force in disproportionate numbers. Their civilian labor force participation rate increased from 38.7% in 1964 to 44.7% in 1973 and then to 55.3% in 1985.[39] Women not only tend to earn less than men in full-time jobs, but also take a disproportionate number of part-time jobs in which they also tend to earn less than men. The apparent shift in roles assumed by men and women at home and in the labor force could be contributing to the growth in low-wage jobs.[40] Similarly, the growth in the use of contraception and abortion (with the critical Supreme Court decision on abortion rendered in 1973); the expansion of the service economy, which allows for contracting-out of household services; improved employment opportunities at higher wages (but still low wages); and improvement in the efficiency of household work could all be contributing to the relative expansion of part-time jobs — and to the relative growth of low-paid jobs.

The relative growth of low-wage jobs could also be explained by a number of other changes in demographic patterns — for example, the tendency toward smaller families, the growth in nontraditional households, the increase in single-parent homes, and the general shift in jobs from high-cost to low-cost areas of the country. The number in an average-size family fell from 3.33 in 1960 to 3.14 in 1970, to 2.76 in 1980, and to 2.67 in 1986, a decrease that may have reduced the necessity of some workers to seek higher-income jobs. This decrease may have encouraged other workers to enter the labor force on a part-time basis.[41]

The aging of the population has often meant, for many people, a gradual retirement from the work force by moving from full-time to part-time employment. The growing divorce rate has increased the number of single-family homes and may have added to the pressure on single parents to obtain employment, even if the job is low-paying. The growing dependence on nontraditional households, including unmarried couples and two or more independent individuals, could also have added to the need for additional jobs, since in such households incomes might not be shared.

The growing tendency of young adults to delay marriage may have tempered the combining of incomes and, therefore, the growth in the number of moderate-income families. At the same time, it may have also increased the discretionary incomes of many households since the unmarried people were not then saddled with fixed costs associated with mortgages and children (which tend to be positively associated with marriages).[42]

The shift in the nation's population toward the South and Southwest could, for many workers, result in a reduction in measured income from employment. At the same time, the resulting increase in real spendable income (after allowing for differences in cost of living and taxes) might mean an actual increase in living standards. Although no single demographic factor may explain a statistically significant share of the shift in job creation, no factor can be totally ignored or dismissed either, especially when these factors are taken together.[43]

The decline in worker productivity growth. Economic improvement in the long run depends inevitably upon productivity increases, which implies more goods and services produced and more income distributed. Wages tend to move, with lags, coincident with productivity, as evident in Figure 5.8, which plots rates of growth in worker productivity and real compensation per hour. What is also readily apparent in Figure 5.8 is the downward trend, over the 1964–85 period, in the rate of growth in worker productivity, accompanied by a decline in real growth in earnings per hour. While a decline in *average* worker productivity and real earnings need not indicate a relative growth in low-wage jobs, we should not be too shocked to observe an inverse relationship between growth in average productivity and the proportion of low-wage jobs. The increasing number of new entrants going into the labor force through part-time

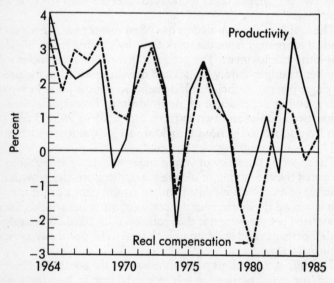

Fig. 5.8 Changes in productivity and real compensation per hour in nonfarm business sector (percent). (*Source: Economic Report of the President*, 1987.)

employment could be helping to pull down the growth in average worker productivity.[44]

Growing environmental and business regulation. The environmental movement gathered full force in the 1970s, resulting in the passage of much legislation intended to clean up the country's air and waterways. The legislation also increased the cost of doing business and retarded the relative growth of many American regions and industries, especially the *smokestack* industries.[45]

Without question, these greater environmental costs decreased the relative output of goods-producing industries—and the relative number of high-wage jobs. These environmental costs also provided a competitive advantage to many personal and business services, which do not use environmental resources subjected to the new controls but which do employ many low-wage workers. Also without much question, on world markets the environmental legislation handicapped many American firms.

The net result has been a relative contraction of several "basic" industries, established manufacturing jobs, and the monopoly power of unions (which have historically had their greatest influence in the basic industries). These consequences were broadly advertised and understood by Congress when the environmental legislation was passed. In that limited sense, a part of the relative growth in low-wage jobs has been intended—even legislated, albeit indirectly—by Congress!

Business regulations of all kinds, involving matters of safety, health, energy consumption, and market entry, have also raised the cost of doing business, reduced employment in some industries, and increased employment in other industries. Overall, the regulations have often contributed to a reduction in the nation's measured, if not actual, real income, and probably have been translated into a downward shift in worker wages and to the relative growth of low-wage jobs.

The decline in the real minimum wage. Many critics of current social politics are painfully aware that the minimum wage has been held constant at $3.35 an hour throughout the Reagan administration, which has meant a deterioration of the earnings of low-income workers. However, the decline in the real purchasing power of the minimum wage did not begin with the advent of Ronald Reagan to the presidency. Indeed, the real minimum wage peaked in 1986 at $5.04 an hour (in terms of 1986 dollars). As economists have predicted since the inception of the minimum wage, a decrease in the real value of the minimum wage should lead to greater employment opportunities for those covered by (or, depending on perspective, afflicated with) the minimum wage.[46]

While the debate over exactly how many low-income jobs should have been created as a result of the one-third decrease in the real minimum wage since 1968, few dispute an assessment that the decline has contributed to the growing count of low-income jobs. Since slightly more than half of the decrease in the real minimum wage occurred since 1981, much of the low-income job creation associated with the decrease should also have come in the first half of the 1980s. Again, low-income-job creation can be viewed as a very positive force in the economy.

Unfortunately, social critics think they know how to remedy the expansion of low-income jobs: raise the minimum wage back to, or almost to, its 1968 peak.[47] The solution may work, but, at best, only to a limited extent and only at the cost of reduced employment opportunities for low-wage American workers. (More is said about minimum wages in Chapter 9.)

The growth in the rate of inflation. Traditionally, growth in wages tends to lag behind the growth of prices. This is especially true when the inflation is unanticipated and increasing at accelerating rates. Workers must negotiate adjustments in their pay to account for the deteriorating value of the dollars they receive, and the time absorbed in negotiation accounts for some of the observed lag in wage adjustments. The 1960s and 1970s (especially the late 1970s) were a period of progressively higher rates of inflation. Under conditions of an inflationary spiral, one should not be especially surprised to observe some deterioration in average real wages and, thereby, even some relative growth in low-wage jobs. The political forces in charge of the inflationary throttle can simply outwit workers by making the inflationary change unpredictable.

Granted, the inflationary spiral was truncated in the first half of the 1980s by a reversal of expansionary monetary policies by the Federal Reserve in late 1979. However, the resulting instability in prices and inflation rates has probably led many employers to be more cautious in their employment policies. After all, many were caught in the early 1980s with employment commitments that they could not keep or could not keep without reductions in profits or outright losses. When employers begin to believe that future economic activity is more uncertain and risky, they can be expected to respond by switching to shorter-term commitments in all areas of business, including their employment plans. This probably means that they will move marginally to greater reliance on part-time and low-wage employment. High-wage employment might require longer-term wage and capital commitments.

In addition, higher and more unpredictable inflation rates can cause an increase in interest rates to compensate for the deteriorating value of the dollar loaned and for the greater risk incurred. With relatively higher interest payments, many firms can be expected to control their product costs by more carefully containing labor costs.

Growing instability in the economy In general, growth in real income is dependent upon macroeconomic stability, which has been absent during much of the past decade. The economy has moved from a period of rapid inflation to a period of two recessions in sequence and then recovery. In 1984 (the last year covered by the initial Bluestone–Harrison study), the economy had not yet fully rebounded from the recessions of the early 1980s. (Indeed, the economy was still recovering sluggishly in 1987.) During a period of recovery, especially when recovery is slow (and 1984 was only the second full year of recovery), we should expect a disproportionate count of low-wage jobs.

The Income Paradox

The purpose of the foregoing section has not been to cover comprehensively all possible explanations for the observed U-turn in worker earnings and the measured restructuring of the labor force. The direction of the movement in earning power and the structure of the income distribution are certainly the end-products of a multitude of economic and social forces, most of which are probably impossible to categorize and describe, much less measure in any meaningful way. Rather, the purpose has been to indicate that there are a number of very powerful, if incomplete, explanations that are sometimes overlooked or ignored in discussions of the U-turn and restructuring theses.

Nonetheless, the U-turn and missing middle may not be as big a mystery as might be thought; they may be problems of money measurements. What has gone practically unnoticed in the statistical and policy debate is an apparent paradox in income data: real per-capita personal and disposable incomes have continued to trend upward at the same time that per-capita hourly and weekly earnings have been going into a modest tailspin. This means that, regardless of

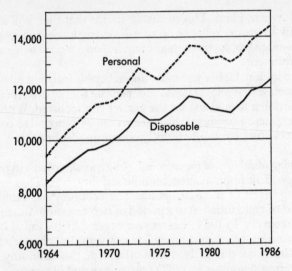

Fig. 5.9 Per capita personal and disposable income (1986 dollars). (*Source: Economic Report of the President*, 1987).

what has happened to worker earnings, there has been progressively more income to go around and more consumable goods and services—even over the years that Professors Bluestone and Harrison chart a growth in low-wage jobs and a U-turn in earnings.

The Contrast in Income Data

Reconsider Figures 5.3a and 5.3b, which cover average hourly and weekly earnings. Then, consider Figure 5.9, which contains plots of real per-capita personal and disposable income (measured in 1986 dollars). Real median hourly and weekly earnings in Figures 5.3a and 5.3b decline irregularly after 1973, whereas real per-capita personal and disposable incomes in Figure 5.9 continue to rise throughout the graph, broken only by recessions. If there is any change evident in Figure 5.9, it is that the rate of *growth,* not the absolute *level,* of per-capita personal and disposable income appears to have slowed in the late 1970s.[48]

How can it be that real personal income rises when earnings do not?[49] An obvious answer is that personal income includes nonwage forms of income—profits, for example—and nonmoney forms of income—in-kind benefits, for example—not captured in worker earnings.[50] However, profits cannot be the explanation because, as evident in Figure 5.10, real corporate profits cycled widely over the 1964–85 period with a trend that is more or less flat. That means that corporate profits tended to become a relatively smaller source of income over the period. Indeed, the ratio of real profits to real wages and salaries declined markedly during the period, a point evident in Figure 5.11

A part of the explanation for the divergence of measures of worker earnings and per-capita income is that worker earnings do not always account for many nonmonetary payments—for instance, fringe benefits, or for transfer payments.

Supplemental Benefits

Consider Figure 5.12, which reports real wages and salaries and total compensation (including supplemental benefits) per employed worker.[51] Two points evident in the figure are noteworthy. First, the plot of per-worker wages and salaries follows much the same pattern of hourly and weekly earnings (Figures 5.3a and 5.3b). Real per-worker wages and salaries rise until 1973 and fall during the next decade.

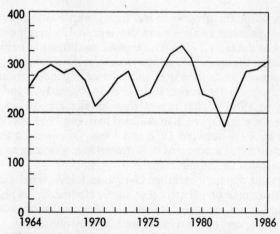

Fig. 5.10 Corporate profits with inventory valuation and capital consumption adjustments (billions of 1986 dollars). (*Source: Economic Report of the President, 1987.*)

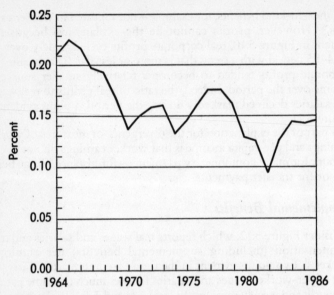

Fig. 5.11 Ratio of corporate profits to wages and salaries. (*Source: Economic Report of the President*, 1987).

Second, while the growth in real total compensation per worker slows during the late 1970s, it turns down primarily in response to the recessions of the early 1980s. The expanding difference between the two curves in Figure 5.12 is the growth in real nonwage income. In fact, the supplements to wages and salaries expanded from 9% of wages and salaries per worker in 1964 to 14.7% in 1973 and upward to 20.5% in 1986.[52] That means that supplements to wages as a percentage of wages more than doubled between 1964 and 1986 and increased by 40% between 1973 and 1986. Of course, many other forms of nonwage income that have grown in importance to workers are not included in "supplements."[53]

In short, the apparent earnings U–turn and downward shift in the jobs structure may be partially (but surely not totally) explained by what is and is not measured by "earnings." Even the "supplemental income" of workers covered in Figure 5.12 may not include all forms of nonmoney payments received by workers—for example, more relaxed work schedules, personal travel at company expense, subsidized lunches, time off for exercise, and use of office telephones and supplies. *The point is that "real effective income" (money and nonmoney forms of pay-*

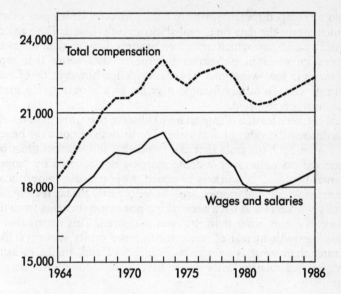

Fig. 5.12 Total worker compensation and wages and salaries per employed worker (1986 dollars). (*Source: Economic Report of the President*, 1987.)

ments) to workers may not have deteriorated as rapidly as money measures indicate. The growth in "low-wage" jobs may not be nearly as large as that measured and documented by Bluestone–Harrison because their "low-wage" statistics may not (and, very likely, do not) capture all of the income.

Because "real effective income" is so difficult, if not impossible, to measure, we cannot be certain what has happened to this income. At the same time, we should not be surprised that people, since the 1970s, have sought to take a growing portion of their "real effective income" in nonmoney forms *simply because these forms cannot be readily measured.* That which cannot be measured cannot be taxed. During the period tax rates at virtually all levels of government were rising, partly because of discretionary actions by government and mostly because of inflation and "bracket creep." The rise in per-capita personal income portrayed in Figure 5.14 must have been claimed by someone. Proponents of the U-turn/missing-middle theses maintain that the income did not go to high-income families. If this is true, then, where did it go? There are only two possible answers: the extra personal income escaped measurement in family income, or it never existed, which means the data on personal income are flawed. Then again, it is difficult to say which are more severely flawed: data series that report increases in per-capita income or data series that report increases in low-wage jobs. There is evidence, however, that Census Bureau data on family income may be, to a progressively greater extent, underreported.[54]

At the very least, it is important to observe that growth in tax rates can destroy the value of data series. The growth of nonwage benefits in Figure 5.12 suggests that tax avoidance and evasion must have occurred on nonmoney-income margins not covered by "supplemental benefits." If workers obtained proportionally more income from firm-provided supplemental benefits partly for tax reasons, then surely workers must have been taking nonmoney benefits from their work in forms other than the ones measured. This means that the actual growth in real effective income per capita was very likely greater than what is evident in Figure 5.12 and, unlike measured "wages and salaries," may never have turned downward after the late 1970s.

Government Transfers

The apparent divergence in personal income and worker earnings may also be partially explained by the growth in government transfers—major federal social programs such as unemployment compensation, Social Security, and welfare payments. On a per-capita basis, transfer payments also began in 1964 to expand relative to wages and salaries. As a percentage of real wages and salaries per employed worker, government transfers increased from 11.5% in 1964 to 18.3% in 1973 and then to 24.8% in 1986. That dramatic growth in the transfers very likely had three effects:

1. It decreased the after-tax value of work, thereby reducing the after-tax value of seeking, obtaining, and retaining higher-income jobs.
2. It increased the economic cushion available for people in lower-income jobs.
3. It encouraged people to give up their higher-income jobs and retire—accepting lower-income, less-demanding jobs (especially in the case of Social Security, which imposes restric-

tions on the amount of income that can be earned without penalties).

In general, the growth in transfers tended to discourage people from taking higher-income jobs and encouraged them to take lower-income jobs, just to make sure they could qualify for the transfers. How important the effects of transfers have been in augmenting the course of real family income and the structure of jobs simply cannot be determined with precision. Although the subject has not been studied exhaustively, much evidence is beginning to mount in support of the hypothesis that government-aid programs have had a variety of perverse effects: increasing the number of displaced workers, extending the length of unemployment, and increasing the poverty rate. David Blau and Philip Robins estimate that welfare benefits have had the expected perverse effects on employment, making employment a less attractive alternative to unemployment or to nonparticipation in the labor force.[55] According to preliminary findings in a study on the sources of worker displacement across states, the author has found that the availability of unemployment benefits increases the rate of worker displacement within state labor forces; the higher the unemployment compensation, the longer the unemployment.[56] This finding has been supported by other research, including a study concluding that a $20 increase in weekly unemployment compensation will extend a worker's average unemployment period by approximately a week. Making unemployment compensation taxable, which has been the case since 1979, has been a factor in reducing the average length of unemployment from 11 to 8.5 weeks.[57]

It appears that expanding benefits can initially reduce the poverty rate, but there also appears to be some threshold level of benefits so generous that benefits exceeding this threshold will actually expand the poverty rate. Ohio University economists Lowell Gallaway and Richard Vedder have estimated that the perverse effects of federal welfare benefits emerge at a per-capita-benefit level of approximately $150. As a point of interest, this $150 was surpassed in 1972, the year before weekly and hourly earnings and median family income turned downward.[58] But, in the absence of more extensive research on the subject, such findings should cause policy commentators to pause before concluding, as one journalist has concluded, "The general perception of a shrinking middle is correct. Over the last decade or so, real family income has declined, and its distribution has become more unequal."[59]

Price Indexes

The movement in measures of *real* (or constant-dollar) income can, of course, be affected by the exact price index used to adjust for price changes. Measures of real worker total compensation and wages and salaries, for example, adjust for price changes as measured by the consumer price index (CPI). However, the CPI has never been viewed as anything other than a rough approximation of the actual price level. This is because the CPI is founded on a given market basket of goods, the prices of which are measured each month, and the collection of goods priced may or may not be representative of what any given groups of workers actually buy. Because of the impact of inflation on interest rates and the way interest rates are treated in the computation of the CPI, many researchers believe that the CPI may seriously overstate how much prices actually rise during some inflationary periods.[60] This means that when the index is used to adjust worker incomes for inflation, an overadjustment may result; real incomes as adjusted by the CPI may have risen faster than what is portrayed in the constant-dollar income measures. In short, the U-turn in worker

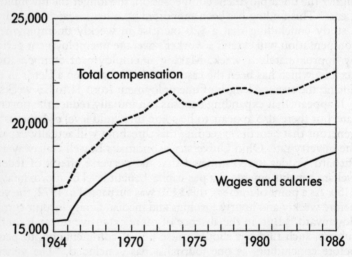

Fig. 5.13 Total worker compensation and wages and salaries per employed worker adjusted by personal consumption deflator (1986 dollars). (*Source: Economic Report of the President,* 1987.)

wages that began to appear in the data may be partially a product of statistical manipulation of the data, not a real phenomenon.

The problem of measuring real worker income can be illustrated by looking at adjustments in worker total compensation and wages and salaries and exploring the use of the much broader implicit price deflator used in calculating real personal consumption expenditures (a major component of real gross national product). Between 1973 and 1986, the CPI increased by 147%. However, in spite of the price increases that were uneven across products, the CPI presumes that wage earners do not change their buying habits among a relatively small number of items, substituting those goods with prices rising less rapidly for those whose prices are rising more rapidly.

The substitution problem is particularly acute with the CPI, since it covers so few items whose prices have been rising faster than products outside the CPI. The implicit price deflator for personal-consumption expenditures, for example, increased 130% in the 1973–86 period.[61] The difference between the increase in the two indexes is not dramatic, but it is also not a trivial difference (amounting to 13%), a point that is evident when real total-worker compensation and wages and salaries per worker (first reported in Figure 5.12) is

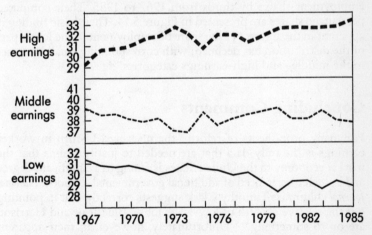

Fig. 5.14 Employment shares based on current-year medians, 1967–1985 (percent). (*Source:* Marvin H. Kosters and Murray N. Ross, "The Distribution of Earnings and Employment Opportunities: A Re-examination of the Evidence," *AEI Occasional Paper* [Washington: American Enterprise Institute, September 1987.] p. 18.)

recomputed using the implicit price deflator (Figure 5.13). What is interesting is that, contrary to what is observed in Figure 5.12, the new measure of wages and salaries per worker never turns downward.

Again, this evidence suggests that at least some part of the measured U-turn in income is very probably a consequence of the index used. The Bureau of Labor Statistics of the Department of Labor, which collects the personal-income statistics, uses the personal-consumption-expenditure deflator, while the Bureau of the Census of the Department of Commerce, which collects family-income data, uses the Consumer Price Index.[62]

Kosters and Ross have clarified the problem of using the conventional CPI in assessing changes in the distribution of employment.[63] Following Bluestone and Harrison, they also divide people in employment shares, but with slightly different cut-off income levels. Anyone earning less than 50% of the median income is in the "low-earnings" group, and anyone earning 150% of the median income is in the "high-earnings" group. Anyone earning between 50% and 150% of the median income is in the "middle-earnings" group. They then use an experimental consumer price index that seeks to correct for the inflation distortion due to the way changes in owner-occupied housing were treated prior to 1983 to compute the employment shares by thirds from 1967 to 1985. Their computed percentage shares are presented in Figure 5.14. Their basic finding is apparent in the figure: "[T]he share of employment in the lower part of the distribution has declined, with corresponding small increases in the middle- and high-earnings categories."[64]

Concluding Comments

For many proponents of reform, the measured U-turn in worker earnings is the only data that are needed to justify claims that the market economy in the United States is failing to a significant degree and is, therefore, in need of additional governmental supports. *National Journal* columnist Timothy Clark suggests correctly that in pointing out the relative growth of low-wage jobs, "Bluestone and Harrison are on to something."[65] Unfortunately, however, in their apparent eagerness to discredit uncontrolled labor markets, they fail to appreciate fully the complexity of what they are on to, other than what they see on the statistical surface. Their analysis is limited and their policy conclusions, misguided. Contrary to what Bluestone and Harrison may want to think, the observed slowdown in wage growth cannot be directly attributed, to any significant degree, to the changing industrial structure or (what is worse) the "deindustrialization of America."[66]

In this regard, Robert Kuttner was never more candid than when he suggested that the missing-middle (as well as the economic-reversal) "debate, though partly technical, is also deeply ideological"[67] — and, it might be justly added, deeply political. For that reason, the debate is extraordinarily important; the course of public policy hinges on what the polity ultimately believes the numbers are saying.

From the evidence covered in this chapter, four conclusions are warranted. First, the analytical integrity of key studies supporting the missing-middle and U-turn theses must be seriously questioned.

Second, the employment and earnings problems faced by American workers are not as serious as may be believed from a review of the crude statistical measures of family income and worker earnings currently available. Family members may still have growing access to more goods and services even though measures of their family incomes report a decline in income. Journalist Michael McFadden summarized the views of a growing number of researchers when he wrote,

> A small group of economists have been advancing the argument of the disappearing middle class for several years, starting in the early 1980s when recession was playing havoc with employment and income growth. Every such claim has evaporated when put to rigorous examination, and the Bluestone–Harrison thesis is proving no exception.[68]

Third, the existence of many low-wage jobs in the economy is not, in and of itself, a mark of a faltering economy. The creation of low-wage jobs can mean improved opportunities for many American workers. After reviewing the findings of a number of empirical studies of the composition and controlling forces of low-wage labor markets funded by the U.S. Department of Health and Human Services, three Clemson University economists conclude:

> Occupants of jobs in these [low-wage] markets tend to be relatively young (their median age is 22, have at least a high school education, and have relatively little work experience). Broadly speaking, workers in these markets are motivated by one of four factors in accepting low-paying jobs: (i) lacking prior work experience, they are using the jobs to accumulate the training and experience that

will enable them to move on to higher paying positions; (ii) they are pursuing further education and are using the jobs to supplement income from other sources (e.g., relatives); (iii) they are "second earners" seeking to enhance total family income; or (iv) they do not wish to undertake the investment required for a higher-paying, permanent job, and so accept low-paying positions that are accompanied by the flexibility to move into and out of the labor force.[69]

Fourth, important employment and earnings problems for some workers cannot be fully denied. However, many of these problems were anticipated long ago when policymakers began to use government transfers and market controls to relieve a variety of existing social problems without regard to long-run consequences. The country is now suffering through the long-run consequences of past policies. If reform is needed, the country had best reevaluate past policies.

Policymakers should also remember how Robert Samuelson sums up his assessment of the exaggerated claims of those who see the U.S. market economy as faltering and in need of government help. Samuelson concludes:

> Our economic system is imperfect. "Hard core" unemployment is more unyielding than it seemed in the inflationary 1960s and 1970s. For other workers, some job security is lost in return for a flexibility that allows companies to hire, fire and reduce pay to adjust to changing circumstances. The process is messy and often cruel, but in a profit-making economy jobs cannot be saved by forcing companies to do unprofitable things. The American job machine has not created a utopia, but it works. Those who think they can make it work better bear a heavy burden of proof.[70]

Notes

1. Otis Port, "Making Brawn Work with Brains," *Business Week,* April 20, 1987, p. 57.
2. Richard C. Michel, Urban Institute, as quoted in Aaron Bernstein, "Warning: The Standard of Living Is Slipping," *Business Week,* April 20, 1987, p. 52.
3. As quoted by Timothy B. Clark, "Economic Focus," *National Journal,* February 2, 1987, p. 399.
4. Lance Compa, "So We Have More Jobs—Low-Paid, Part-Time Ones," *Washington Post,* March 15, 1987, p. C2.

5. According to Professors Bennett Harrison and Barry Bluestone, the "U-turn" thesis will be developed in *The Great U-Turn: Rising Inequality, Low Wages, and the Shattered American Dream* (New York: Basic Books, forthcoming).

6. The literature with the "missing-middle" theme has begun to mushroom. See Robert Kuttner, "The Declining Middle," *Atlantic Monthly*, July 1983, pp. 60–72; Lucy S. Gordon, *Are Middle-Level Jobs Disappearing?* (Washington: Industrial Union Department, AFL–CIO, 1983); Bruce Steinberg, "The Mass Market Is Splitting Apart," *Fortune*, November 28, 1983; Barry Bluestone, "Industrial Dislocation and Its Implications for Public Policy," in *Displaced Workers: Implications for Educational and Training Institutions*, edited by Kevin Hollenbeck, *et al.* (Columbus, Ohio: National Center for Research in Vocational Education, Ohio State University, 1984), pp. 45–68; Lester Thurow, "The Disappearance of the Middle Class," *New York Times*, February 5, 1984, p. F3; *Deindustrialization and the Two Tier Society* (Washington: Industrial Union Department, AFL–CIO, 1984); Thomas B. Edsall, "More than Ever, the Electorate is Polarized on Economic Lines," *Washington Post National Weekly*, January 6, 1986, p. 23; Katherine Bradbury, "The Shrinking Middle Class," *New England Economic Review*, September/October 1986, pp. 44–55; Larry Mishel, *The Polarization of America: The Loss of Good Jobs, Falling Incomes and Rising Inequality* (Washington: Industrial Union Department, AFL–CIO, 1986); Bennett Harrison, Chris Tilly, and Barry Bluestone, "Wage Inequality Takes a Great U-Turn," *Challenge*, March/April 1986, pp. 26–32; Barry Bluestone and Bennett Harrison, *The Great American Job Machine: The Proliferation of Low Wage Employment in the U.S. Economy* (Washington: Joint Economic Committee, U.S. Congress, 1986); Gary Burtless, "Inequality in America: Where Do We Stand?", *Brookings Review*, Summer 1987, pp. 9–16; and Frank Levy, "The Missing Middle: Is It Really Vanishing?", *Brookings Review*, Summer 1987, pp. 17–21.

7. "The American Dream Denied?" *Industry Week*, January 26, 1987, p. 32.

8. Of course, with rising tax rates over the 1970s and 1980s at practically all levels of government, the after-tax real income has tended to deteriorate more rapidly than total earned income. Median family income after deducting only federal personal income and Social Security taxes fell in real terms by nearly 13% between 1976 and 1981, the year that the Reagan tax-cut package was passed (Tax Foundation, "U.S. Family's Purchasing Power Climbs for Fifth Year in a Row," *Tax Features*, August 1986, p.1).

9. The civilian labor-force participation rate (the civilian labor force as a percent of the civilian noninstitutionalized population) rose from 58.7% in 1964 to 60.8% in 1973 to 64.8% in 1985 and finally to 65.3% in 1986.

10. In all instances where 1986 figures are reported, the data are preliminary.

11. In a perfectly normal, bell-shaped distribution, the mean, median, and mode income levels will be identical.

12. Bluestone, "Industrial Dislocation" (see note 6), p. 52.

13. Ibid.

14. Kuttner, "The Declining Middle" (see note 6). The data are drawn from Bureau of Labor Statistics, U.S. Department of Labor, *Economic Projections to 1990,* Bulletin 2121 (Washington: U.S. Government Printing Office, March 1982).

15. This growth rate in manufacturing employment assumes a "moderate" growth rate for the economy as a whole between 1984 and 1995. If the economy grows at a "low" rate, the average annual rate of growth in manufacturing employment is projected to be 0.1%; however, if the economy grows at a "high" rate, manufacturing employment may grow as rapidly as 1% a year. Assuming a moderate growth for the economy as a whole, total private employment is expected to grow at an average annual rate of 1.4% between 1984 and 1995 (Valerie A. Personick, "A Second Look at Industry Output and Employment Trends Through 1995," *Monthly Labor Review,* November 1985, p. 28).

16. This point is developed in more detail in Richard B. McKenzie, *The Good News About Production Jobs* (St. Louis: Center for the Study of American Business, Washington University, 1985).

17. Barry Bluestone, Patricia Hanna, Sarah Kuhn, and Laura Moore, *The Retail Revolution: Market Transformation, Investment, and Labor in the Modern Department Store* (Boston: Auburn House, 1981).

18. Neal H. Rosenthal, "The Declining Middle Class: Myth or Reality?" *Monthly Labor Review,* March 1985, pp. 3–10.

19. Rosenthal, "The Declining Middle Class," p. 6. The BLS researcher also adds that decline of the smokestack industries during the 1970s could not have materially affected the earnings distribution, even if all of the workers in those industries had been clustered in the middle third.

20. Robert Z. Lawrence, "Sectoral Shifts and the Size of the Middle Class," *Brookings Review,* Fall 1985, pp. 3–10.

21. Patrick J. McMahon and John H. Tschetter, "The Declining Middle Class: A Further Analysis," *Monthly Labor Review,* September 1986, pp. 22–27.

22. Bluestone and Harrison, *The Great American Job Machine* (see note 6).

23. The authors report that changing cutoff wage rates to 75% of median and 300% of median did not change the thrust of their findings (Ibid., p. 20).

24. This does not mean that no high-wage jobs were created during the latter period, only that there were more high-wage jobs destroyed than created.

25. Bluestone and Harrison, *The Great American Job Machine,* pp. 21–22.

26. Robert J. Samuelson, "The American Job Machine," *Newsweek,* February 23, 1987, p. 57.

27. As reported in Michael McFadden, "Protectionism Can't Protect Jobs," *Fortune,* May 11, 1987, p. 124. Of course, it needs to be remembered that 33% of the nation's jobs were initially classified as low-income, meaning that the jobs created were only 11 percentage points above an even distribution of newly created jobs by income strata.

28. Of interest is the fact that Robert McIntire, an economist with the

Bureau of Labor Statistics who sought to duplicate the findings of Bluestone–Harrison with BLS data, found the Bluestone–Harrison study included groups not normally included in work-experience tabulations of wage and salary workers. These groups are members of the military, persons who were primarily self-employed or unpaid family workers but who received some wage and salary income, and persons who did not work at all but received some wage and salary income during the year. The inclusion of such groups, accompanied by a failure of Bluestone and Harrison to use the revised weighting of the March 1980 supplement file based on the 1980 census, may exaggerate somewhat the relative growth of low-wage jobs (Robert McIntire, comments accompanying data on the distribution of jobs [Washington: Bureau of Labor Statistics, U.S. Department of Labor, December 30, 1986]).

29. The data for Figure 5.6, which was developed by BLS economist Robert McIntire, was obtained from the BLS. The Bluestone–Harrison data were only approximately (not exactly) duplicated by McIntire (McIntire, comments accompanying data on the distribution of jobs, December 30, 1986).

30. The BLS data also reveal a much larger increase in low-wage jobs between 1979 and 1984 than between 1973 and 1979. However, a significant part of the disparity is corrected by an extension of the period of analysis from 1984 to 1985.

31. See the social agenda developed in the last chapter of Barry Bluestone and Bennett Harrison, *The Deindustrialization of America* (New York: Basic Books, 1984).

32. Robert Kuttner writes, "Public policy exacerbated this maldistribution. Under the Reagan Administration, income transfers to the poor were sharply reduced. The income tax load was lightened, most notably for the rich, while the working poor faced higher Social Security taxes. Public sector employment, a source of jobs paying better-than-average wages, began to decrease. The minimum wage, a major income protection for the lowest-paid workers, fell further and further behind the average wage. In the face of growing resistance from industry and a hostile National Labor Relations Board, unions organized few low-wage workers and concentrated on defending the gains of the relatively well-paid" ("The Shrinking Middle Class Is a Call for Action," *Business Week*, September 16, 1985, p. 16).

33. Marvin H. Kosters and Murray N. Ross, "The Influences of Employment Shifts and New Job Opportunities on the Growth and Distribution of Real Wages," in *Contemporary Economic Problems: Deficits, Taxes, and Economic Adjustments,* edited by Phillip Cagan (Washington: American Enterprise Institute, 1987), p. 230. Kosters and Ross actually observed a very small increase in average hourly earnings, but focused their research on the impact of key variables on the slowdown of the increase in wages. After adjusting for the age, sex, and education of the work force, Kosters and Ross estimate that the net impact of changes in the employment structure on wage rates and worker hours (when the two were combined) was to reduce real average hourly earnings by a scant "two-thirds of a penny a year per year" (Ibid., p. 226). The authors were unable to specify exactly why the slowdown in wage-rate

growth occurred after 1972. At the same time, they were able to conclude that government policies designed to manipulate the economy's future industrial and employment structures would add to the cost of doing business in the United States and slow further the real rate of wage growth (Ibid., p. 236).

34. The presumed fading economic prospects of the "baby-boomers" are discussed in Frank S. Levy and Richard C. Michel, "An Economic Bust for the Baby Boom," *Challenge,* March/April 1986, pp. 33–39.

35. Kosters and Ross, "The Influences of Employment Shifts," p. 229.

36. Research on income distribution often relies heavily on the "Gini coefficient" as a measure of income inequality. Without going into how the coefficient is constructed, it might be noted that since the late 1960s the Gini coefficient has risen to a relatively minor extent (from approximately .035 in 1967 to .38 in 1985), reversing the trend of the coefficient of the 1950s and early 1960s and indicating growing inequality. However, the raw coefficient does not adjust for changing-age composition of labor. When the coefficient is adjusted for changing-age distribution, it is not at all clear that inequality of income is rising; it may in fact be falling. See Morton Paglin, "The Measurement and Trend of Inequality: A Basic Revision," *American Economic Review,* September 1975, pp. 598–609.

37. Rosenthal, "The Shrinking Middle Class," p. 5.

38. Rosenthal reports that the percent of the labor force in part-time employment for "economic reasons" rose from 3.1 in 1973 to 6.5 in 1982. A part of the increase may have been due to the recession under way in 1982. However, when Rosenthal adjusted his jobs distribution for part-time employment, the missing middle does not emerge. The percent of jobs in the low-wage stratum still falls (Rosenthal, "The Shrinking Middle Class," p. 5).

39. By contrast, the civilian labor force participation rate for men fell from 81.0 in 1964 to 76.3 in 1986.

40. At the same time, the growth in the labor force participation rate of women could be increasing the mean income of families and reducing the actual drift of families from the "middle class," a point noted by Katherine Bradbury in "The Shrinking Middle Class" (see note 6), p. 51.

41. The average-size family was 5.04 in 1880, and it is projected to continue its decline, reaching 2.48 at the turn of the century (based on a Census Bureau survey as reported in Robert Pear, "Household Size in the U.S. Declines to Record Low," *New York Times,* April 15, 1987, p. 1).

42. This point has been made by Frank Levy, "The Middle Class: Is It Really Vanishing?" (see note 6), p. 18.

43. Federal Reserve economist Katherine Bradbury argues that "demographic changes are not responsible for the bulk of the 1973–84 decline in the size of the middle class or in median family income" (Bradbury, "The Shrinking Middle Class," p. 52). That is not the same as saying that demographic factors are not responsible for less than the "bulk" of the observed changes, or that they do not contribute at all to our understanding of the relative growth in low-wage jobs. Again, low-wage jobs may or may

not be accompanied by a fall in the median income level.

44. Of course, the decline in worker-productivity growth, over time, could reflect the rise of the labor-force participation rate of women, as well as other demographic factors. In addition, the actual decline in productivity growth may be, at least partially, a product of flaws in statistics on worker productivity. This is especially true of measurements of productivity in services, which have been expanding in terms of employment.

45. For an analysis of the impact of environmental regulation on regional growth, see Bruce Yandle, "Environmental Control and Regional Growth," *Growth and Change*, July 1984, pp. 39–42. For an examination of the employment effects, see Office of Policy Analysis, U.S. Environmental Protection Agency, *Final Report: The Cost of Clean Air and Water, 1984* (Washington, May 1984). The contractors for this latter EPA study found that between 1971 and 1987, firms reported that environmental regulations were a significant factor in the closure of 155 plants involving nearly 33,000 workers (Ibid., p. 18). How many jobs were lost because of environmental regulations that forced production reductions is not reported. What is reported is that by 1987 environmental regulations may have added on balance over a half-million jobs to the work force. How the implied reshuffling of jobs occurred across occupations, industries, and regions is unclear. Also, even though more jobs may have been created through environmental regulation, it does not follow that higher *measured* real incomes—per capita or family—should be expected. If there have been any benefits at all to environmental regulation (a proposition seriously debated), income has been changed, from many measurable forms to many nonmeasurable forms.

46. These points are more fully explored in Chapter 9.

47. Legislation to raise the minimum wage to $4.65 an hour by 1990 (S. 837) by Senator Edward Kennedy (D-Massachusetts) and to $5.05 an hour by 1990 (H.R. 79) by Representative Mario Biaggi (D-New York) was introduced in spring 1987 ("Unfreezing the Minimum," *National Journal*, March 14, 1987, p. 648).

48. Of course, the economy suffered through several recessions during the 1964–86 period. The most recent short-run drop in income between 1978 and 1982, which greatly influences the Bluestone-Harrison findings, is evident in Figure 5.9. The important point about Figure 5.9 is the upward direction of the trend that has tilted downward since at least the middle of the 1970s.

49. This important question was first addressed directly by Paul Ryscavage, "Reconciling Divergent Trends in Real Income," *Monthly Labor Review*, July 1986, pp. 24–29.

50. Personal income includes wages and salaries (cash and in-kind payments); employers' contributions to private pension, welfare, workers compensation funds; proprietors' income; income from rental properties; dividends and interest; and business and government transfer payments (Social Security, food stamps, corporate cash prices, etc.). Family-income series developed by the Bureau of Census, on the other hand, exclude wages received

in-kind, food stamps, Medicare and Medicaid, the net rental value of owner-occupied houses, goods produced and consumed at home, and fringe benefits (Ibid., pp. 25–26).

51. Supplemental benefits in the calculations below are limited to employer contributions for social insurance and to private pension, health, and welfare funds; workers' compensation; directors' fees; and a few other minor items.

52. Based on national income accounting definition of wages and salaries and supplemental benefits as reported in *Economic Report of the President: 1987* (Washington: U.S. Government Printing Office, 1987), p. 270.

53. A far more inclusive definition of income supplements—including, for example, salary continuation, vacations, paid lunches, and rest periods—devised by the U.S. Chamber of Commerce makes "employee benefits" equal to 36.6% of payroll (or $7,842 per year per employee) in 1984 (Economic Policy Division, Chamber of Commerce of the United States, *Employee Benefits: 1984* [Washington: Chamber of Commerce of the United States, 1985], pp. 13 and 15).

54. The Bureau of Census, which collects its family-income data based on surveys of 60,000 households (supposedly representative of all households), has faced a growing problem of nonreporting of income—that is, a growing tendency for people interviewed in the surveys to refuse to report their incomes. In 1958 only 7% of the people interviewed refused to divulge their incomes. In 1968, the percentage of nonreporters was up to 11.2%. By 1986, the percentage had risen to 26.6%. The nonreporters are disproportionally represented by high-income earners in high-income professional jobs. According to one study, the Census Bureau fails to fully correct for the growing problems of nonreporting and tends, as a consequence, to underreport income (Lee Lillard, James P. Smith, and Finis Welch, "What Do We Really Know about Wages? The Importance of Nonreporting and Census Imputation," *Journal of Political Economy,* June 1986, pp. 489–506).

55. David Blau and Philip Robins, "A Study of Turnover in Low-Wage Labor Markets" (Washington: U.S. Department of Health and Human Services, Grant No. 113A-83, 1985).

56. The study, using Bureau of Labor Statistics counts of "displaced workers" across states, was under way when this book was being finalized. Using cross-sectional data, the econometric evidence, however, indicated a significant positive relationship between the amount of unemployment compensation and the prevalence of displaced workers.

57. Gary Solon, "Work Incentive Effects of Taxing Unemployment Benefits," *Econometrica,* March 1985, pp. 295–306. A number of other government-funded studies on the impact of government benefits on low-wage labor markets are reviewed in Daniel Banjamin, Mark L. Mitchell, and John T. Warner, *Synthesis of Policy Implications from Studies of Low Wage Labor Markets,* a monograph prepared for the Assistant Secretary for Planning and Evaluation, U.S. Department of Health and Human Services (February 1987).

58. Federal public aid per capita in 1980 dollars was $100.19 in 1970; $153.18 in 1972; $227.19 in 1978; and $197.54 in 1983 (Lowell Galloway and Richard Vedder, *Poverty, Income Distribution, The Family and Public Policy* [Washington: Joint Economic Committee, U.S. Congress, December 19, 1986], p. 37). The authors draw their conclusion about the perverse impact of federal public aid based on a variety of specifications of econometric equations in which public assistance is almost always negative and significant at the 5% level. They conclude, "Thus, in general, the public aid variable in the various forms of the estimating equation tend to confirm the hypothesis that transfer payments eventually become counterproductive when used as a policy device to reduce the incidence of poverty in the economy" (Ibid.).

59. Bradbury, "The Shrinking Middle" (see note 6), p. 41.

60. An important problem with the CPI is that it presumes that all householders have to endure the decrease in real income implied in higher interest rates on home mortgages (which tend to go hand-in-hand with higher inflation rates). However, many home owners are unaffected by higher interest rates, since they negotiated their loans in previous, noninflationary periods.

61. Other price indexes that adapt to changes in consumer buying patterns indicate slightly smaller price increases over the 1973–86 period than the personal consumption expenditure deflator. For example, between 1973 and 1983 (the latest year for the indexes), the Fisher 53 (Laspeyres) price index increased 104%, and the GFT-TCLI(1) index increased by 100%. The CPI-U, on the other hand, increased during the 1973–83 period by 121%, and the personal-consumption expenditure deflator increased by 110%. See R. L. Basmann, C. A. Diamond, J. C. Frentrup, and S. N. White, "Variable Consumer Preferences, Economic Inequality, and the Cost-of-Living Concept: Part Two," *Advances in Econometrics: Economic Inequality: Survey, Methods, and Measurements,* edited by R. L. Basmann and George F. Rhodes, Jr. (Greenwich, Conn.: JAI Press, 1985), pp. 10–11.

62. See Paul Ryscavage, "Reconciling Divergent Trends in Real Income" (see note 49), p. 26.

63. Marvin H. Kosters and Murray N. Ross, "The Distribution of Earnings and Employment Opportunities: A Re-Examination of the Evidence," *AEI Occasional Papers* (Washington: American Enterprise Institute), September 1987).

64. Ibid., p. 17.

65. Clark, "Economic Focus," p. 399.

66. See Kosters and Ross, "The Influence of Employment Shifts" (see note 33), pp. 209–42.

67. Kuttner, "The Shrinking Middle Class Is a Call for Action" (see note 32), p. 16.

68. McFadden, "Protectionism Can't Protect Jobs" (see note 27), p. 124.

69. Benjamin, Mitchell, and Warner, *Synthesis of Policy Implications from Low Wage Labor Markets* (see note 57), p. iii.

70. Samuelson, "The American Job Machine" (see note 26), p. 57.

CHAPTER 6

American Competitiveness

No matter how it is measured, America's balance of international trade has deteriorated dramatcially during the 1980s. Few internaitonal analysts think that it will go away in the near future; some predict that large (if not progressively larger) trade deficits will linger into the 1990s. Most Washington policy pundits worry that the country's worsening trade balance signals a degeneration of the country's "competitiveness," the new Washington buzzword made so prominent by the Reagan administration that it is sometimes called the "C-word" in Washington policy circles.

Unfortunately, too many policymakers fret that the presumed loss of America's preeminence in world trade is not transitory and self-correcting through normal market forces. Rather, they say, the trade deficit, still expanding in the late 1980s, is more evidence of a fundamental weakness in the American job machine—in Americans' capacity to cope with the ongoing structural changes in their own economy and to meet on an equal footing competitors from around the globe. "Getting more Americans to realize that it pays to make things in the U.S. is the heart of the competitiveness issue," concludes a *Business Week* reporter after surveying the dimensions of the competitiveness debate.[1]

Stephen Cohen and John Zysman, who direct the University of California's Berkeley Roundatable on International Economy, tell us that no matter how it is measured (but especially when measured by the trade deficit), "American industry confronts a severe problem of competitiveness, which it has never known before. Each measure has its limitations and can, perhaps, be explained away, but taken together they defy dismissal and portray a serious long-term problem."[2]

Following the media drumbeat of economic decline, as noted in all earlier chapters, policymakers often conclude that the country's economic salvation lies in a plethora of interventionist policies, including greater government expenditures on research and development, remedial education, and job retraining, all of which have been enthusiastically endorsed by President Ronald Reagan.[3] At the same time that they "bash" Japan for its unusually large contribution to U.S. trade woes, many policymakers recommend that the United States become more like Japan, both in terms of the personal attributes of the labor force and the content of public policy. Mainly, however, many policymakers tell us that the only certain way Americans can ever hope to compete effectively in world markets is through the elimination of the federal budget deficit via a tax increase or through the passage of protectionist legislation that would hamstring the foreign competitors.

Accordingly, pushed by a variety of labor and business interest groups, members of both the Reagan White House and the 100th Congress have readied their own legislative agendas on trade reforms.[4] "To the trade professionals, competitiveness is a buzzword," comments a trade lawyer. "For the Democrats, it's a way to say, 'We're not protectionists,' as they write their protectionist legislation. For the Republicans, it's a way to say, 'We are not single-minded free traders.'"[5] Political leaders have juxtaposed the C-word itself with various measures of large trade deficits in order to cast a favorable light on politically inspired restrictions on competition. As Senator Lloyd Bentsen (D-Texas), an ardent advocate of protectionism, confidently declared, the 100th Congress is "going to pass [trade legislation] and put [a measure] on the President's desk with him or without him."[6]

Before more people join the competitiveness bandwagon toward higher taxes or greater protectionism, the nature of the "trade deficit"—a necessarily artifical and arbitrary accounting convention—must be understood both as a concept and as a statistical construct. When understood as a statistical artifact, subsumed within the overall balance of *payments,* the balance of *trade,* even when in deficit, is not nearly so revealing of the country's competitiveness as has been widely assumed. Indeed, there are good conceptual reasons for believing that the trade deficit that emerged in the early 1980s mirrors, at least partially, a growing competitiveness within the domestic economy that was only fortified by the growing international aggressiveness of firms in other countries.

The Magnitude of the Trade Deficit

The presumed trade problems of the United States are measured in several ways, but the most easily understood measure is the balance on *merchandise trade*, which covers only U.S. exports and imports of goods.[7] Figure 6.1 vividly portrays the striking growth of the U.S. merchandise trade deficit in the period from 1982 to 1986. In 1981, the United States had a modest trade surplus of nearly $12 billion, measured in 1986 dollars. By the following year, the trade balance on exports and imports had switched to a deficit of under $9 billion in constant (1986) dollars. By 1986, however, the merchandise trade balance had grown in real terms by 1500%, to a whopping deficit of more than $146 billion.[8]

During the 1982–86 period, relative to real gross national product (GNP), the trade deficit also grew substantially. In 1982, the deficit was just above 0.2% of GNP. In 1986, the deficit represented slightly less than 3.5% of GNP. Other measures of the deficit on goods and services and current account grew both absolutely and relatively in concert with the merchandise trade deficit.[9]

Does the United States face a competitive crisis? Commentators considering the raw trade figures certainly think so. The country has

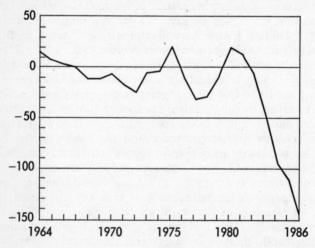

Fig. 6.1   Balance on U.S. merchandise trade: real exports 1964–1986 (1986 dollars). (*Source: Economic Report of the President*, 1987.)

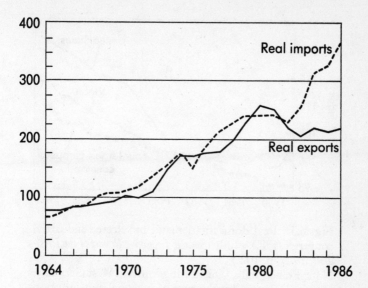

Fig. 6.2 U.S. merchandise exports and imports, 1964–1986 (billions of 1986 dollars). (*Source: Economic Report of the President,* 1987.)

had persistent trade deficits in its history, for example, in the late 1960s and early 1970s, but never as large as the ones reported in 1984 through 1986. The deficit in 1986 was, in real terms, more than four times the size of the previous peak deficit in 1977. Nevertheless, an answer to the competitiveness question is not as clear as might be imagined on first appraisal of the deficit record. The answer depends on how the export and import data—which encompass economic opportunities as well as problems—are viewed.

Taken by itself, the trade deficit can be misleading because it is the *net* of exports and imports. The total rise in the deficit in the 1980s could, therefore, have been due only to a fall in exports. A $160-or-so billion drop in exports between 1982 and 1986 might have, indeed, been a major policy concern, since it would have meant a virtual collapse (more than a 70% reduction) in exports during a four-year period. (U.S. exports in 1982 were only $219 billion, measured in 1986 dollars.)

However, as evident in Figure 6.2, the rapid rise in the trade deficit between 1982 and 1986 was actually due to a combination of export and import forces. Real imports grew by 52% between 1981 and 1986, while real exports fell by slightly more than 13%.

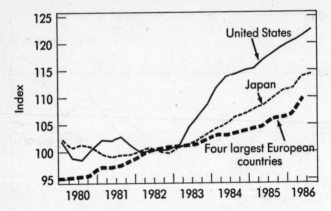

Fig. 6.3 Real domestic demand in selected industrial countries (1982 = 100). (*Source: Economic Report of the President,* 1987, p. 102.)
Note: France, Italy, United Kingdom and West Germany. Domestic demand is the sum of personal consumption expenditures, gross private domestic investment and government purchases of goods and services.

Obviously, some exporters were being outcompeted in foreign markets, but focusing on exports and imports, instead of on the *net* of the inflows and outflows of goods, is important for two reasons. First, the shift in imports relative to exports could be largely attributed, as it has been, to a relatively more rapid rate of economic growth in the United States. In fact, after inspecting data like that contained in Figure 6.3 on the relative growth of aggregate demand in the 1980s, President Reagan's Council of Economic Advisors concluded,

[T]otal demand grew much more rapidly in the United States than in other countries during the first six quarters of the expansion (through mid-1984). Since then, differentials between U.S. and foreign demand growth have narrowed considerably, but a large cumulative gap in domestic demand growth remains. This gap reflects the fact that the current recovery of U.S. domestic demand is one of the strongest of the postwar period. It also reflects the fact, however, that the recovery of domestic demand abroad has been one of the weakest.[10]

Clearly, the Reagan economists have political reasons for empha-
sizing the importance of the relatively faster growth rates of domestic
demand in the United States than in other countries. Yet they actually
managed to underplay its importance in explaining the downturn of
U.S. exports.[11] The growth in U.S. demand has, as recognized, led to
an expansion of imports because more foreign resources need to be
bought in order to produce more domestic output. In addition, more
foreign goods will be bought with the rise in domestic income. But
the growth in domestic demand has also led to a contraction of the
ability of the U.S. economy to export. The growth in domestic
demand has pulled resources away from export production.

Seen from this perspective, the balance-of-trade deficits could have
been moderated. Barring an expansion of foreign demand, however,
correction in the balance of trade would have called for a reduction
in domestic demand. This, in turn, would imply a lower rate of growth
in domestic production and income and higher unemployment at a
time when unemployment rates were already high by historical
standards—hardly a means of improving domestic competitiveness.

Second, as evident in Figure 6.4, between the late 1970s and 1985,

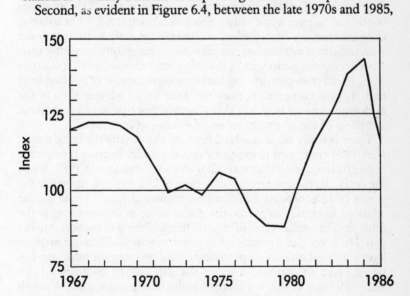

Fig. 6.4 The multilateral trade-weighted value of the U.S. dollar,
1967–1986 (March 1973 = 100). (*Source: Economic Report of the President,* 1987.)

the U.S. dollar appreciated in value more than 30% against a trade-weighted index of 15 other currencies; this means that U.S. exporters were, during the period, facing stiffer price competition in foreign markets. Given the rise in U.S. export prices in foreign markets and the relative rise in U.S. domestic demand, it may be deemed somewhat remarkable that U.S. exports did not drop by more than 13% in the period and that they were actually moving gradually upward after 1983 (refer to Figure 6.2)[12] One reason why exports did not fall by a greater percentage must be that, during the period, many (but, of course, not all) U.S. exporters were becoming more aggressive—more competitive, not less so. Improvement in the competitiveness of American industries has been reflected in their reductions of production costs.

On the import side, the rapid appreciation of the dollar meant a rapid decrease in import prices, which, of course, caused competitive problems for several domestic industries. U.S. firms were having to fend their market positions against lower-priced foreign goods, but at the same time, most U.S. industries were not being pushed out of their markets. The sales and employment levels in most U.S. industries continued to rise, while only a few levels contracted.[13] On balance, once the recovery from the last recession of the early 1980s was under way, industrial production and manufacturing output generally rose. Also during the period, most domestic import-competing industries were, in effect, demonstrating that they were capable of holding their own against competition made tougher by an adverse shift in the exchange rate—an outcome that is hardly descriptive of a systematic crippling of the competitiveness of American industries.

There is really no unresolved mystery about why the trade deficit after 1984 continued to expand when the dollar began a precipitous depreciation, a drop that was still under way throughout 1987. When the dollar depreciates rapidly, the prices of U.S. imports rise while the prices of U.S. exports fall. Because trading channels could not be adjusted as rapidly as prices, the dollar value of imports rose at the same time the dollar value of exports fell, widening the export–import gap. However, once producers in the domestic and foreign markets have sufficient time to adapt to new exchange rates, the trade gap can be expected to narrow. Whether the gap will be eliminated is an uncertain issue, as well as a fundamentally unimportant issue, although a point to which we will return.

Even if we could agree that the decline in the nation's competitiveness is evident in the balance-of-trade stratistics, we must wonder why the country's competitiveness fell so precipitously after

1981. The dollar began to appreciate rapidly on international money markets coincidentally with the appearance of rising trade deficits, but the high correlation between the dollar appreciation and the trade deficit must make us wonder about the source of the exchange appreciation. A rising U.S. demand for imports caused by, say, a slack in U.S. competitiveness or a greater aggregate demand in the domestic economy could not be the culprit. The reason is obvious: the greater demand for foreign currencies (or the rising supply of dollars) on international money markets that must accompany an exogenous rise in imports would imply a depreciation, not appreciation, of the dollar. Hence, the cause(s) of the balance of trade deficit in the first half of the 1980s must be found elsewhere in the country's international transactions—namely, in the little appreciated balance-on-capital account, the subject of a later section in this chapter.

Bilateral-Trade Follies

Discussions of the impact of trade deficits never become more misguided than in treatments of U.S. bilateral trade with identified countries, most prominently, Japan. In 1986, the U.S. trade deficit with Japan was approximately $60 billion—a figure which many presume can be readily corrected by the imposition of tariffs and quotas on U.S. imports from Japan. What is often forgotten is that Japan employs the dollars received from its bilateral surplus with the United States to buy goods and services from other countries around the world, and these countries use dollars received from the sale of their goods to Japan to buy goods from the United States.

Recognizing that point, solutions to U.S. bilateral-trade deficits are not so simple. Efforts to restrict U.S. imports from Japan, or any other country for that matter, can throttle U.S. exports.

The trade deficit with Japan, or with all other countries in the world, might be marginally improved by protectionist measures, but U.S. competitiveness certainly will not be.[14] Because less costly Japanese resources and parts must be used, protectionist measures can increase the cost of U.S. goods and can reduce the demand for U.S. goods since Japan will be less able to buy goods from other countries—in turn, less able to demand U.S. goods.

What is also overlooked in discussions of bilateral-trade deficits is that the United States is a much larger country in terms of people, income, and wealth than almost all of its principal trading partners. That means that the United States buys more goods from many of its trading partners simply because it has more people with higher incomes to do the buying. This point was explained with unusual clarity by Robert Mottice, an economist for the National Association of Manufacturers. He noted that in 1985 the United States had a $5-million merchandise-trade deficit with the Comoros, but he stressed that it is absolutely absurd to think that the deficit is indicative of the relative competitiveness of the two countries because

> Comoros is a tiny nation, both in terms of population and wealth. There is only one Comoran for every 480 Americans, and the U.S. per-capita gross national product is 40 times that of Comoran per-capita GNP. If every American spent a mere $2 a year on Comoran products while every Comoran spent his entire income on American goods, the U.S. would still have a trade deficit with Comoros.[15]

If it makes any sense at all to compare bilateral-trade deficits, the comparisons should at least be reduced to per-capita spending on foreign goods as a percentage of per-capita income, which is done in Table 6.1. That table reports the bilateral merchandise-trade deficit that the United States had with 17 countries in 1985 [column (1)]. It also reports the percentage of per-capita income Americans spent on the designated countries' goods [column (2)] and the percentage of per-capita income foreigners spent on U.S. goods [column (3)].

If Americans were truly noncompetitive with any country, Americans would have spent in 1985 a higher percentage of their incomes on foreign goods than foreigners spent on American goods. However, aside from Japan, foreigners spent a greater percentage of their incomes on U.S. goods than did Americans on foreign goods. The percentage gap between Japan and the United States was relatively modest, 1.81% for Americans versus 1.70% for the Japanese.

On the other hand, the percentage gaps for all the other countries was rather dramatic. Americans spent 1.74% of their per-capita income on Canadian goods, whereas Canadians spent 14.26% of their per-capita income on American goods. Even the Taiwanese, who supposedly are "blessed" with a competitive edge due to their low-wage labor, spent 18 times the proportion of their income on American goods that the Americans spent on Taiwanese goods.

The Overlooked Capital-Account Surplus

Policy commentators often discuss U.S. international-trade flows in goods as if they are the only meaningful transactions in the nation's

Table 6.1 Merchandise Trade Accounts with Various Countries, 1985

Country	U.S. Trade Deficit (in millions of dollars)	U.S. Spending on Foreign Goods (percent)	Foreign Spending on U.S. Goods (percent)
Japan	$49,749	1.81	1.70
Canada	22,176	1.74	14.26
Taiwan	13,061	0.44	7.82
West Germany	12,182	0.53	1.45
Hong Kong	6,208	0.23	8.23
Mexico	5,757	0.49	9.26
Italy	5,756	0.26	1.29
Brazil	5,007	0.20	1.47
South Korea	4,756	0.27	6.91
United Kingdom	4,300	0.39	2.54
France	3,864	0.25	1.19
Switzerland	1,291	0.09	2.49
South Africa	975	0.05	0.46
Philippines	955	0.06	0.42
Singapore	937	0.11	17.78
India	837	0.06	0.86
Chile	175	0.02	3.55

Source: Robert N. Mottice, "The U.S. Hasn't Lost Its Competitive Edge," *Wall Street Journal,* April 3, 1987, p. 32 (which was based on data obtained from the U.S. Department of Commerce and the International Monetary Fund).

balance of international payments, which, of course, is hardly the case, but which does permit policy discussions to proceed in terms of a deficit. A *deficit* cannot exist in the context of the entire balance of payments. Because of double-entry bookkeeping methods employed in recording international transactions, *the (full) balance of payments must balance!* An import entry in the trade account of the balance of payments, for example, must be exactly offset by another entry somewhere else in the balance-of-payments accounts. If this entry is not made with an export, then it may be made with a capital flow, a part of the capital account (a subsection of the full balance of payments).

Double-entry bookkeeping is used to accommodate the unbreachable principle that trade is a two-way exchange. What is bought from abroad by Americans or from the domestic market by foreigners must be paid for in some way—either in terms of dollars, other goods or services, securities, or trade credit (or some combination of all these payment methods). Recognizing the double-entry nature of the nation's international books makes two points evident. First, a trade deficit must be offset by a surplus in some other balance-of-payments account. As a matter of fact, as shown in Figure 6.5, the United States had a sharply rising capital-account surplus beginning in 1982, the same year that the balance-of-merchandise-trade deficit surfaced (see Figure 6.1). Furthermore, as is obvious in Figure 6.6 (and as expected), the merchandise-trade and capital-account balances moved between deficits and surpluses in almost identical countercycles (to each other) throughout the period covered by Figure 6.5.[16]

Second, the data on trade and capital balances say nothing about causal effects—what caused what. Policymakers who worry about the trade deficit seem to believe that trade deficits are directly caused by increases in imports or reductions in exports. This convinces some observers that the deficits are due to the growing (relative) aggressiveness of foreign producers who are able to outcompete American producers both in foreign and domestic markets.

From this perspective, the trade deficit is seen as a major (if not the only) cause of the capital-account surplus, not the other way around. Americans buy more from foreigners than foreigners buy from Americans, inadvertently leaving foreigners with more dollars than

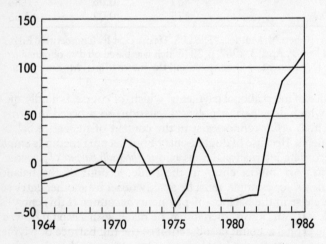

Fig. 6.5   Balance of U.S. capital outflows and inflows. 1964–1986 (billions of 1986 dollars). (*Source: Economic Report of the President,* 1987.)

they can use on American goods. Foreigners store the dollars (practically by default) in American bank accounts or in securities (all forms of capital inflows).

The causal connection between the trade-and-capital account balances is hardly so neat and self-revealing. Clearly, foreigners do sell goods to Americans and do hold onto some of the dollars they receive in exchange, but the dollars must also be valued and demanded (for a variety of reasons) by foreigners; otherwise, they would not give up their valuable goods for the dollars. Both parties must value the things received in exchange, or else the exchange across national boundaries would not happen (at least, not on a continuing basis).

Having acknowledged that obvious point, it is a leap of extraordinary perception for observers to conclude that the trade of foreign goods for U.S. dollars is motivated exclusively by the Americans' demand for the goods. It could be just as forcefully argued that the exchange is motivated by the foreigners' demand for the dollars — which can reflect their demand for U.S. cash balances, securities, or future goods and services.

This line of argument is elementary but crucial to an appreciation of just what trade deficits do — or, more accurately, do not — tell us about the competitiveness of the U.S. economy. Indeed, the argument

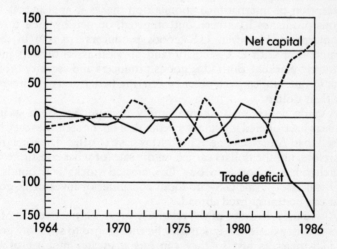

Fig. 6.6 Balance of merchandise trade and capital flows, 1964–1986 (billions of 1986 dollars). (*Source: Economic Report of the President, 1987.*)

casts considerable doubt on any proposition that a U.S. merchandise-trade deficit mirrors a lack of competitiveness among Americans. Clearly, the trade deficit indicates that Americans find foreign goods attractive, competitive. But, it indicates that in the Unites States forcigners find something—cash, securities, physical assets, or future goods and services—attractive and competitive.

Whether the foreign goods are *more* attractive to Americans than American cash and securities are to foreigners absolutely cannot be determined because the relative (subjective) values to the different people involved in the exchange cannot be measured. In addition, the question of relative attractiveness is irrelevant. What is important is that the exchange made across national boundaries is mutually beneficial to the people (not countries) involved.

The problem of assessing the relative competitiveness of Americans with reference solely to the balance of merchandise trade is made more difficult when it is understood that all Americans—goods producers and security brokers—actually compete with one another for the dollar claims held and obtained by foreigners through the sale of their goods and services in the United States. In other words, domestic goods producers are often perceived to be competing directly with their counterparts in other countries for domestic and foreign sales. When U.S. imports rise and exports fall and trade deficits result, this perception of international competition makes it appear that U.S. goods producers have been outcompeted, on net, by their foreign counterparts. However, U.S. goods producers are also in direct competition with U.S. security (and physical asset) brokers in the domestic markets. Both U.S. goods producers and security brokers seek to outcompete each other by offering better deals to foreigners for their dollars.

A trade deficit may emerge simply because American security brokers have offered foreigners a better deal on the securities they have to sell than American goods producers have to offer. The foreigners, therefore, use the dollars earned on the sale (of what constitute U.S. merchandise imports) to buy U.S.-created stocks and bonds (or physical assets), not U.S.-produced consumer or investment goods that can be transported abroad.

Alternately, because of the relatively greater attractiveness of the U.S. security deals, foreigners may be encouraged to sell more goods in U.S. markets just so they can buy a greater number of U.S. securities. However the capital inflow is ignited, the more competitive U.S. security brokers, offering improved deals on U.S. investments, can cause a rise in foreigners' demand for U.S. dollars. This leads to an appreciation of the dollar on international exchange markets and, in turn, to more attractive prices of foreign goods in U.S. markets and to less attractive prices of U.S. goods in foreign markets. In the process, economic life may be made more troublesome for U.S. export- and import-competing industries; but trouble for the non-competitive wherever it is found is endemic to market competition.

The principle is straightforward. The shift in the relative attractiveness of U.S. goods in international markets may appear to be due to deteriorating U.S. competitiveness (or, what amounts to the same thing: improving foreign competitiveness). In fact, the shift in relative competitiveness may be totally within the United States—among American producers.

The Presumed Loss of Jobs and Control

It may be understood that the troubles of U.S. goods producers may have their source in the attractiveness of U.S. investment. Yet the fear may linger that the surplus on the U.S. capital account implies a loss of jobs in the U.S. economy and a takeover by foreigners of the country's productive and financial assets. The fear of foreign takeover of the economy also cannot be summarily dismissed. After all, foreigners do not always have the same economic, cultural, and national objectives as do Americans. At the same time, the fear of foreign takeover is probably grossly exaggerated. Most foreign investors—for example, Canadians—have economic motives for their investments that are the same as Americans'. Many are no less inclined to use their control in American firms to further their private (as opposed to nationalistic) economic interests than are Hawaiians, for instance.

Furthermore, it is not at all clear that the United States would be economically stronger, more vibrant, and more independent if exports of real goods—for example, trucks and looms—were substituted for the export of financial assets—for example, stocks and bonds. When foreigners buy stocks and bonds, they have some limited control over U.S. productive assets. However, when they buy U.S. trucks and looms, they also have some limited control over U.S. productive assets. The principal difference is that when foreigners buy U.S. stocks and bonds, only a few sheets of paper are exported; the real productive assets remain in the country to be used to produce other things in this country. Because of their location, if for no other reason, the United States retains some control over the productive assets partially or totally owned by foreigners.[17] Conversely, when foreigners buy U.S. trucks and looms, the U.S.-produced assets are lifted out of the country with all U.S. control over them relinquished.

Foreigners investing in this country decide (implicitly or explicitly) that keeping the assets in this country is more productive than trucking, shipping, or airlifting them abroad for use elsewhere. That is, they decide that the assets can be more competitively employed in the United States than in their own country or in another country. By the same token, artificial inducements to promote exports from the United States would amount to a concerted effort to restrict foreign investment in the United States; artificial inducements to restrict imports would shift productive assets to less productive national venues.

The Destruction of Jobs Through Protectionism

Supporters of protectionism constantly remind voters that their favored artificial trade restrictions—that is, tariffs and quotas—can "save" and "create" American jobs. What they forget to tell voters is that artificial restrictions on specific imports invariably have secondary market effects that, on balance, can reduce American "competitiveness" and decrease American job opportunities.

Granted, by shifting domestic demands from foreign to domestic producers, tariffs and quotas may increase jobs in the protected industries. At the same time, the trade restrictions increase the prices of the protected products *and* the prices of American goods that use the protected products. For example, a quota on steel imports can drive up the price of American and foreign steel, increase the cost of producing cars and electrical equipment in the United States, and increase the prices of American-produced cars and toasters. To the extent that automobile jobs in the country are related to sales, jobs in the automobile and appliance industries (and in all other American industries that use steel) can be expected to fall because of the steel import quotas.

To illustrate with a real-world example, in 1984, the Reagan administration announced "voluntary export restraints" (VER)—that is, quotas—on the imports of steel, designed to reduce steel imports, as a percentage of total domestic sales, from 26% to 22% and to increase American jobs in the depressed domestic steel industry. According to Washington University economist Arthur Denzau, by 1986 the "VER" had in fact accomplished its objective and had increased steel employment by approximately 17,000.[18] At the same time, however, the VER had reduced employment in "steel-user" industries by more than 52,000: metal fabrication, 26,000 job losses; nonelectrical machinery, 11,800 job losses; electrical machinery, 4,600 job losses; and transportation equipment, 7,600 job losses.[19] The estimated net employment effect of the VER: 35,600 job losses. That empirical fact caused Professor Denzau to conclude (understandably), "To put it bluntly, trade protection is no friend of manufacturing jobs."[20]

Capital Surpluses and Trade Deficits, Once Again

A major implication of the foregoing discussion is that a source of the trade deficit lies in the dramatically rising capital-account surplus of the early 1980s. This is true because the rising trade deficit was accompanied, at least through 1985, with an appreciation of the dollar. An exogenous increase in import demand in the United States would have caused the dollar to depreciate.

As can be seen in Figure 6.7, a major source of the capital-account

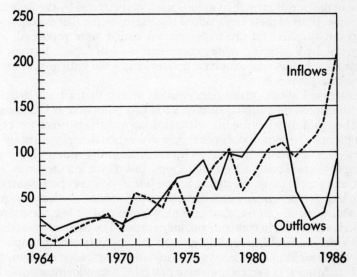

Fig. 6.7 U.S. capital outflows and inflows, 1964–1986 (billions of 1986 dollars). (*Source: Economic Report of the President,* 1987.)

surplus was the precipitous fall-off in U.S. capital outflows. At the same time capital inflows into the United States changed very little, capital outflows from the United States fell, in constant 1986 dollars, from $140 billion in 1982 to $25 billion in 1984, a drop of 82%.[21] After 1984, both capital inflows and outflows expanded. Inflows expanded more rapidly than outflows, however, resulting in a growing capital-account surplus—and a growing trade-account deficit.

The locus of the nation's trade woes in the 1982–85 period can, therefore, be found in the drop in U.S. foreign investment. Two important forces affecting U.S. capital outflows are especially worth mentioning. In the early 1980s, a number of underdeveloped countries, including Mexico and Brazil, began to face a debt crisis, raising the specter of default and, no doubt, causing many U.S. investors to reappraise the risks of foreign investment. Investors also cut back their loans and investments, at least until they understood the prospects of default and higher taxes in the foreign countries.

In addition, the U.S. economy began to develop more rapidly after 1982, partially in response to the 1981 tax-cut package that intentionally favored domestic investment (through more generous capital-depreciation schedules for computing taxes) and partially through a rise in the rate of growth in money stock orchestrated by the Federal Reserve. Both of these explanations suggest, however, that the capital-account surplus and the trade-account deficit were produced, in general, by a growing *relative* competitiveness of U.S. industries, a point that has been developed at greater length and with greater care by other authors.[22]

As noted above, many policymakers worry that a trade deficit accompanied by a capital surplus leads to a reduction in U.S. jobs. Although it may be true that identified labor markets (steel, for example) may be hurt, it does not follow that national employment suffers. This is because the foreign investments in the country are not simply financial; they are real in the sense that they affect the demands for, and supply of, goods and resources. Just as foreign export demand can lead to more employment because more goods are needed, foreign capital demand can translate into more employment because more goods are needed in construction, for example. The elimination of the trade deficit would, accordingly, mean the elimination of the capital surplus, resulting in, at best, a shift in national employment among U.S. industries, not an enhancement of total U.S. employment opportunities. If the trade deficit were "corrected" by trade barriers, as many have recommended, the logical long-run consequence would be a deterioration of aggregate employment opportunities. Mutually beneficial exchanges would be missed and national income would, in the aggregate, fall.

The Tale of Two Deficits: The Tenuous Connection

The search for explanations for the growing balance-of-trade deficit has led many commentators to a patently simple conclusion: the offender is Ronald Reagan. Or a better conclusion is that Reagan's improvident fiscal policies have given rise to huge deficits in the federal budget. Was it Reagan and his policies? Probably so, at least to some degree. It is hard to imagine a president's fiscal policies, which account for a quarter of the nation's expenditures, not having a minor, if not major, influence on national economic conditions.[23]

By the same measure, blame for the rise in the trade deficit cannot be attributed solely to the budget deficit (inspired by the 1981 tax-cut package), as has been widely presumed. According to much conventional financial wisdom, the likely connection between the budget deficit and trade deficit is apparent in Figure 6.8. The two deficits do not move in close synchronization, but they do move in concert. Causation cannot be determined solely from only two statistical series, but proponents of this line of argument maintain that there is a

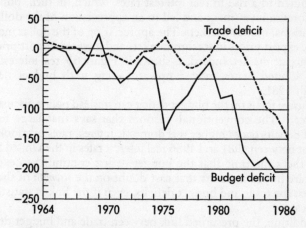

Fig. 6.8 Real federal budget deficits and real merchandise trade deficits 1964–1986 (billions of 1986 dollars). (*Source: Economic Report of the President, 1987.*)

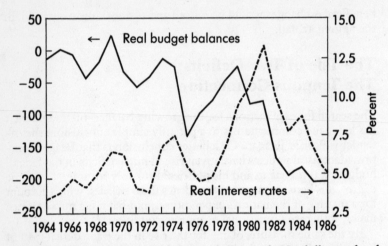

Fig. 6.9 Real federal budget balances (billions of 1986 dollars and real interest rates on three-month U.S. Treasury bills, 1964–1986. (*Source: Economic Report of the President, 1987.*)

theoretical sequence of connections between the budget deficit and the trade deficit. The $200 billion-plus budget deficits experienced during the Reagan years increased the demand for loanable funds and contributed to a rise in real interest rates, which, in turn, pulled in more foreign investment and led to an appreciation of the dollar on international money markets. The appreciation of the dollar increased U.S. export prices in foreign markets and lowered import prices in the domestic market. Indeed, as shown in Figure 6.9, real interest rates in the United States moved upward along with budget deficits through 1981.

Exclusive focus on the budget deficit can mislead policy discussions, however.[24] The conventional wisdom that says that large federal budget deficits *caused* higher real domestic interest rates overlooks the fact that between 1981 and 1986 real interest rates in the United States fell at the same time that the budget deficit continued to expand. These are important facts that cast doubt on the *strength* of the link between the trade and budget deficits, even if the link is statistically significant.[25]

In addition, the presumed link between trade and budget deficits suggests that the trade-deficit problem could have been avoided by the elimination of the federal-budget deficit (through a tax hike or the defeat of the 1981 tax-cut package). Supposedly, a tax hike would lower the federal deficit, reduce the government's demand for loanable funds, lower real interest rates, and reduce net-capital inflows.

There are two problems with the tax-hike solution. It presumes that a tax hike would cure the deficit problem, which may not be the case at all, given Congress's proclivity to spend whatever revenues are received. In addition, while a tax hike would reduce the demand for loanable funds from the federal government, it would also decrease the supply of loanable funds through the reduction in people's disposable incomes and savings. It is not at all obvious that real interest rates would have been materially different with the wholesale elimination of the deficit, given the federal-expenditure record.[26]

This latter point leads to the suspicion that the source of both deficits may be partially, if not totally, attributed to the growth in federal expenditures — a fiscal trend established during the Carter presidency and continued under Reagan.[27] Federal expenditures have continued to grow in both absolute real terms and as a percentage of gross national product during the Reagan years. Regardless of how they are financed, federal expenditures drain resources from the private sector, effectively containing the ability of American producers to expand private production with domestic resources alone. The federal growth in expenditures, not simply budget deficits, can thereby induce an expansion of imports and a contraction of exports and can contribute to an increase in the capital-account surplus.

The Confusion over Competitiveness

The United States, as a country, is often engaged in direct conflict and competition with other countries around the world. The United States has a notorious conflict of interest with the Soviet Union, Iran, and Libya, to name just three countries. With aligned and unaligned countries, the United States competes with these and other countries in terms of military might and influence. Conflicts with the Soviet Union, for example, are appropriately viewed as "national" problems because, to a greater or lesser degree, collectively established goals are at stake. But the overwhelming bulk of international trade is a matter of neither national goals nor collective means. International trade is, for the most part, the consequence of individuals, not nations, voluntarily acting alone and with others. If there is any international competition involving the United States, it is competition among *people* in the United States and between *people* in the United States and *people* in the rest of the world.

Herbert Stein, former chairman of the Council of Economic Advisors, succinctly captured a central point of this chapter when he noted that the U.S. trade deficit is a "metonymy," a figure of speech that conveys an idea by association but cannot be taken literally.[28] People speak of the New York Mets winning the World Series, suggests Professor Stein, when, in fact, they realize that a group of men who play for the Mets organization actually won the series. Similarly, people loosely talk of the U.S. running a trade deficit when, in fact, all fully understand that countries do not run trade deficits; people do. People actually do the buying and selling in foreign markets, almost always to their mutual advantage.

Although admitting that verbal precision was never the central object of his comments, Professor Stein goes on to ask "why any of us should worry about this particular statistic [the trade deficit], and why the U.S. government should take any responsibility for it. The people who have the trade deficit—who are buying more abroad than they are selling—are dong so voluntarily. If they were worried much they would stop. I had a trade deficit in 1986 because I took a vacation in France. I didn't worry about it; I enjoyed it."[29]

Unfortunately, in policy discussions "trade deficit" has been juxtaposed with discussion of the country's "competitiveness" so often that far too many people have begun to assume that international trade is some kind of ongoing Olympic game in which the United States is losing. Knowing little about balance-of-payments statistics, they imagine the trade deficit to be an official count of medals awarded for individual events, when, in fact, the *country* is not competing with other countries in the sense presumed.

A major point of this chapter is amazingly simple: Contrary to the popular view, international trade is not (and should not be perceived as) a set of ongoing transnational games in which the countries receive medals and the spoils of victory, while the losers get nothing. Trade, whether domestic or international, is a continuing economic process conducted, for the most part, at the individual-consumer level and firm level in which all parties gain ("medals" are given to all participants). All parties are ultimately responsible for their own transactions.

There is little that government should or could do directly to correct the country's "trade deficit" and, at the same time, correct the country's "competitiveness." Protectionist measures have been offered as solutions to both problems. Protectionism hardly corrects the country's—meaning individuals' and firms'—competitiveness. Competitiveness is, fundamentally, the ability of people to adapt, outwit, outmaneuver, and outproduce market rivals. And protectionism does absolutely nothing to improve the ability of Americans to adapt, outwit, outmaneuver, outproduce, and underprice foreigners or other Americans. Instead of fostering competition, protectionism obstructs it by reducing the capacity of foreigners to adapt, outwit, outmaneuver, and outproduce Americans. And it reduces the long-run incentives Americans have to learn how to compete more effectively in a global marketplace. Competitors, whether in sports or business, do not advance their skills by shackling their rivals. Rather, they improve—become more competitive—facing their present rivals head-on, and even seeking out more pressing contenders.

Comparative Advantage and Competitiveness

Competitiveness, especially when applied to the interaction among foreign and domestic rivals, loses much of its meaning as a nationalistic notion. Firms and industries can become more competitive, but not countries. Countries can change policies that influence the productivity and total output of industries, but it is the firms or industries, not countries, that compete with their rivals.

The problem of "American competitiveness" as a national phenomenon can be understood only by first realizing that absolute levels of productivity of individual firms or industries have nothing directly to do with their ability to export and/or to fend against import competition. As recognized since the early 19th century (the days of David Ricardo), economists have understood that what matters in determining the direction of trade across national borders is the structure of *comparative*, not *absolute*, advantage of industries within countries. Comparative advantage depends on the relative trade-off (or cost) of goods and services in production within countries. Just because an industry in one country is more productive than the same industry is in another country does not guarantee that the former industry will have a comparative advantage over the latter industry, meaning that the former does not have to face foreign competitors. Because *comparative* productivities are involved, the direction of trade also depends upon the productivity of domestic industries and how their relative productivities compare with the relative productivities in other countries.

The point is that government policies designed to improve the productivity of *all* sectors of American business will not insure that *all* will be in a better position to compete in international or domestic markets. Again, this is because the direction of trade depends upon comparative, rather than absolute, advantages of industries within countries. An even, across-the-board improvement in all sectors may simply upgrade the productivity of all industries. It may not change at all their relative productivities and, as a consequence, the trade-offs: their comparative advantages and disadvantages. It may only change the overall productive capacity of the economy, which could lead to more imports and exports.

Should policymakers and political leaders be concerned about the competitiveness of American industries? Surely, they should. Improvements in the living standards of Americans is contingent on increases in productivity and in the aggressiveness of people in product and resource markets. At the same time, policymakers should not ignore the trade deficit. They must recognize the relevance of the nation's policies—taxes, expenditures, and rules—to determine how they may be obstructing the ability of Americans to adapt, outwit, outmaneuver, and outproduce their domestic and foreign competitors. Competitors need the opportunity to compete, which means the freedom to find their own way in markets unconstrained, as much as possible, from external controls and directions.

Concluding Comments

The political attractiveness of "competitiveness" is magnified by its ambiguity. It means so many different things to so many different people. To that extent, it offers many political leaders a verbal banner around which they mistakenly believe they can unite. This is because agreement over the use of a single word proffers the pretense of agreement. Much of the current political interest in competitiveness will surely dissipate when political opponents realize they are talking at cross purposes—when they realize that they have radically different goals in mind that give rise to opposing policy solutions. The pretense of agreement may dissolve altogether when it is recognized that across-the-board improvement in productivity for all business sectors may not change the *relative* ability of firms to compete with foreign producers.

However, the vagueness of the term might allow those who want to restrain competition in U.S. markets to work their political wills, which is the advancement of their private economic interest at the expense of the general population. Proponents of protectionism have already been successful in making many voters believe that the trade deficit is a *national* problem subject to direct *national* remedies that all too often translate into market controls, which, in reality, are the antithesis of competitive policies.

Notes

1. Norman Jones, "Can America Compete?" *Business Week,* April 20, 1987, p. 47.

2. Stephen S. Cohen and John Zysman, *Manufacturing Matters: The Myth of the Post-Industrial Economy* (New York: Basic Books, 1987), p. 61. The authors are especially concerned that key manufacturing industries, which they believe are vital to the future health of the U.S. economy, are in serious decay: "Unfortunately, the evidence is substantial that the competitiveness of the American economy is eroding, and manufacturing is taking the brunt of the downward shift" (Ibid.).

3. Ronald Reagan, Speech to business leaders on the administration's competitiveness initiative, East Room of the White House (Washington: Office of the Press Secretary, Executive Office of the President, February 17, 1987).

4. The principal legislative actions in 1987 revolve around two comprehensive trade bills, H.R. 3, introduced by House Speaker Jim Wright (D-Texas), and S. 1860, introduced by Senator Lloyd Bentsen (D-Texas). See Jonathan Fuerbringer, "Toned-Down Bill to Widen Exports Offered in House," *New York Times,* March 11, 1987, p. A1; Monica Langley, "House Panel Approves Bill Covering Trade," *Wall Street Journal,* March 13, 1987, p. 5; and "Compromise Textile Bill Introduced," *Greenville* (S.C.) *News,* February 20, 1987, p. 1A.

5. As quoted in Bruce Stokes, "Setting the Stage," *National Journal,* January 17, 1987, p. 119.

6. Ibid.

7. Two other commonly cited measures of U.S. "trade" problems include the balance on goods and services (which adds net military transactions, investment income, travel, transportation, and other services to merchandise trade) and balance on current account (which adds remittances, pensions, and other unilateral payments to the balance on goods and services).

8. All trade and deficit figures for 1986 are preliminary, based on annualized figures for the first three quarters.

9. The deficit on goods and services and on current account tended to be lower in all years than the deficit on merchandise trade. This was generally because of the net inflow of investment income and the surplus in trade of services.

10. Beryl W. Sprinkle, chairman; Thomas Gale Moore; and Michael L. Mussa, Council of Economic Advisors, *Economic Report of the President* (Washington: U.S. Government Printing Office, 1987), pp. 101–2. Between

1982 and 1985, real domestic demand in the United States grew at an average annual pace of 5.6%; aggregate demand in Japan grew 3.1%; in Canada, 4.2%; in France, 0.8%; in Italy, 1.5%; in Germany, 1.9%; and in the United Kingdom, 3.1% (Ibid., p. 104).

11. Reporting on econometric work by six contributors to a Brookings Institution workshop on the current account imbalance, Brookings senior fellows Ralph Bryant and Gerald Holtham conclude that the rise in the current account deficit in the first half of the 1980s was not unexpected, given the relative rise in U.S. income and the appreciation of the dollar. In fact, using historical data, the econometric models represented at the workshop predicted the actual deficits for each year fairly closely, causing them to write that such a fact "is strong evidence against the assertion that there has been a break in historical relationships" (Ralph C. Bryant and Gerald Holtham, "The External Deficit: Why? Where Next? What Remedy?" *Brookings Review*, Spring 1987, p. 29). The authors estimated that about one-fourth of the current account deficit could be attributed to the relative rise in U.S. income and three-fourths to the appreciation of the dollar. The Brookings researchers were unable to attribute any of the deterioration in the U.S. trade balance to growing protectionism abroad, a frequently asserted, but unsubstantiated claim of advocates of expanded protectionism in the United States (Ibid.).

12. Bryant and Holtham conclude "paradoxically that the deficit is 'too' easy to explain" (Ibid.).

13. Norman Fieleke notes in a study of the impact of rising trade deficits on industry, "A common view is that rising import competition signifies unemployment and plant closings. In fact, no such simple correlation prevails" (Norman S. Fieleke, "The Foreign Trade Deficit and American Industry," Federal Reserve Bank of Boston, *New England Economic Review*, July/August 1985, p. 52). Fieleke explains that import penetration can be misleading when aggregate demand is rising. While American industries may have done better, if the dollar had not appreciated, "it is clearly premature to lament the downfall of American industry" (Ibid.).

14. The improvement in the trade deficit will not be equal to the reduction in imports. This is true because exports will also be reduced.

15. Robert N. Mottice, "The U.S. Hasn't Lost Its Competitive Edge," *Wall Street Journal*, April 3, 1987, p. 32.

16. The reason that the two account balances do not *exactly* offset each other is that several transaction categories, mainly services and remittances, are left out of the trade balances.

17. If ownership of firms is shared by Americans and foreigners, the American owners still retain a voice in the firm's operations. Even if foreign ownership is complete, Americans still retain controls through legislated policies.

18. Arthur T. Denzau, *How Import Restraints Reduce Employment* (St. Louis: Center for the Study of American Business, Washington University, June 1987), p. 5.

19. Ibid., Table 2, p. 6.

20. Ibid., p. 4.

21. Capital outflows include all U.S. investments in foreign assets and securities, whereas capital inflows include all foreign investments in U.S. assets and securities.

22. See *U.S. Competitiveness: Perception and Reality* (New York: New York Stock Exchange, 1984); Murray L. Weidenbaum with Richard Burr and Richard Cook, *Learning to Compete: Feedback Effects of the Non-Linear Economy* (St. Louis: Center for the Study of American Business, Washington University, 1986); John Tatum, "Domestic vs. International Explanations for Recent U.S. Manufacturing Developments," *Review* (St. Louis Federal Reserve Bank), April 1986, pp. 5–18; and Norman S. Fieleke, "The Foreign Trade Deficit and American Industry" (see note 13).

23. However, it is easy to exaggerate a president's influence, especially since as much as 75% of the federal budget cannot be changed from year to year.

24. Unfortunately, the author has, in the past, accepted the conventional connection between budget and trade deficits.

25. The link between the trade and budget deficits by way of real interest rates has been studied by John Tatum, "Domestic vs. International Explanations for Recent U.S. Manufacturing Developments"; David Bowles, Holley Ulbrich, and Myles Wallace, "Default Risk, Interest Differentials, and Fiscal Policy: A New Look at Crowding Out" (Clemson, S.C.: Economics Department, Clemson University, 1986); and Nathan Childs, *International Trade Explanations for Farm Troubles in the 1980s* (Clemson, S.C.: Agriculture Economics Department, Clemson Univesity, Ph.D. dissertation, 1987). These authors conclude that the link could not be satisfactorily detected in their econometric studies.

26. In fact, it is not at all clear whether interest rates would rise, fall, or remain the same, given the directional shifts in supply and demand for loanable funds.

27. For an analysis of how the federal expenditure pattern during the Reagan presidency compares with the expenditure pattern that would have been projected along the Carter trend, see Richard B. McKenzie, "Taking Stock of the Federal Budget," *Occasional Paper* (St. Louis: Center for the Study of American Business, Washington University, March 1986).

28. Herbert Stein, "Leave the Trade Deficit Alone," *Wall Street Journal*, March 11, 1987, p. 36.

29. *Ibid.,* Stein's thesis is more fully developed in Herbert Stein, "A Primer on the Other Deficit," *AEI Economist* (Washington: American Enterprise Institute, March 1987).

CHAPTER 7

The Demise of Textile and Apparel Jobs

Proponents of protectionism claim that the major adjustment problems American industries face is, to a major degree, due to foreign competition. In order to save American jobs, they say, American firms must be protected with tariffs, quotas, and voluntary export restraints by foreign countries. The textile and apparel industries have made such claims for decades, and the validity of protectionist claims can be partially assessed by comparing the rhetoric and reality of the employment records of the textile and apparel industries.[1] This chapter is, in effect, a case study of how these two industries justify their political drive for protectionism and how the facts square with the reality of lost American jobs.[2]

The Protectionist Claims

Backers of the vetoed Textile and Apparel Trade Enforcement Act of 1985 sought to reduce textile imports by as much as 36% and apparel imports by as much as 20% from their 1985 levels.[3] According to one estimate, if the bill had been enacted, it would have raised wholesale prices for textile imports by 33% and wholesale prices for apparel imports by 16%.[4] It would have also added at least $3.4 billion to the annual consumer cost of textile protectionism already estimated at more than $20 billion a year.[5]

These proposed textile and apparel trade restrictions have been tendered on the proposition that expanding textile and apparel imports have caused the closing of as many as 250 plants since 1980 and have robbed American textile and apparel workers of hundreds of thousands of jobs during the past decade.[6] Indeed, the drafters of the bill estimated that in 1984 the total volume of textile and apparel imports into the United States represented "over 1 million job opportunities lost to the United States workers."[7]

Ellison McKissick, president of the American Textile Manufacturers Institute, argued that "our markets have been overwhelmed by imports... Since 1980, more than 300,000 fiber, textile and apparel workers have lost their jobs."[8] "[I]f the rate of growth of imports of textiles and textile products into the United States that occurred since 1980 continues," wrote the backers of the 1985 textile and apparel bill, "plant closings will continue to accelerate, leaving the United States market with reduced domestic competition for imported products."[9]

Senator Fritz Hollings (D-South Carolina) called the textile and apparel bill "sensible protection."[10] Hollings was concerned about plant closings in his home state caused partially because shirts can be made in "downtown Shanghai, China for 18 cents an hour." He and other supporters of protection maintained that they want only to return "fair trade, to make the table level again."[11]

Now that the textile and apparel bill has been vetoed by President Ronald Reagan, the purpose of this chapter is to assess the impact of changes in textile and apparel imports as well as in domestic textile and apparel productivity on U.S. textile and apparel employment. While the findings are mixed, the research reported here (which is unavoidably technical at times) should prove useful in what appears to be a perennial public debate over textile and apparel protection. (In spite of their political defeat in 1986, the textile and apparel industries were once again lobbying hard in 1988 for additional import protection.)

In summary, we found that the total number of people employed in the textile and apparel industries would have decreased substantially (by possibly more than 200,000 jobs) during the 1973–84 period even if there had been no textile imports at all. Contrary to the contentions of protection components, textile imports have not, in any systematic and predictable manner or to any statistically significant extent, adversely affected U.S. textile employment between 1960 and 1985. However, apparel imports appear to have had an important negative impact on both textile and apparel employment.

Textile employment losses can, to a meaningful degree, be attributed to improvements in productivity. (Determining the extent to which these improvements may have been spurred by textile and apparel import competition and by domestic textile and apparel competition is, however, beyond the scope of the study reported in this chapter.) On the other hand, improvements in productivity have not been a statistically significant factor of employment losses in the apparel industry.

The findings of this chapter help explain why many textile firms have remained profitable, even in the face of employment cutbacks. Another more predictable conclusion of the analysis is that employment in both the textile and apparel industries is significantly influenced by changes in real personal disposable income in the United States.

The first section of this chapter briefly describes developments in the textile and apparel industries during the period from 1960 to 1984. The following section presents the model and analyzes the effects of imports, personal disposable income, and productivity on textile and apparel employment. The final section summarizes the results and conclusions drawn from the findings.

Industry Descriptions

In many respects, the textile and apparel industries are of similar size and have confronted similar employment, production, and import

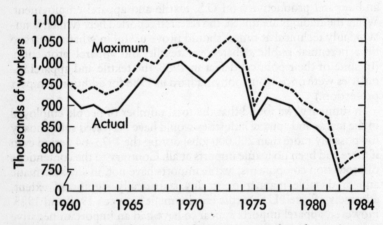

Fig. 7.1 Textile industry employment, actual and maximum, 1960–1984. (Note: Maximum employment assuming that imports are replaced by domestic production.) (*Source:* U.S. Bureau of Labor Statistics, *Employment, Hours, and Earnings: 1909–1984*; and *Employment* and *Earnings,* July 1985.)

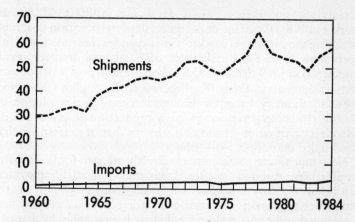

Fig. 7.2 Textile industry real domestic shipments and imports, 1960–1984 (billions of 1984 dollars). *Source:* U.S. Department of Commerce, *U.S. Industrial Outlook* [various annual editions].)

patterns during the 1960–84 period. During these two and a half decades, both industries faced mounting imports, productivity increases, and relative price declines.[12]

The Textile Industry

Between 1960 and 1973, employment in the textile industry—identified by standard industry classification (SIC) 22—rose from 924,000 to slightly more than 1 million, but by 1984 industry employment had fallen to 746,000, or by slightly more than a quarter of the 1973 peak employment level. (See Figure 7.1, which shows the irregular but decreasing shift in employment figures.)

Total industry shipments in constant-dollar (1984) terms nearly doubled between 1960 and 1973, rising from just over $29 billion to almost $53 billion.[13] (See Figure 7.2.) After declining for two years, real shipments rose until 1978, peaking at nearly $65 billion. Textile shipments then began to fall again during the recessions of the early 1980s. However, by 1984 industry shipments had climbed back to just under $58 billion in spite of a continuing drop in textile employment and increase in textile imports.

During the 1960–84 period, worker productivity, defined as monetary value of real shipments per worker, increased 147%, rising in real (1984) dollars from \$31,407 per worker in 1960 to \$77,526 per worker in 1984. Constant-dollar textile imports more than quadrupled during the period, yet market share expanded more modestly. Imports grew from \$922 million (or 3.2% of total domestic textile shipments) in 1960 to nearly \$3.8 billion (or nearly 6.5% of domestic textile shipments in 1984). (See Figure 7.2.) Throughout the period, the textile industry was going through a technological revolution, including the computerization of many production processes and the introduction of water-jet and air-jet looms that, at times, more than quadrupled output per worker hour.

How much have textile imports directly affected textile-industry employment? A rough estimate of maximum potential employment can be obtained by assuming that textile-industry employment is proportional to sales and then computing industry employment assuming that the import share would have been supplied by domestic firms.[14]

In the absence of imports, textile-industry employment naturally would have been higher in every year between 1960 and 1984. (Compare the actual and maximum employment patterns in Figure 7.1.) However, it is important to note that between 1973 and 1984, textile employment would still have fallen by virtually the same amount

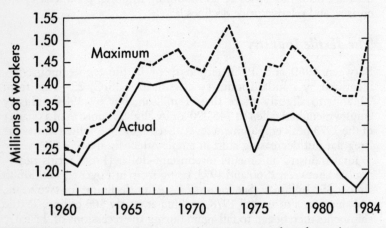

Fig. 7.3 Apparel industry employment, actual and maximum, 1960–1984. (Note: Maximum employment assuming that imports are replaced by domestic production.) (*Source:* U.S. Bureau of Labor Statistics, *Employment, Hours and Earnings: 1909–1984;* and *Employment and Earnings,* July 1985.)

(267,000) as the actual decline (264,000) even if imports could have been totally replaced by domestic production.[15] This happens to be the case because the elimination of textile imports would have led to approximately the same increase in employment—about 50,000—in both 1973 and 1984.[16]

Practically the same conclusion can be reached about the impact on textile employment of eliminating textile imports between 1980 and 1984. During that four-year period, textile employment actually fell by 102,000, whereas industry employment would have fallen by 98,000 in the absence of imports. However, as will be discussed later in this chapter, the substantial rise in real apparel imports, incorporating foreign textiles, did contribute to declining employment in domestic textiles, during both the 1973–84 and 1980–84 periods.

The Apparel Industry

In 1960, there were approximately 1.2 million apparel workers in the country. Employment in the apparel industry (SIC 23) also peaked in 1973 at more than 1.4 million workers, fell to 1.2 million by 1975, and then rose to 1.3 million by 1979. In 1980, apparel employment began a steady decline, dropping to a level just under 1.2 million workers by 1984. (See Figure 7.3.)

However, industry shipments in constant dollars moved irregularly

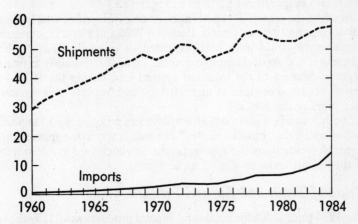

Fig. 7.4 Apparel industry real domestic shipments and imports, 1960–1984 (billions of 1984 dollars). (*Source:* U.S. Department of Commerce, *U.S. Industrial Outlook,* various annual editions.)

upward from over $29 billion in 1960 to more than $57 billion in 1984. (See Figure 7.4.) Unlike the textile industry, however, the value of industry shipments in apparel was greater in 1984 than in any previous year since 1960. Given industry rhetoric about the devastating impact of imports, the fact that domestic-industry shipments was at an all-time high in the mid-1980s is, indeed, startling.

Worker productivity doubled in real terms from $23,649 per worker in 1960 to $47,858 per worker in 1984. However, the productivity increase was slightly less than 70% of the productivity improvement in textiles. Constant-dollar apparel imports surged dramatically during the 1960–84 period, rising more than twenty-fold—from under $600 million (or 2% of domestic apparel sales) in 1960 to over $14 billion (or nearly 25% of domestic apparel sales) in 1984.[17] (See Figure 7.4.)

Did the rise in apparel imports adversely affect employment? If we again assume that apparel employment is proportional to sales and that apparel imports could be replaced by domestic production during the period 1960–84, apparel employment would have been 2% higher in 1960 and 25% higher in 1984.[18] The computed maximum apparel employment would have dropped 35,000 between 1973 and 1984, whereas actual employment decreased by 241,000. In other words, between 1973 and 1984, apparel imports may have resulted in the loss of as many as 200,000 apparel jobs. (Compare the actual and maximum employment patterns in Figure 7.3.)

Much of the impact of apparel imports on employment was, indeed, felt during the 1980–84 period. Between 1980 and 1984, U.S. apparel employment could have been expected to grow by 77,000 jobs, whereas actual apparel employment fell by 67,000. Possibly as many as three-quarters of the losses in apparel jobs during the 1973–84 period occurred because of increased apparel imports over the first four years of the 1980s.[19]

In other words, if there was an employment problem due to imports in the "textile and apparel industry" as a unit, it was in the apparel segment. However, domestic apparel production continued to rise in spite of the import-induced loss of apparel jobs.

Prices of Textile and Apparel Products

The 1984 price index for textile and apparel products was 111% above its 1960 level. However, the prices of other goods and services during the 1960–84 period rose much more rapidly, especially during the late 1970s. As a consequence, prices of textile and apparel products (relative to the consumer price index) declined by one-third during the period.[20]

However, it is difficult to say how much of the relative decline in textile and apparel prices is due to imports. The textile and apparel industries, by all accounts, are highly competitive, and technological developments internal to the domestic industries could have played a major role in reducing costs and driving down prices. Contrary to what the industries might want to think, domestic competitors could be responsible for many of their pricing, production, and employment woes. Many of the 250 domestic plants that closed, over the past decade or so, may have gone out of business due to mismanagement and due to domestic competition, which is likely to be strong even in the absence of imports. An associate dean of a major textile school once made an important, rarely admitted insight when he once told the author in private, "Every time I hear that textile executive [of a major American company] get up and rant and rave about how imports are killing the American textile and apparel industry, I think to myself that his company, by its aggressiveness in markets, has probably caused the elimination of more American textile jobs than all of the imports combined." In short, it is not always the foreigners who are competitive, and it appears to be the height of policy folly to suggest otherwise (which the facts do not support).

Statistical Models and Results

The loss of jobs in the textile and apparel industries is probably due to many factors, which is a way of admitting that the foregoing discussion, focusing on simple time-series data, has important limitations. The actual impact of textile and apparel imports on domestic employment can be more accurately assessed through regression analysis, which is a statistical technique for separating the impact of several variables.

Domestic textile and apparel employment can be influenced by many factors, including productivity change, real textile and apparel imports, and real disposable personal income. Textile and apparel employment may be expected to vary directly with real disposable personal income. The greater the real disposable personal income (representing the buying power of consumers), the greater the demand for textile and apparel products and the greater the number of workers in the industries.

However, the directional impact of the other three variables is less certain. Productivity improvements can increase or decrease textile and apparel employment, depending on the elasticity of demand for textile and apparel products.

Similarly, textile and apparel imports can increase or decrease textile and apparel employment, depending on the relative magnitudes of the substitution and income effects of textile and apparel imports. Imports may substitute for textile and apparel products of U.S. firms because of either lower prices or higher quality.[21] In addition, imports—especially textile imports—can lower production costs of textile and apparel firms and prices of U.S. goods that incorporate tex-

Table 7.1 Log-Linear Regression Equations for the Textile and Apparel Industries

Independent Variables	Dependent Variables	
	Total Employment in the Textile Industry	Total Employment in the Apparel Industry
Intercept	0.731	2.222
	(0.666)	(2.766)
	[.5131]	[.0119]
Productivity	−0.455	−0.076
	(−2.123)	(−0.400)
	[.0464]	[.6937]
Real disposable personal income	1.143	0.789
	(5.381)	(5.659)
	[.0001]	[.0001]
Real textile imports	0.166	0.159
	(2.243)	(3.198)
	[.0364]	(.0045)
Real apparel imports	−0.257	−0.245
	(−3.659)	(−4.715)
	[.0016]	[.0001]
Adjusted R^2	.756	.742
F value	19.541	18.266
	[.0001]	[.0001]

(T statistic)
[Significance level]

tile and apparel products, expanding sales and demand for U.S. or imported textiles and apparel.

The effects on real income of textile and apparel imports can be expected to be positive; however, the substitution effects of imports — especially textile imports — are more ambiguous. On one hand, apparel imports, *ceteris paribus,* can be expected to reduce domestic apparel and textile employment. On the other hand, textile imports can make more competitive domestic apparel goods, and textile goods that incorporate imported unfinished textiles. As a consequence, textile imports may have a positive effect on both domestic textile employment and domestic apparel employment.[22]

To test the employment effects of textile and apparel imports, we had to resort to regression analysis. Separate log-linear least-squares regression models for the textile and apparel industries have been developed with total employment in the respective industries as the dependent variable. The time-series models cover annual data for the period 1960 to 1984. The four independent variables used in the regression equation are:

Industry labor productivity = the current-dollar value of total annual industry (textile or apparel) shipments adjusted by the textile and apparel price index divided by total industry employment[23]

Real disposable personal income = current-dollar annual disposable income adjusted by the consumer price index

Real textile imports = current-dollar value of annual textile imports adjusted by the textile and apparel price index

Real apparel imports = current-dollar value of annual apparel imports adjusted by the textile and apparel price index.

The Effects of Imports

The results of the least-squares analysis are presented in Table 7.1. As can be seen, the four variables explained nearly three-quarters of the variance in employment for both textile and apparel equations. As indicated by their high F values, both equations offer robust explanations of textile and apparel employment over the 1960–84 period.

Textile imports. During the 1960–84 period, real textile imports had a relatively small but statistically significant *positive* impact on both domestic textile and apparel employment levels, suggesting that textile imports may well have enabled some, but, of course, not all, domestic producers to be more competitive through the use of cheaper unfinished textile imports. (The significance level of textile imports is lower for the apparel equation than the textile equation.) The two equations indicate that a 1% increase in real textiles will lead to an approximately 0.16% increase in both the domestic textile employment and domestic apparel employment.[24]

Apparel imports. The coefficient for real apparel imports is negative and highly significant in both employment equations. The size of the negative apparel–import coefficient, roughly the same in both equations, is also substantially higher in both equations than the positive coefficient for textile imports.

The statistical tests indicate that a 1% increase in real apparel imports will lead to approximately a 0.25% reduction in both textile and apparel employment. However, it should be noted that if both textile and apparel imports expand by 1%, the increase in textile imports will partially offset the negative impact of the increase in apparel imports.[25]

The Effect of Income

As expected, during the 1960–84 period, real disposable personal income had a significant and positive effect on both textile and apparel employment. A 1% increase in real annual disposable personal income can be expected to lead to a 1.14% increase in textile employment and to a 0.79% increase in apparel employment. These findings reveal that, in terms of 1984 employment levels, a 1% increase in real disposable personal income can be expected to add approximately 8,500 textile jobs and 9,500 apparel jobs.[26]

The Effect of Productivity

Changes in worker productivity had different effects in the textile and apparel industries, perhaps reflecting a difference in the ability of the two industries to adjust to competitive pressures. Productivity changes did not have a statistically significant impact on apparel employment, whereas they did have a statistically significant and relatively strong negative influence on employment in the textile industry. A 1% increase in productivity in textiles can be expected to lead to a 0.46% reduction in textile employment.

The 1973–84 period. As noted, textile employment peaked in 1973.

However, between 1973 and 1984, textile employment decreased by 264,000 workers while, at the same time, worker productivity rose by 49%. According to the regression results, that productivity increase had the potential of reducing textile employment by approximately 225,000 jobs (about 85% of the actual decrease of 264,000 in textile employment).

The 1980–84 period. The textile and apparel industries have been especially concerned with employment trends in their industries during the 1980–84 period. The findings of this statistical investigation suggest that the 21% increase in worker productivity in the textile industry during the 1980–84 period led to a decrease in textile employment of about 81,000 (or approximately 80% of the actual employment loss).

Production and Peak Employment

Some of the productivity increases experienced by the textile and apparel industries has resulted from the closing of inefficient plants, as well as from technological advances and competitive pressures brought on by imports. For this reason, as for any projection of size of a labor force, the production capacities of the textile and apparel industries must remain rough estimates. Nevertheless, it is useful to observe that, given the 1984 productivity of textile workers, had textile employment been magically returned to the 1973 industry peak, the output of textiles in 1984 would have been 35% greater—nearly $17 billion higher than the total of constant-dollar domestic production plus imports.

Similarly, it is interesting to note that at current productivity levels, if apparel employment should return to the 1973 industry peak, the apparel industry's output would be 20% greater than in 1973. This figure is only $3 billion less than the total amount of constant-dollar industry shipments and imports.

The point is that a return to the 1973 employment peaks in the textile and apparel industries is unlikely, even with drastic cutbacks in imports (as contemplated by the backers of the Textile and Apparel Trade Enforcement Act of 1985). Given the increased productivity in the two industries, the supply of products at the peak employment levels would approximately equal consumer demand for apparel or greatly exceed consumer demand for textiles.

The Industry Impact of Imports

The impact of textile and apparel imports may indirectly affect domestic textile and apparel employment through competitive pressure on prices and productivity. An expansion of imports can place downward pressures on textile and apparel prices and upward pressures on productivity. Those firms that lead the way in expanding productivity in the face of price declines can maintain—and even expand—employment and profitability. However, those industries that face declining relative prices without compensating increases in worker productivity can be forced to cut employment or close altogether.

Regression equations not reported here indicate that the relative price decline of textile and apparel products has had an impact on textile and apparel employment.[27] However, the exact amount of the price effect caused by import competition is unclear because the price, productivity, and employment effects are tightly entangled. Textile and apparel prices can also be affected by domestic, as well as foreign, supplies that, in turn, can be affected by productivity changes. In addition, the productivity changes can be a response to import pressures on prices.

Concluding Comments

Several important conclusions can be drawn from the findings reported in this chapter. First, the findings cast doubt on the charge that textile imports are directly to blame (virtually to the exclusion of any other consideration) for job losses in both the textile and apparel industries. Job losses in the textile industry are not directly attributable to increases in textile imports during the early 1980s. If textile imports during the period had any negative effect at all on textile and apparel employment, it was likely an indirect effect. Competitive pressures forced U.S. textile firms to innovate and improve productivity. Even those persons speaking for the industry are beginning to recognize the role of productivity in eliminating textile jobs, a point on which this chapter is closed.[28]

Nevertheless, the findings do support apparel industry claims that employment has declined as a result of imports. In fact, both the textile and apparel industries have been affected by apparel imports. The chapter also reaffirms the commonly acknowledged proposition that textile and apparel employment is strongly influenced by fluctuations in real disposable income. The connection between general economic activity and textile production and employment was, in fact, obvious in the continuing (albeit sluggish) recovery in 1987: textile and apparel employment was rising in 1987.

Second, this research indicates that during the past two-and-a-half decades, net job losses in the textile industry have been due to substantial increases in productivity. The same cannot be said about the apparel industry. One explanation is that opportunities for fending off imports by using labor-saving machinery appear to be much greater in textiles than in apparel, where labor-intensive "cutting and sewing" operations remain a significant part of the production process. Also, it needs to be noted that a nontrivial part of the apparel employment losses due to imports has been due, not to foreign firms, but to aggressive American firms who have transferred production to the Caribbean or Far East. It is also due, in part, to the export of American textiles to foreign-apparel plants, meaning that, to some extent, the domestic apparel-job losses are offset by domestic textile-employment gains.

Third, the research suggests that much of the financial distress confronted by many domestic textile and apparel firms may be the consequence of expanded supplies of textile and apparel products. Increases in productivity have, in part, expanded supplies, and many firms that have closed or reduced operations have done so because they have been unable or unwilling to keep pace with industry productivity improvements.

The analysis presented here helps explain why some major textile firms have been able to maintain rates of return on equity in excess of 10% (sometimes significantly above 20% and even 30%) at a time when many textile and apparel plants are closing and employment is declining.[29]

In summary, proponents of trade restrictions maintain that import protection is justified because of the presumed connection between textile and apparel imports and domestic employment. The presumed connection has been shown to be applicable to apparel imports but not applicable to textile imports. Yet in neither case does the magnitude of the employment loss come close to approaching 1 million lost jobs — the number advertised by protectionists.

Futhermore, as Will Rogers once said, "If a business thrives under a protective tariff, that don't mean that it has been a good thing. It may have thrived because it made the people of America pay more for the object than they should have, so a few got rich at the cost of the many."

If apparel and textile imports are restricted to a greater degree, the prices of textile and apparel goods to consumers will likely rise, resulting in a hidden transfer of income from consumers to textile and apparel producers. As stressed before in earlier chapters (especially Chapter 6), such curbs will also likely discriminate against lower-income groups because quantity controls typically cause a disproportionate reduction in lower-priced goods usually purchased by lower-income groups.

Nor are the effects of quotas necessarily all positive for the textile and apparel industries. Increased prices for domestic and imported textiles will increase the cost of textile and apparel production. The main long-run effect of curbs on textile and apparel imports seems to be some retardation of productivity improvements, the result of reduced competitive pressures. Ultimately, slower-productivity growth means that many U.S. textile and apparel firms will be less able to compete in the global marketplace. Finally, we noted at the start of this chapter that employment in other domestic industries — for example, retail trade — will be adversely affected by textile and apparel restrictions. On balance, protectionism can be expected to reduce American jobs.

Maybe some textile and apparel industry leaders are beginning to understand this central message. Wilburn Newcomb, editor of *American Textiles International,* took a courageous industry stand in 1987 when he acknowledged in an editorial that additional textile protectionism may do nothing more than protect domestic producers who continue to operate with "50-year-old fly shuttle looms." He then added,

> The screaming and yelling for a new textile bill can only fall on dead ears right now, especially if the screamers really only want to "protect" their totally outmoded plants. Now is the time to buy and build. Sales and profits are high. Stock values are higher. Consumers want to "buy American." Let's give them the best products at the best prices. But that can only be done with the latest technology. We can't keep crying "imports!" to cover up large pockets of inefficiency remaining. Instead we need to make ours one of the most modern manufacturing industries in the nation — modern throughout![30]

What the American job machine needs now, more than ever, is a few more industry leaders who will call a spade a spade in the protectionism debate—with the interest of the country, not their industries, in mind.

Notes

1. Protectionist claims for other industries are evaluated in Morris E. Morke and David G. Tarr, Bureau of Economics, Federal Trade Commission, *Effects of Restrictions on United States Imports: Five Case Studies and Theory* (Washington: U.S. Government Printing Office, June 1980); Arthur T. Denzau, "How Import Restraints Reduce Employment" (St. Louis: Center for the Study of American Business, Washington University, June 1987); and Robert W. Crandall, "Import Quotas and the Automobile Industry: The Costs of Protectionism," *Brookings Review,* Summer 1984, pp. 8–16

2. Unfortunately, the analysis in this chapter is, at times, highly technical (involving regression analysis). The nontechnical reader may want to stop reading at the section headed "Statistical Models and Results."

3. U.S. Congress, Senate, "Textile and Apparel Trade and Enforcement Act of 1985," S. 680 (February 26, 1985). For a review of the history of textile and apparel import restrictions and features of the Textile and Apparel Trade and Enforcement Act of 1985, see Edwin Hudgins, "Why Limiting Textile Imports Would Hurt Americans," *Backgrounder* (Washington: Heritage Foundation), September 30, 1985.

4. Laura Megna and Thomas Emrich, "An Analysis of the Impact of the Textile and Apparel Trade Enforcement Act of 1985," (Washington: International Business and Economic Research Corporation, June 1985).

5. Ibid.

6. "Textile Industry Imports, Too," *New York Times,* October 10, 1985, p. 33.

7. Ibid., p. 5.

8. Ellison S. McKissick, Jr., "Sweatshirts and Sweatshops," *Wall Street Journal,* September 4, 1985, p. 23.

9. U.S. Senate, "Textile and Apparel Trade and Enforcement Act of 1985," p. 8.

10. Fritz Hollings, "We're in a Trade War," *Reports* (Washington: U.S. Senate Offices), July 1985.

11. McKissick, "Sweatshirts and Sweatshops," p. 23.

12. Employment data are taken from U.S. Bureau of Labor Statistics, *Employment, Hours and Earnings: 1909–1984* and *Employment and Earnings* (July 1985); industry shipments and import data are taken from U.S. Department of Commerce, *U.S. Industrial Outlook* (various annual editions). The 1984 industry shipment and import figures are estimates. The actual figures are reported in Tables A1 and A2.

13. Constant-dollar textile and apparel shipment and import figures were obtained by deflating the current-dollar figures by the textile and apparel price index (1984 = 100).

14. These estimates of the direct impact of textile imports are necessarily tentative because they do not account for other variables that can directly influence textile employment or the indirect effects of imports on employment through pressures on prices and productivity. The econometric work that follows partially remedies these problems.

15. It is very unlikely that domestic production could ever fully supplant imports. The higher prices of the domestically produced goods would cause total sales to drop below the level achieved with imports.

16. In 1973, the elimination of imports, which represented 5% of domestic shipments, would have led to an increase in textile employment of about 50,000. In 1984 the elimination of imports, which then represented 6.5% of domestic shipments, would have led to an increase in employment of approximately 49,000.

17. Some of the surge in apparel imports could have been in response to quota restrictions on the importation of textiles.

18. As with the textile industry, imports would have further reduced apparel employment through the indirect effects of imports on industry prices and productivity.

19. Of course, lower-priced textile imports very likely enabled domestic-apparel firms to lower their costs and compete more effectively with apparel imports and very likely kept apparel employment from falling as much as it otherwise would have.

20. In 1984, the textile and apparel index (1967 = 100) stood at 211, whereas the consumer price index was 311.

21. Textile and apparel imports may also contribute to an expansion of real U.S. income via expanded purchasing power of consumer dollars that, in turn, may marginally expand the demand for U.S. textile and apparel products.

22. Finally, an increase in textile and apparel imports may be caused by a rise in income and may accompany a rise in imports of a wide range of foreign goods and services (including textile and nontextile machinery and materials). Lower-priced and higher-quality imports of many goods and services can make American industries more competitive and can support the continued expansion of real income and employment in the U.S. economy. Of course, as noted in the text, textile and apparel imports can spur domestic firms to become more productive, which can indirectly lead to job losses in the textile and apparel industries.

23. The results of the empirical analysis should be evaluated with one caveat in mind. Since industry employment is used as the dependent variable and as the denominator in the measure of productivity, a measurement error for employment can introduce a negative bias in the coefficient for worker productivity.

24. Conversely, the regression equation using 1984 figures suggests that reducing textile imports to zero could theoretically *reduce* textile employment by almost 125,000 jobs and reduce apparel employment by almost 200,000 jobs.

25. Put in more concrete terms, our statistical analysis indicates that, using 1984 data, reducing apparel imports to zero would at most increase textile employment by 191,000 jobs and apparel employment by 293,000 jobs.

26. Future employment in the textile and apparel industries is significantly dependent on the general health of the U.S. economy. If these estimates of the impact of income changes hold for the remainder of the 1980s and if real personal disposable income rises by 3% a year throughout the remainder of the 1980s, textile and apparel employment combined could increase over 18%, or nearly 350,000 jobs, during this 1984–90 period. These combined employment gains in the textile and apparel industries can be expected to be tempered by productivity and import increases.

27. Indeed, when the ratio of textile and apparel prices to the consumer price index is introduced into each of the two equations as a fourth independent variable, the price ratio is positive, as might be expected, and highly significant. Imports are then statistically insignificant.

28. Wilburn Newcomb, "New Textile Bill—Protecting our Outmoded Plants?" *American Textiles International,* February 1987, p. 6.

29. In 1984, among the 21 major Southeastern textile firms evaluated, 12 had rates of return on equity in excess of 10%; 5 of the 12 had rates of return on equity in excess of 15%. One firm had a rate of return on equity of more than 46%. Only two major textile firms on the list of 21 had losses in 1984 ("Guilford Mills, Carriage Industries Rated Tops in Textile Survey," *Jenks Southeastern Business Letter,* June 24, 1985, pp. 4–5).

30. Ibid.

CHAPTER 8

The Seductive Appeal of Government Retraining

The political search for a national *industrial* policy—emerging rapidly and fading just as quickly during the first half of the 1980s—began to reappear in the late 1980s as a search for a new national *labor* policy. The old national-industrial-policy movement was predicated in part on the presumed need to target various forms of governmental relief on ailing industries.[1] The new labor-policy movement is founded partially on a similar presumption: the need to target governmental aid on ailing worker groups, mainly "displaced" or "dislocated" workers.[2] These have been important themes in preceding chapters.

Some supporters see a new labor policy simply as a means of expressing a humanitarian concern for distressed workers. Other supporters seek to reduce government welfare and unemployment expenditures caused by worker displacement. Still others seek to brake the political bandwagon for protectionist trade policies that began to roll at an accelerating pace in the mid-1980s. The country has been told repeatedly that either something must be done to ease the economic pain suffered by displaced workers or else U.S. citizens must incur the greater costs associated with higher taxes or trade protection.[3]

If achieved, these lofty objectives would increase federal intervention in labor markets and (presumably) allow for industrial restructuring, but would not overlook the economic pain of workers caught in the throes of the restructuring process. As one reform group explained, "There is a need for a balance between the preservation of the necessary flexibility of the American enterprise system and the cushioning of human and economic dislocation."[4]

In spite of relatively good news regarding growth in industrial production and a decline in unemployment in the mid–1980s, proposals for labor-policy reform abound.[5] By institutionalizing "economic democracy" at the level of the firm, several radical proposals would transfer fundamental managerial decision-making on investment, reinvestment, disinvestment, and divestment.[6] Other slightly less radical reform proposals would restrict managements' rights to close their plants without warning or without worker and community compensation. These so-called "plant-closing laws," though considered and rejected several times since 1970, have been reconsidered in revised form in several bills in the 99th Congress.[7] Still other proposals would require companies to become social agents of the state, mandating, for example, company-sponsored child-care facilities and maternity and paternity leave.[8] Most of these policy proposals will be considered in following chapters. This chapter focuses on one of the most often-mentioned (and difficult to question) policy concerns, worker retraining.

Most labor-reform proposals advocate, in one form or another, greater governmental efforts to retrain workers displaced by structural changes in the domestic economy and growing competitiveness in world markets. As stated by William Brock, secretary of labor in the Reagan administration, the central purpose of the retraining reforms is, generally, to "ameliorate the impact on workers dislocated by adjustment."[9] The purpose of this chapter is to explore in more detail conventional arguments for greater governmental retraining efforts, to explain the political appeal of these arguments, and to assess the likely value of government-sponsored retraining programs. However, analytical points related to government retraining programs are often applicable to a variety of other worker benefits provided by government. Again, several points raised here will reappear in following chapters on mandated wages and fringe benefits for workers.

The Appeal of Training

Among reform advocates, training and retraining programs have considerable appeal. Proponents base their support on the following line of reasoning:

• Workers and their families are hurt when displaced by structural change, that is, by plant closings and permanent layoffs. As covered in Chapter 5, studies made by the Bureau of Labor Statistics (BLS) and the Government Accounting Office (GAO) reveal that workers often suffer a loss of wealth when they become unemployed. When unemployed, the annual income of workers falls by an average of 10% to 15% of their pre-displacement income. (The actual income loss depends on the worker's age, industry, and time and place of dislocation.)[10] Displaced workers must endure personal and family crises and, as a result of their displacement, are more likely than the rest of the population to face problems associated with mental disorders, divorce, child and spouse abuse, and even suicide.[11]

• Worker displacement increases government expenditures and taxes because of a greater need to provide unemployment compensation and a variety of welfare benefits, ranging from cash payments to food stamps to medical care. Even government expenditures on police protection can increase because worker displacement often gives rise to a higher incidence of murder and robbery. Furthermore, "losing experienced employees from the work force further weakens overall U.S. productivity."[12]

• Retraining programs enable workers to reenter the work force more quickly and with improved job opportunities. Without outside governmental help, workers are ill-equipped to meet their own retraining needs. The retraining expenses must often be incurred at the worst possible time, when workers are out of work and have little or no income.

• Government can ease the pain of dislocation and smooth the transition process by providing worker retraining through subsidies to workers or their employers or by forcing workers to save for their retraining needs through tax-exempt "Individual Retraining Accounts."[13]

• To the extent that government-sponsored retraining prevents displacement or reduces the length of unemployment, total government expenditures and taxes can be reduced and the national income can be increased. Because of reduced government expenditures and increases in national income, effective tax rates on earned income can also decrease, resulting in an additional boost to economic efficiency and growth. "The problem, therefore, is not one for industry, or labor, or government, alone. Rather," writes a Labor Department task force, "it is the concern of every citizen. Protecting the country's investment in human capital ensures a more productive, more fully employed society for all."[14]

While the foregoing line of argument prominently undergirds efforts to expand government retraining programs for displaced workers, such arguments could be readily applied (as they have been) to an array of government activities that might speed the adjustment process or ease the pain of transition for workers. Examples of other forms of recommended adjustment assistance could include:

- severance pay,
- continuation of health and life insurance,
- early retirement,
- supplementary unemployment benefits,
- pay in lieu of plant-closing notice, and
- outplacement and reemployment services, such as job-market information and testing, personal and career counseling, time off for job search, job clubs, worker buyouts, company transfer options, and relocation expenses.[15]

All of these benefits might be financed by government or costs might be imposed on the firms involved. The foregoing line of argument regarding retraining could even be applied to expanding the "rapid-response" capability of government through any given collection of labor-market services. After all, any governmental capacity to speed the adjustment process could conceivably reduce the social costs of adjustment incurred by workers and by government.[16]

Hence, our concern cannot be totally restricted to the efficacy of "worker retraining," *per se,* but also with the efficacy of an array of government activities that can be justified by the same line of argument. We need, in other words, to assess the value of the *principles* that undergird policies, as well as the value of any specific policy under consideration.

Defects in the Arguments

Unfortunately, the retraining logic is not as compelling as it might at first appear, at least not for workers who are not poor or disadvantaged. We might agree, for sake of argument (if nothing else) that sound social and economic reasons exist for helping the truly disadvantaged worker, not the least of which are altruism and the need to provide people with an equal opportunity to compete in the labor marketplace.[17] However, the logic is myopic at best, counterproductive at worst, when applied to a substantial majority of working Americans with reasonable incomes.

Yet just because workers are hurt at the time they are dislocated, it does not follow that they are harmed on balance and over the long run by a labor-market *system* producing occasional dislocations.[18] Through unfettered flexibility, workers can gain over the long run through improvements in their own wages, reduced prices, and improved choice in the products they buy. Required adjustments can be quite painful, but workers can benefit from all of the similar (and even painful) adjustments made by others in the economy. These commonly shared adjustments, faced by a multitude of others, can improve overall economic efficiency, reduce the real prices of goods and services bought by workers in general, and increase the real incomes of workers.

Policymakers pay considerable attention to wages after workers have been reemployed and compare these new wages with old wages (prior to their dislocation). A Labor Department report stressed that

> Econometric studies based on the 1984 displaced worker survey showed average real earnings losses of 10 to 15 percent upon reemployment for all workers displaced from full-time jobs. Nearly 30 percent of reemployed blue collar workers and 24 percent of reemployed white collar and service workers had losses of 25 percent.[19]

In the narrow terms of their own displacement, workers may be

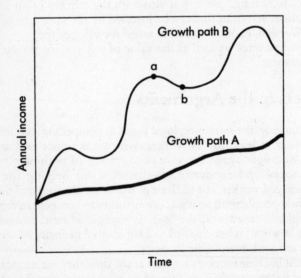

Fig. 8.1 Alternative income growth paths of hypothetical worker.

"worse off." However, the relevant question is whether, over the course of time, labor markets deliver real wages (accounting for occasional dislocation) that are higher or lower than they otherwise would have been. The point unrecognized by reform advocates is that, even after allowing for dips caused by occasional dislocation, the income path followed by workers, over time, can be higher than the path that would have been followed if the blows of dislocation had been cushioned.[20] In short, comparing wages before and after dislocation contributes little or nothing to an evaluation of the performance of the labor-market *system.*

Consider Figure 8.1, which shows two hypothetical income-growth paths for a representative worker. One of the income-growth paths (labeled A) is smooth and upward sloping but at a lower incline than path B. Income-growth-rate A reflects a lower growth rate than path B, but income-growth-rate B is much more irregular. BLS and GAO researchers measuring worker incomes before displacement and after reemployment may be doing nothing more than measuring points *a* and *b* on income path B, merely measuring dips in income growth that are normal, expected, and unavoidable—given the dynamic nature of the economy. A goal of governmental retraining programs may be to prevent the dips in worker incomes due to displacement. However, elimination of dips in worker incomes may come at the price of shifting income-growth path B to path A.

Seen from this perspective, the policy debate over retraining programs is partially a question of how effectively these programs smooth the income path (a point to be considered later in this chapter). Yet it is also partially a debate over the long-run consequences on actual worker income-growth paths. Proponents imagine that workers' income paths will be smoothed and raised. Opponents fear that income paths may be made smoother (if retraining programs are even marginally effective) but that income paths may be shifted downward—over time.[21]

For several reasons, such fears cannot be dismissed. First, the retraining program can result in higher taxes, which can dampen incentives people have to work, to improve their skills (human capital), to save, and to invest in plant and equipment (physical capital).

Second, retraining subsidies can reduce the competitive drive of workers and their employers to control production costs and raise product quality. This is true because all workers can count on government retraining benefits to cushion the economic blow of their competitive failures. The result can be greater government expenditures on retraining than may have been originally expected.

Third, the retraining programs may not be effective in accomplishing their intended goal: improving the ability of workers to adapt to economic change. In fact, government retraining programs may reduce the ability of workers to adapt. The programs may encourage workers to develop skills that are no longer very productive and may encourage the development of skills that are not transferable among firms and industries. This happens when the retraining programs are guided by the interests of employers—developing and maintaining firm-specific labor forces: labor forces that cannot readily move and be reemployed in other jobs.

Admittedly, while such arguments may not conclusively demonstrate the superiority of unfettered labor markets, they certainly cast doubt on the facile conclusion that worker-retraining programs will necessarily raise the welfare of workers by cushioning their temporary adjustment problems. Such arguments certainly demand that the effectiveness of the retraining programs be demonstrated.

The Retraining Record

The federal government has been in the worker-training and retraining business for at least half a century, since the Great Depression and the experience of the Work Progress Administration, commonly known as the WPA. However, government involvement in job training and retraining began to escalate in the 1960s. Since the 1960s more than 50 federal training programs have been developed (with familiar and not-so-familiar call letters), including:

- MDTA (Manpower Development Training Administration),
- CETA (Comprehensive Employment and Training Act),
- YEDTP (Youth Entitlement Demonstration and Training Program)
- JTPA (Job Training Partnership Act),
- AYES (Alternate Youth and Employment Strategies),
- STEADY (Special Training and Employment Assistance for Disadvantaged Youth),
- STIP (Skill Training Improvement Program),
- BEST (Basic Essential Skills Training Program),
- YIEPP (Youth Incentive Entitlement Pilot Projects),
- YACC (Youth Adult Conservation Corps),
- SCSEP (Senior Community Service Employment Program), and
- HIRE (Help through Industry Retraining Employment Program).

Now, many policy groups want to go one step further and establish a much more comprehensive training and retraining program. For example, President Ronald Reagan proposed in his 1988 budget an "entirely new program," one that "would assist all dislocated workers without regard to whether they were unemployed because of increased imports, or because they were permanently laid off, lost their farms, or were long-term unemployment insurance recipients."[22] In this "new" program (as in several of the existing programs), workers would be provided counseling, job-search assistance, basic education, and job-skill training, all of which would be controlled by the federal government but administered by state governments.[23]

However, the question of why the federal government is undertaking an expanded retraining program must be answered. The social goal of the training program may be laudable. Nevertheless, after a review of the federal-training record, researchers have repeatedly found success of federal-training efforts to be questionable at best, very likely counterproductive, and almost always a waste of federal tax dollars. After reviewing the federal training record, James Bovard, in blunt terms, concluded,

> Federal job-training programs have harmed the careers of millions of Americans, failed to impart valuable job skills to the poor, and squandered billions of dollars annually. For 25 years, government programs have warped work ethics, helped disillusion generations of disadvantaged youth, and deluged America with fraudulent statistics. After spending over a hundred billion dollars on manpower programs, we have learned little or nothing: today's programs merely repeat the mistakes of the early 1960s.[24]

The training and retraining efforts of the federal government have been criticized for not affecting worker wages and employment,[25] for not providing the right worker skills,[26] and for counting trivial accomplishments (teaching recruits to count money) as training successes,[27] not to mention "having no meaningful statistics on the effectiveness of these programs."[28] Of all the federal job-training programs, CETA has probably been most prominently condemned for its ineffectiveness and outright corruption. As Bovard notes,

> CETA spent $53 billion—yet only 15 percent of its recruits got unsubsidized jobs in the private sector. In 1982, when CETA was winding down, GAO found that 50 percent of laid-off CETA

workers were unemployed and that 55 percent of those were receiving one or more forms of government handouts. Only 25 percent had permanent, full-time jobs.[29]

However, while Joint Training Partnership Act (JTPA) has been touted as "one of the greatest achievements in the history of government social policy,"[30] the real wages of JTPA graduates in 1983 averaged only 4% more than the real wages of CETA graduates. The wage difference might be explained by the relatively higher education levels of JTPA recruits.[31]

In addition, the way in which training funds are allocated across states and groups of workers can have unintended, perverse effects on worker displacement and unemployment. For example, as in the case of CETA, JTPA continues to allocate retraining funds across states partially on the basis of state unemployment rates. The higher the state unemployment rate, the higher the funds allocated to the states.

Unfortunately, state unemployment rates are far from a perfect measure of state "need" for federal assistance, if that is the objective the JTPA is designed to serve. Unemployment may not be a major problem for persons in households with other employed workers and may be less of a problem for higher-income families than for lower-income families. Many people's unemployment can be voluntary or can be the result of workers' high-wage demands or their unwillingness to make wage concessions in order that production can continue on a cost-competitive basis.

Interestingly, economists James Ragan and Daniel Slottje have found that state unemployment rates are highly and positively correlated with wages, which means that higher wages are significantly associated with higher rates of unemployment across states.[32] This means that retraining funds have tended to favor the high-wage states at the expense of low-wage states. To the extent that state policies (for example, unemployment compensation) have aggravated their worker displacement and unemployment, federal retraining funds could indirectly (and perhaps inadvertently) be subsidizing state policies that worsen the displacement and unemployment problem—at a nontrivial cost to other (typically, lower-income) states.

The debate over the effectiveness of federal job-training programs cannot be fully settled by empirical studies, such as the ones cited. Studies abound; political interests of researchers invariably color the ways data on the effectiveness of training programs are gathered and interpreted. Even if it is demonstrated that federal job training has not increased employment opportunities and wages of covered workers, it can be argued that the programs kept the employment opportunities and wages of recruits from falling (or from falling as much as they might have, otherwise). Although the measured costs of the training programs might be greater than the measured benefits, proponents of extended federal job training can also point to a variety of nonquantifiable benefits (for example, worker self-esteem and community stability and security). These benefits could, possibly, more than close the gap between measured costs and benefits and could, thereby, justify the training programs.

In the absence of conclusive data, we can only conceptualize what problems may emerge from federal retraining efforts. Admittedly, in a static economy federal job planners might be reasonably competent to train workers. In fact, "all" the job planners have to do (which is actually a Herculean task) is figure out the distribution of existing jobs, determine skills, and train people for the jobs that are available. Official measures of the existing characteristics and distribution of jobs might not be available for scrutiny by policymakers for months, or even years, after the surveys are taken. Such delays between measurement and action, inevitable in government, would pose no serious problem, since the characteristics and distribution of jobs would remain the same over a period of years.

However, the world is hardly static. Jobs and worker skills change — often dramatically and rapidly. Indeed, the displaced-worker problem has emerged in public-policy debates because the world has, supposedly, become highly dynamic.

Unfortunately, in a dynamic economy there is no good reason to expect government policymakers and officials to be able to figure out, effectively, the retraining needs of workers or to be able to match, accurately, workers' needs with their preferences and abilities. The more dynamic the economy, the larger the displaced-worker problem, or so proponents argue. However, it also follows that the larger the displaced-worker problem, the greater the task the training planners must face in measuring the existing distribution of jobs, projecting future distributions, marshalling training forces, and (actually) matching skills with jobs that may not now exist.

As a result, mistakes in policy and program should be common. The reason for the mistakes is not necessarily that the training planners are any less competent than other people; the planners may be quite competent in their own right. Rather, the reason is that the difficulty of discerning the precise circumstances of future employment and the preferences of workers will increase exponentially with the number of displaced workers. Consequently the federal planners will not then know where the job changes are going to occur and how federal dollars should be spent to meet the changes.

The important fact is that federal job planners are not a part of the adjusting market economy and cannot, to that extent, know clearly or in detail where the economy is heading and what types of skills are needed. Their knowledge is bounded by the surveys they conduct and by econometric techniques, all of which have considerable limitations when dealing with nonmeasurable characteristics of jobs and skills. In other words, official job classifications, which are devised for purposes of the government, very often have no meaning in the real workaday world. Complicated job characteristics that defy class-ification may be grossly out of date in terms of specific needs of employers and workers by the time they are available for policy decisions. Of course, increases in both the sophistication and internationalization of production will further complicate the projection problems faced by federal training planners.

In short, federal job planners may know a great deal about labor markets—more than anyone else—but there is much that they cannot know. There is much about training—what types of training should and should not be secured—that only the employers and workers in the "trenches" can know. Under the circumstances, we should expect federal training planners to reduce coordination problems to manage-able proportions. Coordination problems are all too frequently re-duced in part by training workers for past or current employment needs (which may soon become irrelevant) and in part by passing training decisions to the actual managers of the training programs. Of course, "passing the [training] buck" may only invite abuse and misuse of federal training funds by the managers of the federal funds and the workers who receive them. With only loose bureaucratic incentives for effective use of government funds, waste and outright corruption in training programs should be no surprise. The costs of waste and corruption can be imposed on many groups—for example, the general taxpayers—who are not able to supervise the training programs directly.

Policymakers often maintain that the size of the displaced-worker problem and the pervasiveness and accelerating pace of change are persuasive arguments for federal intervention. The point of this chapter is quite the opposite: such factors should point to greater, not less, reliance on market principles. Recent proponents of an expanded retraining effort have argued that the administration of the programs should be decentralized: undertaken by the states. They insist that state officials know more than federal officials about what types of training are needed in their areas. This is, no doubt, true. However, even state officials do not know as much about what types of training are needed as private individuals and firms, an important point that suggests that individuals should (to the extent that is at all practical) shoulder responsibility for making and covering the cost of their own training decisions. There is no particular reason to stop at the state level in decentralizing decisions — at least when concerned about the needs of the public in general. Why not decentralize all the way the most important people in training, the individual employer and employee?

The Need for Individual Responsibility

Most proposed worker-retraining programs, of course, are not intended to be cost effective, *per se*, but rather are intended to create cross-subsidies from all workers to identified displaced workers.[33] The argument in support of cross-subsidies is relatively straightforward: workers affected by labor-market forces should not be held responsible for the costs associated with changes in the economy beneficial to the economy as a whole. A part of monetary gains (lower prices and higher real incomes) and nonmonetary gains (more efficient allocation of resources, security, and improved products) garnered by the general population from labor-market adjustments should be taxed away and used to compensate workers for the costs they incur in acquiring new skills — or so it is argued.

A critical flaw in the argument lies in an unstated assumption: in the absence of government intervention in labor markets, workers are systematically uncompensated for their retraining expenditures through normal market forces. However, the private costs of training should restrict the supply of workers with given skills and lead to higher wages (including a premium for the training expense incurred). In making the case for government training programs, it is also assumed that the adjustments workers have to make and the attendant costs are more or less unaffected by the governmental-adjustment compensation provided dislocated workers. However, a greater supply of government-trained workers should lower the wages of not only the workers who take the government training but also the workers already in the market with the skills developed in the training programs.[34]

The case for having workers retain individual responsibility for their own retraining is founded on the time-tested assumption that individuals tend to respond to personal incentives and that the proposed governmental solution can make the observed problem worse. As noted earlier, to the extent that retraining subsidies are permitted, workers and their employers can be expected to be less attentive to keeping their skills current and readily applicable to a variety of employment opportunities. And workers can also be more inclined to take greater risks when they are making noncompetitive wages. Of course, the taxes that are required to finance the training programs can provide further disincentives for workers and their employers to keep skills current and in tune with changing market forces. As a consequence, government adjustment subsidies can make the worker-displacement problem worse, over time, requiring a further expansion of public efforts to help workers make necessary adjustments.[35]

Individuals have information that can be possessed by no one else about their employment circumstances, needs, and preferences. An often unrecognized social purpose of imposing on private individuals responsibility for their own retraining needs is to insure that individuals have the necessary incentives, both positive and negative, to use the information they have. Imposing employment responsibility on individuals is also intended to suppress the natural inclination of individuals to pass off to others through the tax system their employment costs.[36]

Arguments against using public funds for retraining many, if not most, displaced workers who may be far removed from poverty (and quite capable of planning their own retraining needs) are not applicable with equal force to lower-income workers. The latter may be down on their luck and have little or no backup support when they are displaced. They may lack the intelligence to figure out what they should learn to do and may be unable to take responsibility for their own actions. In effect, such unfortunate workers cannot solve their problems of unemployment, and government training planners could hardly do worse in providing for their training needs.

To insure that those people have a reasonable chance to earn as much of their living as possible, few would deny that such people need a public (training) safety net. In addition, truly unfortunate workers probably represent a trivial part of the displaced-worker problem.[37] The real political debate, therefore, is really over whether the much-better-educated and intelligent workers (who are quite capable of fending for themselves by reeducating themselves and relocating when necessary) should be the beneficiaries of government largess, which will probably be financed, in part, by less-fortunate workers.

Concluding Comments

Charlayne Hunter-Gault, anchorwoman on the McNeil–Lehrer News Hour, began a 1987 report on the displaced-worker problem with the question, "What should the federal government do for hundreds of thousands of workers who lose their jobs each year *through no fault of their own*?" (italics added)[36] The way the question was posed is exceedingly interesting because of the phrase "through no fault of their own." That phrase suggests strict limits on which workers and how many workers will be helped by enacted federal programs. The phrase also represents an appeal to reasonableness. After all, who could possibly be against helping workers who do not cause their own displacement — those who are "victims" of the adjustment process? When workers are not at fault, their displacement may amount to an injustice that should be rectified by whatever federal means are available.

Unfortunately, "through no fault of their own" has no clear meaning for defining the limit of federal retraining responsibility. This is especially the case when the constraining definition is dependent upon politics. Are workers who are displaced because of foreign imports at fault? What about the workers who lost their jobs because they raised their wages or reduced their productivity to uncompetitive levels? Are workers at fault who lose their jobs because newly developed domestic products and services caused their firms to go out of business? Suppose the displaced workers had the opportunity to develop those same new products and services but resisted taking the opportunity?

For example, a computer company located in South Carolina in the early 1960s produced what was, at the time, a very fine 64-K personal computer (with two disk drives) that employed the CPM operating system. So long as personal computers had limited capabilities and were CPM-based, the company and workers prospered. However, the computer business changed. The machines rapidly increased in power, and many companies switched to the MS-DOS operating system. The South Carolina company resisted the trend, preferring to make marginal improvements in its machines and to stick with the old CPM system. The company is now defunct. My purpose in raising the above queries is that bankruptcy and worker displacement are not always beyond the control of firms and their workers. Many firms make bad decisions, and one of the functions of the market system is to screen out the bad decision-makers from the good ones. In general, the screening process should help improve decisions overall because the bad decision-makers are removed from their markets and because decision-makers will in fact be forced to face at least some of the consequences of their decisions, good or bad.

In general, how do federal policymakers and program organizers determine who is at fault for worker displacement? (Is it even possible to find fault when job losses are the consequence of literally thousands, if not millions, of interactive forces that cannot be specified, much less measured?) The answers are self-evident. In effect, the question raised by the television anchorwoman does not harbor the stringent checks on the scope of federal training effort that might first appear to be the case.

The U.S. Labor Department Task Force on Economic Adjustment and Worker Dislocation (which has been the concern of analyses in several of the previous chapters) had the phrase "through no fault of their own" in their preliminary declaration that displaced workers should be helped by federal programs. However, in their deliberation on government policies, the task force subsequently took out the qualification. It did so partially because of the difficulty of drawing the lines between those who are at fault and those who are not at fault and, in part, because any likely definition of "fault" might exclude worker constituencies of task-force members from the programs.

A fundamental problem with government programs is that all too often policymakers and program directors cannot or will not make the necessary judgments. Consequently, government programs tend to become excessively large and wasteful—necessarily becoming entitlement programs that are much too frequently put on automatic pilot. The task force's deliberations on the issue are an interesting case study of the politics of training. In taking out reference to fault for displacement, the task force settled on a program that would "meet the needs of *all* displaced workers" (emphasis in the original), regardless of their personal and household income and wealth, regardless of whether employee wages carried a premium accounting for the risk of being displaced, and regardless of whether the workers caused their own displacement.[39] What could be more reckless?

Especially to currently displaced workers and to the politicians who represent their immediate interests, proposed government-backed training and retraining programs are politically tempting, even irresistible. Currently displaced workers can be expected to favor the implementation of new or expanded government training programs. They receive the benefits of the program but do not have to bear any of the costs in terms of higher taxes or curtailment in their own private income-growth path. However, it is questionable if employed workers would be willing to bear, through the tax system, the costs of the programs or would even be eager to favor the programs. Employed workers would have to pay the taxes (and suffer a deterioration in their income path, over time) with only the expectation that someday they might need to take advantage of the training programs. They, too, could imagine the extra costs incurred by the expanded number of displacements induced by the programs and the waste in the programs.

Unfortunately, the case against extended displaced-worker programs is grounded in something of an abstraction, the prospects that workers themselves would not approve of the programs if they understood the (likely) political and economic consequences and if they knew they could not escape paying the government tab on the menu of expected benefits. The case for relying on market forces to handle the country's training needs is founded on the prospect that the broad-spectrum of people at work in the American job machine are sufficiently intelligent to handle their own training needs — at least, they are more competent to do so than government officials who are far removed from the country's diverse places of employment.

The truth is that workers will pay the training bill. The question is how they will pay it: through taxes or through personal savings for those periods of displacement in their lives?

Notes

1. Proponents of a national industrial policy advocated grants and subsidized federal loans distributed through a revived Reconstructed Finance Corporation, import protection of ailing industries through tariffs and quotas, and subsidies for worker buyouts of their plants slated for closing. These policies are reviewed in Richard B. McKenzie, *Competing Visions: The Political Conflict over America's Economic Future* (Washington: Cato Institute, 1985).

2. Concern for displaced workers has been expressed by business groups as well as government study groups. See Policy and Research Committee, *Work and Change: Labor Market Adjustment Policies in a Competitive World* (Washington: Committee For Economic Development, December 1986); Office of Technology Assessment, U.S. Congress, *Plant Closing: Advance Notice and Rapid Response* (Washington: U.S. Government Printing Office, September 1986); and Task Force on Economic Adjustment and Worker Dislocation, *Adjustment Assistance in a Competitive Society* (Washington: Office of the Secretary, U.S.

Department of Labor, December 1986).

3. See the citations in footnote 1, plus Malcolm R. Lovell, Jr., "An Antidote for Protectionism," *Brookings Review,* Fall 1984, pp. 23–28.

4. From a handout from the Office of the Secretary, U.S. Department of Labor, Task Force on Economic Adjustment and Worker Dislocation distributed at the first meeting (December 17, 1986).

5. Such concern led to the introduction of several bills in the 99th and 100th Congresses. Key provisions of these bills include:

- extending displaced workers' group-health and/or life-insurance benefits for up to 18 months past their termination date (Public Law 99–272; H.R. 3128) [The legislation was passed in 1986 and was effective July 1, 1986. The law initially requires beneficiaries to pay the cost of the coverage plus 2% for administrative costs. However, legislation (S. 837) supported by Senator Edward Kennedy (D–Mass.) and Representative Fortney Stark (D–Calif.), if enacted, would require employers to extend the group coverage for up to four months after termination and pay the same portion of the premium they paid before dismissal.];
- making plant closing decisions mandatory subjects of collective bargaining (H.R. 6258);
- targeting federal procurement in "labor surplus areas" (H.R. 1611 and 6096);
- developing public works programs (H.R. 378);
- requiring businesses to cover the relocation expenses of terminated workers (H.R. 6411 and 6412);
- linking additional unemployment compensation to worker participation in training programs (H.R. 5399);
- offering tax credits to firms for their expenditures on worker training (H.R. 4738);
- preventing federal support of firms that cause "unjustified" dislocation (H.R. 1212).

6. Economic democracy "means that those with jobs will have much more to say about the way those jobs are organized; those who live in communities will have more to say about what happens to those communities—even whether a plant can simply up and leave after thirty years" (Martin Carnoy, Derek Shearer, and Russell Rumberger, *A New Social Contract: The Economy and Government after Reagan* [New York: Harper and Row, 1983], p. 2). See also Robert A. Dahl, *Preface to Economic Democracy* (Berkeley: University of California Press, 1985). For criticism of the proposal to transfer managerial rights to workers, see Richard B. McKenzie, *Justice As Participation: Should Workers Be Given Managerial Rights?* (St. Louis: Center for the Study of American Business, Washington University, 1985); and McKenzie, *Competing Visions,* Chap. 6.

7. Plant-closing bills introduced in the 99th Congress include H.R. 1616, 5829, 6411, and 6412. One plant-closing bill (H.R. 1616) was narrowly defeated by five votes in the House in late 1985. For descriptions of proposed plant-closing laws, see Gretchen E. Erhardt, "Summary of Federal and State Proposed Initiatives Introduced in 1983–1984," *Clearinghouse* (Washington:

National Center for Occupational Readjustment), February 1985. For the cases for and against closing restrictions, respectively, see Barry Bluestone and Bennett Harrison, *The Deindustrialization of America* (New York: Basic Books, 1982); Richard B. McKenzie, *Fugitive Industries: The Economics and Politics of Deindustrialization* (San Francisco: Pacific Institute for Public Policy Research, 1984).

8. See the arguments in support of maternity and paternity leave by Sylvia Ann Hewlet, "Feminism's Next Challenge: Support for Motherhood," *New York Times,* June 17, 1986, p. 27; and Edward Zigler, "For Many, Father's Day Is No Field Day," *New York Times,* June 14, 1986, p. 15. In early 1987, the Supreme Court in a 6-to-3 decision, upheld a California law that provides for four months of leave to women who are physically disabled by pregnancy and childbirth (Stuart Taylor, Jr., "Job Rights Backed by Supreme Court in Pregnancy Case," *New York Times,* January 14, 1987, p. 1).

According to Dana Friedman of the Conference Board, "Company support for eldercare is likely to become the new, pioneering employee benefit of the 1990s" (as reported in "Next Comes Eldercare: Help for Workers Looking after Parents," *Wall Street Journal,* June 17, 1986, p. 1).

9. From Secretary Brock's summarized remarks in the minutes of the Task Force's first meeting, December 17, 1985; p. 2.

10. See Marvin H. Kosters, "Job Changes and Displaced Workers: An Examination of Employment Adjustment Experience," *Essays in Contemporary Economic Problems: 1986,* edited by Philip Cagan (Washington: American Enterprise Institute, 1986), p. 300.

11. After surveying the costs and benefits of legislated prenotification for plant closings, the Office of Technology Assessment concluded:

The consequences of involuntary job loss are both painful and long lasting for many displaced workers. Displaced workers are likely to experience prolonged unemployment: one-fourth of all workers displaced between January 1979 and January 1984 were without work for a year or more during the period. Most displaced workers do return to work, but the majority take a cut in earnings, either through lower wages or acceptance of part-time employment in place of a full-time job. Many drop out of the labor force, sometimes after many weeks of discouraging job hunting. Most displaced workers lose benefits; health benefits usually stop with the loss of a job or shortly thereafter, pension benefits suffer, and seniority is usually wiped out. The economic stresses of displacement also take a toll in mental and physical health. Effective adjustment assistance, helping displaced workers to find or train for new jobs, helps to minimize the costs of displacement (Office of Technology Assessment, *Plant Closing,* p. 5).

12. Lovell, *Adjustment Assistance* (see note 3), p. 16.

13. The creation of Individual Retraining Accounts would allow workers to set aside a tax-exempt portion of their incomes. The accumulated funds, which would have an upper limit, could be used to finance retraining expenses without tax penalties.

14. Lovell, *Adjustment Assistance,* p. 17.

15. Most of these displaced-worker benefits are included in a survey of termination benefits conducted by the General Accounting Office (William J. Gainer, "GAO's Preliminary Analysis of U.S. Business Closures and Permanent Layoffs during 1983 and 1984," a paper prepared for presentation at the OTA/GAO Workshop on Plant Closings, April 30–May 1, 1986, p. 22).

16. All of these outplacement services were recommended by the Task Force on Economic Adjustment and Worker Dislocation (Lovell, *Adjustment Assistance*).

17. For a discussion of the case for using government to provide people with equal opportunity in markets, see James M. Buchanan, *Liberty, Market and the State: Political Economy in the 1980s* (New York: New York University Press, 1985), Chap. 12; and Richard B. McKenzie, *The Fairness of Markets: The Search for Justice in a Free Society* (Lexington, Mass.: Lexington Books, 1987), Chap. 9.

18. This point is the central theme of McKenzie, *The Fairness of Markets,* especially Chap. 5.

19. Lovell, *Adjustment Assistance,* p. 14.

20. Current workers can almost always gain from breaking with the market system adopted sometime in the past. They can improve their incomes by effectively drawing on the capital stock built up by the system over time. That is, instead of using current income for reinvestment and replacement of the nation's capital stock through saving, they can use their income for current consumption of goods and services. Of course, the cost of current consumption is a reduction in the growth of the incomes of future generations. Therein lies a major source of temptation for current policymakers to shift policy and cater to the interests of current generations of voters to the detriment of future generations who may be poorer because of changes in current incentives.

21. Some opponents, of course, harbor the nontrivial fear that worker-retraining programs might actually lower the income-growth path and make it even more irregular.

22. Office of Management and Budget, Executive Office of the President, *Budget of the United States Government: Fiscal Year, 1988* (Washington: U.S. Government Printing Office, January 5, 1987), p. II-32—II-33.

23. "New" is in quotes because the principal federal program to be eliminated, if the Congress agrees to the proposed changes, is Title III of the JTPA, which has many of the same benefits as the new program. The principal differences in the old and new programs may be in the delivery approach and in the way "displaced or dislocated workers" is defined. If the Reagan administration adopts the recommendations of its Department of Labor Task Force on Economic Adjustment and Worker Dislocation, all workers with three or more years of tenure on a job from which they are displaced will be entitled to benefits under the new training program.

24. James Bovard, "The Failure of Federal Job Training," *Cato Policy Analysis* (Washington: Cato Institute, August 28, 1986), p. 1.

25. The Congressional Budget Office concluded that "the impact of training [under MDTA] on wage rates has been minimal; the wage rate increases of participants are not substantially different from those of nonparticipants" (Congressional Budget Office, *CETA Reauthorization Issues* [Washington: U.S. Government Printing Office, 1978], p. 15).

26. U.S. Congress, *Congressional Record,* p. 2524.

27. John M. Berry and Art Pine, "19 Years of Job Programs — Question Still is 'What Works?' " *Washington Post,* April 24, 1979.

28. Ibid. The GAO found that "no one knows how many people are being trained, for what occupations they are being trained, or the impact on the demand for skilled workers" (General Accounting Office, *Federal Programs for Manpower Services for the Disadvantaged in the District of Columbia* [Washington: U.S. Government Printing Office, January 30, 1973]).

29. Bovard, "The Failure of Federal Job Training," p. 5. See also General Accounting Office, *Implementation of the Phaseout of CETA Public Service Jobs* (Washington: U.S. Government Printing Office, April 14, 1982).

30. Former Secretary of Labor Ray Donovan, as quoted in the *New York Times,* July 22, 1984.

31. James Bovard, "Son of CETA," *New Republic,* April 14, 1986.

32. James F. Ragan, Jr. and Daniel J. Slottje, "Alternative Measures for Allocating Federal Funds by Geographic Area" (Manhattan, Kansas: Economics Department, Kansas State University, March 1987).

33. Otherwise, government intervention could not be justified. Workers could decide for themselves how much and what kinds of retraining they need and would provide for their retraining expenditures through personal saving.

34. These points are developed in Richard B. McKenzie, *What Should be Done for Displaced Workers?* (St. Louis: Center for the Study of American Business, Washington University, 1985).

35. Indeed, current concern for displaced workers is in part fueled by past governmental efforts to ease transition problems — by providing unemployment compensation, job-training programs, and the like. The values of governmental training and retraining efforts are developed in McKenzie, *What Should be Done for Displaced Workers?*

36. In this regard the case for imposing responsibility for retraining on individuals is symmetrical with the case for imposing charges on the use of environmental resources. Charges on the use of environmental resources prevent pollution. Individual responsibility, which means that individuals suffer costs for their decisions, prevents the excessive use of the federal government's taxing authority.

37. The case for helping the "truly poor" is argued to be consistent with market principles in Richard B. McKenzie, *The Fairness of Markets: The Search for Justice in a Free Society* (Lexington, Mass.: Lexington Books, 1987), Chap. 9.

38. Charlayne Hunter-Gault, McNeil–Lehrer News Hour, January 14, 1987.

CHAPTER 9

Minimum Wages:
Revisions in the
Conventional Wisdom

One of the most startling public-policy stands of the decade was taken in early 1987 when the *New York Times*—bastion of eastern liberal thought and self-appointed protector of working-class Americans—declared in the headline of its lead editorial: "The Right Minimum Wage: $0.00."[1]

For many dedicated readers, the *Times* closed its editorial with an equally profound and confounding statement: "The idea of using a minimum wage to overcome poverty is old, honorable—and fundamentally flawed. It's time to put this hoary debate behind us, and find a better way to improve the lives of people who work very hard for very little."[2]

The *Times* edtiorial is remarkable for other reasons than its break with the newspaper's editorial tradition.[3] First, it was printed just as members of Congress—in particular, Senator Edward Kennedy (D-Mass.), chairman of the Senate Labor and Human Resource Committee—were readying legislation to raise the minimum wage in steps from $3.35 an hour in 1987 to $4.65 an hour by January 1990. If enacted, this proposal might affect the livelihoods of as many as 10 million American workers. Under the Kennedy bill, the minimum wage would be adjusted annually after 1990 to equal no less than 50% of the average hourly wage (presumably, of all nonfarm private production workers).[4] Accordingly, the *Times* editorial signaled a potentially disruptive policy debate among liberals who were expected to make a unified stand on the issue of a higher minimum wage.

Second, the editorial came during the same week that the conservative Reagan administration (represented by then Secretary of Labor William Brock at a hearing of the Senate Labor and Human Resource Committee) was waffling on whether to support or resist the then-mounting political drive for a higher minimum wage.[5] It took the Reagan administration two months after the Kennedy announcement to adopt, more or less, the *Times* position and to acknowledge that an increase in the minimum wage would be counterproductive.

When the Kennedy bill was introduced in March 1987, Secretary Brock was finally able to muster the political courage to say, "We will oppose it. The administration cannot stand by while some in Congress propose an action which will further deny opportunity to America's young men and women."[6] Again, the concern appears to be that the minimum wage is the equivalent of sand thrown into the gears of the American job machine.

The minimum wage debate is now interesting from academic and policy perspectives not so much because the lineup in the debate makes for odd policy bedfellows—with people on the *New York Times* editorial board and in the Reagan administration on the same side against traditional liberal politicians—but because the opponents persist in using the wrong arguments to draw the right conclusion. Minimum-wage laws are now commonly opposed because some workers gain at the expense of others: some workers' wages are raised by minimum-wage laws while other workers' wages are reduced. Yet for almost all the affected workers, this is not true. As empirical studies show, minimum-wage laws do not affect workers' employment opportunities to a substantial extent precisely because they do not affect workers' real incomes (including both money and nonmoney benefits of employment) to a substantial degree.

Before these points are made, the minimum-wage legislative debate needs to be understood in terms of what has actually happened to the minimum wage over the past half-century and in terms of the specific concerns of minimum-wage backers. Using much the same line of analysis developed below, Chapter 10 assesses the impact of proposed "mandated (fringe) benefits" for workers.

The Minimum-Wage Record

The first legal minimum wage, passed as a part of the Fair Labor Standards Act, went into effect in 1938. As shown in Table 9.1, the minimum wage in that year was $.25 an hour. The following year the minimum went to $.40, not breaking $1 an hour until 1956. By 1968,

Table 9.1 The Minimum Wage in History (1938–81)

1938	$0.25	*1968*	$1.60
1939	0.30	*1974*	2.00
1945	0.40	*1975*	2.10
1950	0.75	*1976*	2.30
1956	1.00	*1978*	2.65
1961	1.15	*1979*	2.90
1963	1.25	*1980*	3.10
1967	1.40	*1981*	3.35

Source: U.S. Department of Labor.

the minimum wage had risen another 60% to $1.60 an hour; by 1981, the last year, to date, it has been raised, the minimum wage had again more than doubled.[7] Throughout the five decades of its existence, the coverage of the minimum-wage law — meaning the number of people affected — has risen steadily.

However, since 1938, the purchasing power of the legal minimum wage has been affected as much or more by inflation as by legislative action. As expected from Table 9.1, the value of the minimum wage in nominal money terms in Figure 9.1 rises in distinct steps throughout the period. What is most notable from Figure 9.1 is the long-term decline in the *real* or *constant (1986) dollar* minimum wage. This decline did not start in the 1980s, nor with the advent of the Reagan administration. The real minimum wage peaked in 1968 at $5.04 an hour (1986 dollars). It then declined steadily to approximately $3.95 in 1973, only to rise again in 1974 and oscillate within a range of $4.45 to $4.16 until 1981. After 1981, it began another steady decline, reaching $3.35 an hour in 1986.

The political case for raising the minimum wage has been bolstered by a few simple facts of real deterioration in the minimum wage. The real minmum wage fell by more than a third (or $1.69 an hour) between 1968 and 1986, and 60% of the decrease, or $1 an hour, occurred between 1968 and 1981. In 1986 the real minimum wage was approximately the same as it was in 1950 and was only 43% above the real level of 1940.

The decline in the minimum wage in the late 1970s and early 1980s might be attributed in part to the fact that the average hourly wages of all workers were decreasing, from a constant (1986) dollar high of $9.72 an hour in 1973 to $8.73 an hour in 1986.[8] However, the minimum wage fell slightly more rapidly. As a consequence, it was 56% of average hourly earnings in 1968 and only 39% in 1986.[9]

Proposals to raise the minimum wage to $4.65 an hour by 1990 and to 50% of the average hourly earnings are, therefore, not drastic recommendations by historical standards. These proposals would only return the minimum wage, in relative terms, to levels first achieved in the early 1950s.

So what is the problem? Why do the *New York Times* and the Reagan administration oppose what appears to be a relatively modest proposal in historical terms? Is it that they are simply anti-workers? Anti-poor? Many proponents appear to think so, arguing that they alone have the interests of low-income workers at heart. They appear to believe that the historical decline in the real minimum wage implies that the covered workers are worse off. This is a conclusion that is naturally but incorrectly drawn from misleading economic models of minimum-wage markets conventionally shared by analysts on both sides of the debate.

The Allure of Mandated Poverty Reduction

The political attraction of a minimum-wage law stems primarily from its simplicity. It appears to be a straightforward solution to a persistent problem: low income for many American workers—the so-called

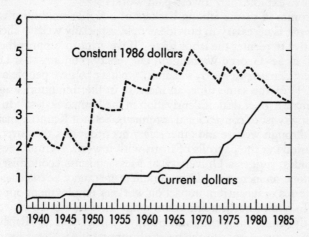

Fig. 9.1 The rise and fall of the minimum wage, in current and constant (1986) dollar terms, 1938–1986. (*Source:* U.S. Department of Labor and author's calculations.)

have-nots of America. An hourly wage of $3.35 provides a year-round, full-time, covered worker with slightly less than $7,000 a year, even if he or she works every week of the year and puts in 40 hours a week.

Only several thousand dollars a year may be more than adequate income for a teenager interested only in supplementing a modest allowance from parents, but, for heads of households, $7,000 a year represents an amount far below the official poverty-income level. However, proponents maintain that perhaps as many as 30% of American workers covered by the legal minimum are heads of households.[10] Protesting the *Times* editorial, Jack Sheinkman, secretary-treasurer of the Amalgamated Clothing and Textile Workers Union, contended that a minimum wage of $3.35 is actually

> far below the official poverty threshold income for a family of three [much less a family of four]. It is even below the income that would be available from welfare and basic food-stamp benefits in New York City. It represents a wage that is exploitive, degrading and a substantial disincentive to work.[11]

Similarly, Senator Kennedy declared when he introduced his bill that the current law "permits unscrupulous firms with significant market power to exploit their lowest-paid workers."[12]

A common theme among backers of a higher minimum wage is that a rise is necessary to provide people, especially welfare clients, an incentive to reenter the labor force. "If we want to support the work ethic," argues George Washington University economist Sar Levitan, echoing Senator Kennedy's claims, "we have to give people a living wage."[13] At the same time, an increase in the minimum wage will "eliminate a great deal of deprivation in the United States."[14] In an interesting twist of conventional arguments, Senator Kennedy maintains that "through welfare and other safety net programs, the government is subsidizing the payrolls of firms with low-wage employees."[15]

Besides, suggests University of Massachusetts economist Barry Bluestone, an increase in the minimum wage cannot be evaluated solely in terms of its current impact on workers' employment opportunities. In and of itself, a minimum-wage increase can be expected to have dynamic, long-run, and positive consequences: "Raising the minimum wage goes to the heart of important problems facing our economy. It will force managers to redesign their production processes and that will, in the long run, produce real wage increases."[16] By raising the minimum wage, Congress will force productivity increases and induce improvement in the international "competitiveness" of the U.S. economy, or so Professor Bluestone appears to argue.

Finally, backers contend that if there is any evidence at all to support the argument that the minimum wage will reduce employment, the effect is quite small—so small that Congress can and should dismiss the problem.[17] They argue that other social problems, which can be partially rectified by minimum-wage increases, are more pressing. In an effort to do the most good for the most people, Congress needs to think about minimum-wage increases, as it must in all areas of social policy, in terms of their effect, on balance, across the targeted labor markets, weighting the positive and negative effects of the increases.[18] These proponents suggest, in effect, that cost-benefit analysis (endorsed by pro-market economists inside the Reagan administration) should be employed in the case of minimum wages, just as it is commonly used in safety, health, or environmental legislation. They propose raising the minimum wage since far more people would be helped than hurt by the increase.

Interestingly, the most-favored argument of opponents of the minimum wage has now been widely accepted by proponents.[19] Opponents have traditionally contended that an increase in the minimum wage would reduce the job opportunities of the affected workers, especially young, uneducated, and inexperienced workers.[20] They maintain that many jobs are simply not worth the specified minimum wage; some workers are not sufficiently productive (do not contribute enough to firm revenues) to justify the legal minimum wage (of, say, $3.35 an hour) even if this wage amounts to a poverty-level income.[21]

As a consequence, the minimum wage effectively outlaws some job opportunities, leaving a smaller number of jobs to be rationed among a larger pool of workers seeking employment. The law, in effect, tells workers and employers that a bargain both consider to be to their mutual benefit is illegal. The law is not only blatantly anti-employers, but anti-workers too!

The purpose of the law—to benefit affected workers—may be noble. Yet, at the same time, conventional market analysis warns that by expunging job opportunities, some workers—those who lose their jobs or are unable to obtain employment—are made worse off because they must then seek a less lucrative job or go on public welfare. Many workers may receive an increase in pay, *because of the minimum wage,* but other workers will receive a decrease in pay, *because of the minimum wage.* In the words of the *New York Times,*

... Senator Kennedy considers raising the minimum wage as "something like an anti-poverty program for the working poor without any federal spending." That last part is especially seductive in a time of budget constraints.

Congress has increasingly been putting more burden on employers, like higher minimum wages...These requirements amount to a hidden tax. In the case of the minimum wage, the tax is on the jobs of those at the lowest rung. . . .

But the increase would come out of the hides of other working poor people. Employers are bound to circumvent a higher minimum wage in two ways: by evading the law through underground, sub-minimum hiring or by letting workers go. A higher minimum wage would probably price many working poor people out of jobs, since they could not demonstrate the productivity necessary to justify the higher wage.[22]

Further, opponents warn that an increase in the minimum wage will mean that employers must discriminate among applicants according to nonmarket tests: age, religion, and sex of workers. In the covered labor markets, the minimum wage will likely encourage discrimination against the very young and the very old, blacks and Hispanics, women, and any particular religious group that might be in current disfavor.[23] In general, the legal minimum wage will tend to give the more productive workers a competitive advantage over the unproductive.

The Limited Wisdom in the Conventional Wisdom

Conventional wisdom on the consequences of minimum-wage laws embrace two principal problems, one relating to politics and the other relating to incorrect assumptions about the restricted forms of worker payment. The first problem is that conventional market analysis fails to consider the political implications of the conclusions drawn.[24] Politicians love to vote for policies that benefit far more of their constituents than they hurt. This is true especially if the constituents who are hurt by the adopted policies do not, or cannot, vote and if the harm of the policies is difficult to attribute to the adopted policies and to the politicians who voted for them.

As a practical matter, many of the people who are likely to lose job opportunities due to a minimum-wage increase are often too young to vote or are not inclined to vote, perhaps because they are poor and live outside the mainstream of the political and economic system (for example, in ghettos). In addition, the conventional analysis predicts that few people will be hurt by a hike in the minimum wage.[25] If there are many people hurt by any *given* increase, then politicians can temper the increase to make sure that the balance shifts in favor of people helped, rather than hurt, by the increase.

Based on studies of the "elasticity of demand" of employers for affected workers, economists can denounce minimum-wage laws all they like. However, politicians may continue to favor mandated wages as long as their own studies of the "elasticity of vote" indicate that their support is politically astute.[26]

At the same time, many government officials charged with caring for people out of work through public welfare may see a higher minimum wage as a mixed blessing. On the one hand, they may be distressed when people are unable to find work because of the minimum wage. On the other hand, the higher minimum wage can be the source of greater public demand for their services, higher budgets, and more opportunities to supervise programs that care for poor people.

Granted, an increase in the minimum wage can result in fewer workers hired, fewer goods and services produced, higher prices for goods and services, and lower real incomes for consumers. However, it is extraordinarily difficult for consumers to sort out the impact of the minimum-wage increase from all the other events in the market that might lead to higher prices and lower real income. What is remarkable about the January 1987 *Times* editorial on the minimum-wage law is that the editors were finally able to draw the connection between higher minimum wages, fewer jobs, and less real incomes for people directly and indirectly affected by the law.[27]

The second problem with the conventional analysis is that it is very likely dead wrong on its principal contention, which is that a higher minimum-wage law actually enhances the long-run incomes of many, if not most, of the covered workers. Contrary to what is normally thought, an increase in the minimum wage probably reduces the long-run *real effective income* — as opposed to the money income — of all (or practically all) covered workers, including those who retain their jobs at the higher legal minimum wage.[28]

The conventional analysis of minimum-wage laws implicitly assumes that workers are paid only in terms of money and/or that employers will adhere, to the best of their ability, to the spirit of the minimum-wage law. Therefore, if the minimum wage expressed in money is raised to, say, $4.65 an hour, employers simply must decide how many workers are worth that wage and, consequently, adjust by nonprice-rationing devices the number of workers needed. The affected employers may be "scandals" in that they are willing to pay less than the new established minimum wage and may discriminate by race, creed, and sex, but these employers do nothing else but abide by the law. Perhaps this is because they have no other options, or so it is assumed.

Granted, incomes of some workers may be increased for a short period of time, until employers have time to adjust their mode of paying workers. However, once employers are given enough time to adjust to the higher money wage by changing their hiring and payment practices, the gains will erode to the point that even those workers who retain their jobs in face of a higher minimum wage will be worse off.

The payment adjustments can be made because few workers—even minimum-wage workers—are paid solely in terms of money. Indeed, workers are commonly paid in a multiplicity of forms, and the variety of payment forms is restricted only by the creativity of the employers in devising nonmoney payments. Accordingly, minimum-wage workers are paid in an assortment of fringe benefits (for example, health and life insurance and vacation). Granted, minimum-wage workers often have few conventional fringe benefits, but they are also paid in terms of working conditions, on-the-job training, rest periods, promises of college educations, courtesy of employers and supervisors, scheduling of work hours, time off, company discounts, recommendations, credit, and opportunities for advancement.

Finally, although it may not be exactly proper to say that workers are paid in terms of the work demands of the job, it is clear that employers seek to make work demands compatible with the other forms of explicit, and implicit, on-the-job payments. Workers are no less concerned about how much is expected of them while on the job as they are about wages and fringe benefits. Similarly, employers understand that if their work demands are raised, other forms of payment will have to be made to compensate for the employee dissatisfaction caused by the increased demands. This also implies that employers can compensate for lack of adequate fringe benefits and other forms of explicit money and nonmoney payments by reducing the work demands imposed on their workers. In this restricted sense, slack work demands can be construed as a form of nonmoney payment.

The important point is that in the absence of mandated wages and benefits, employers and employees will tend to work out "payment bundles" that represent the best mutually beneficial exchanges they can devise, given their circumstances (including tax law applying to various forms of money and nonmoney income). Legally specified minimum-money wages upset many of those mutually beneficial "payment bundles."

Proponents of minimum-wage increases appear to be convinced that, by the stroke of the legislative pen, the bundle is increased by the exact amount of the money-wage increase. The assumption behind Senator Kennedy's 1987 minimum-wage proposal is that if the bill was passed, the affected workers' payment bundles would rise by $1.30 between 1987 and 1990. Why? Because the minimum wage, if enacted, would be raised from $3.35 to $4.65 an hour.

Senator Kennedy and his supporters have forgotten that the money wage is just one component, not always the major component, of workers' payment bundles. There is nothing in the proposed legislation that requires employers to raise or even maintain the same payment bundles; the proposed law talks only about what should happen to the money wage. And there is every reason to expect adjustment in the nonmoney forms of payments.[29]

The first of these reasons is that no one should count on employers who do not voluntarily pay their workers $4.65 to hold the line voluntarily on the other forms of payments when not forced to do so. The very fact that the employers must be forced to raise the money wage is *prima facie* evidence that the employers are willing to keep their workers' total-payment bundles as low as possible.

Second, in a competitive struggle to hold their position in the markets for the goods or services produced, employers will be forced to cut costs to compensate for the required higher money wage. If they do not cut their nonmoney payments, then they can reason that other employers will do so—thereby acquiring a cost advantage and a capacity to underprice.[30]

Third, as conventionally argued, the higher money wage will lead to fewer job opportunities with more people looking for work (given the initial greater monetary incentive). Employers faced with more people wanting to work than jobs they have to offer will be in a market position enabling them to cut nonmoney forms of payment. Employees who do not like the reductions in nonmoney payments can be readily replaced by other unemployed workers knocking on the employers' doors.

In short, faced with an increase in the money minimum wage, employers can cut fringe benefits, reduce on-the-job training, and eliminate employee discounts and prospects of promotion. They can also increase work demands. And there is nothing particularly illegal or reprehensible about these responses by the employers. Indeed, such responses are perfectly legal and, because they reduce the total cost of hiring workers, they partially negate the adverse employment consequences of legislated increases in the minimum wage. (Hence, the employer reduction in nonmoney payments may explain why researchers have been so hard-pressed in calculating the employment impact of minimum-wage laws.)[31]

Nonetheless, the adjustments made by the employers do not place in a better economic position the affected workers who retain their jobs. They may have more money income (which is taxable), but they will have less nonmoney income (which is not taxable). Indeed, because the overall cost of hiring workers is raised by the minimum-wage increases and the subsequent downward adjustments in nonmoney benefits, fewer jobs are, in fact, available. The intense competition among workers for the restricted number of jobs should cause the actual value of the entire payment bundles received by workers to fall below what it was before the minimum money wage was raised.

In concrete (but hypothetical) terms, an increase in the minimum wage of $1.30 over a three-year period can cause a reduction in the total value of the nonmoney payments of, say, $1.50 in the workers' bundles during the same time period. The workers would then be losing $.20 per hour.

Why the expected net decrease in the total payment bundles? Again, the affected workers will have fewer available jobs. Workers who wish to become employed will have to reduce their total payment demands in order to be among the relatively more fortunate persons who actually obtain or retain the restricted number of jobs.

Put another way, the demand for workers is reduced because the imposed higher-money wage forces employers to establish a marginally more costly or less efficient bundle of payments—more money income and fewer nonmoney benefits. The reduced labor demand leads to a payment bundle of lower value to the affected workers (just as a lowered demand for a consumer service reduces the overall price the seller can get for the service).

From the perspective of technical conventional economic models, illustrated with supply and demand curves on a graph, a higher minimum wage results in fewer workers employed because employers are driven up the demand-for-labor curve. That does happen in this revised line of analysis, but only because the overall cost of labor rises (the forms of payment are more inefficient). What is different from this new perspective is that, instead of a higher minimum wage inducing workers to move up their supply-of-labor curve, workers are actually forced down their supply-of-labor curve, since the net benefit of the covered jobs to workers is reduced.[32] The difference between the higher cost of hiring workers (incurred by the employers) and the lower total benefits (received by the workers) amounts to the deadweight loss of the mandated wage—that is, a nonrecoverable cost of legislative action.

The unfortunate consequence of the mandated higher-minimum wage is that a few workers withdraw from the covered markets, only to seek employment in jobs that are then made marginally better than the jobs covered by the minimum wage. Nonetheless, they are still worse off. Practically all of the remaining workers, those who stay with their jobs, are also made worse off. Workers may receive more money but their total payment bundles are worth less than before the legislated money raise.[33] Workers who stay with their jobs, unlike those who leave the markets covered by the minimum wage, do not have a higher-valued opportunity. Once more, because relatively more of their total income is received in money, those workers who retain their jobs will pay more in taxes, either in income taxes when they earn the additional money income or in sales taxes when they spend their higher money income.

The long-run effects of raising the minimum wage can actually be even more perverse than the short-run consequences. This is because of the marginal reduction in on-the-job training for some workers that is likely to accompany the minimum-wage increase. Because of reduced training, many of the affected workers can be expected to follow lower growth in their wage profiles over all, or some portion, of their working lives.

Reversing the analysis, the conclusion can be drawn that a decline in the legal minimum-money wage can lead to an increase in the effective value to workers of their payment bundles. Therefore, the decline in the real minimum wage, evident in Figure 9.1, probably hides real income improvements of workers covered by the minimum-wage laws. The decline has probably increased (albeit marginally) the employment opportunities of the covered workers but, more importantly, has led to an increase in the short-run and long-run overall value of the payment bundles to the covered workers.

Making Workers Worse Off: The Empirical Support

Although still controversial, this new perspective on the adverse effects of minimum wage laws is supported by a growing body of research.

• Writing in the *American Economic Review*, Nori Hashimoto found that under the 1967 minimum-wage hike, workers gained 32 cents in money income but lost 41 cents per hour in training—a net loss of 9 cents an hour in full-income compensation.[34]

• Linda Leighton and Jacob Mincer, in one study, and Belton Fleisher, in another study, came to a similar conclusion: Increases in the minimum wage reduce on-the-job training—and, as a result, dampen growth in the real long-run income of covered workers.[35]

• Walter Wessels found that the minimum wages caused retail establishments in New York to increase work demands. In response to a minimum-wage increase, only 714 of the surveyed stores cut back store hours, but 4,827 stores reduced the number of workers and/or their employees' hours worked. Thus, in most stores, fewer workers were given fewer hours to do the same work as before.[36]

• The research of Belton Feisher, William Alpert, and L. F. Dunn shows that minimum-wage increases lead to large reductions in fringe benefits and to worsening working conditions.[37] For example, in the just-mentioned New York study, many stores reduced commission payments, eliminated year-end bonuses, and decreased paid vacation and sick leave. In his study, Professor Alpert found that for every 1% increase in the minimum wage, restaurants reduce shift premiums by 3.6%, severance pay by 6.9%, and sick pay by 3.4%.

• If the minimum wage does *not* cause employers to make substantial reductions in nonmoney benefits, then increases in the minimum wage should cause (1) an increase in the labor-force participation rates of covered workers (because workers would be moving up their supply-of-labor curves), (2) a reduction in the rate covered workers quit their jobs (because their jobs would then be more attractive), and (3) a significant increase in prices of production processes heavily dependent upon covered minimum-wage workers. However, Wessels found little empirical support for such conclusions drawn from conventional theory. Indeed, in general, he found that minimum-wage increases had the exact opposite effect: (1) participation rates went down, (2) quit rates went up, and (3) prices did not rise appreciably—findings consistent only with the view that minimum-wage increases make workers worse off.[38] With regard to quit rates, Wessels writes,

I could find no industry which had a significant decrease in their quit rates. Two industries had a significant increase in their quit rates... These results are only consistent with a lower full compensation. I also found that quit rates went up more in those industries with the average lowest wage. This shows that the more minimum wages force employers to raise wages, the more full compensation is reduced. I also found that in the long run, several industries experienced a significantly large increase in the quit rate: a result only possible if minimum wages reduce full compensation.[39]

Given the findings of various studies done by himself and other researchers, Wessels maintains that it is reasonable to deduce that every 10% increase in the hourly minimum wage will make workers 2% worse off.[40] This means that an increase in the minimum of $1.30 (equal to the 1987 Congressional proposal) could, on balance, make the covered workers worse off to the tune of 26 cents per hour.

Concluding Comments

The intent of this chapter has been to correct the way economists and policymakers think about minimum wages. The discussion has been developed in terms of everyone, or practically everyone, being made worse off by legislated increases in the minimum wage.

Admittedly, such a position is probably extreme. As noted, some workers may, in fact, be paid only in money terms. There may be, in some employment circumstances, only a very few ways in which employers can adjust the work demands in response to an increase in the minimum wage. However, it is highly unlikely that a significant percentage of employers cannot make adjustments, at least in the long run. If nothing else, employers can change their treatment of their employees by making their employees work harder, faster, and with fewer breaks; employers can impose higher skill demands, acquired at worker expense, on their new employees. The important point is that conventional analysis of minimum-wage laws is grossly misleading when it suggests that all, or even a significant percentage, of the workers who retain their jobs in the face of a higher minimum wage are consequently better off. Unfortunately, that incorrect line of thought has amounted to an inadvertent political endorsement of the minimum wage.

The revised view of the economic consequences of minimum-wage laws developed in this chapter is not particularly new to applied-policy economics. It is, rather, an extension of a line of analysis commonly applied to rent controls. For decades economists have predicted that municipal control over apartment-rental payments can be expected to give rise to deterioration of the controlled apartments. Rent controls reduce the quality of apartments offered and increase the number of renters demanding apartments, leading to a shortage of apartments. The market shortage gives the landlords the power to raise the effective rents by simply not keeping the apartments up or by transferring payment of utilities to renters. If the renters do not like the treatment they receive, they can be replaced by other renters caught in the market shortage.

Unfortunately, economists have not traditionally applied this identical line of analysis to minimum-wage laws, even though such laws are nothing more than forms of price controls. Minimum-wage controls cause a shortage of jobs, and, just as in the case of rent-controlled apartments, employers can be expected to reduce the "quality" of those jobs in response to the policy-induced shortage of jobs. This means that all, or practically all, workers affected by minimum wages should face a reduced living standard precisely because of the wage law.

The best way to make workers better off is to do more than what the *New York Times* says should be done: repeal the minimum-wage laws altogether, not just reduce the minimum wage to $0.00. A minimum wage of zero can still be too high, because even a mandated zero wage can possibly thwart some workers' perceived opportunities. Paying the employer to work and thereby learning the business on the job is a benefit that some workers (as distinct from policymakers) may consider well worth the payments.[41]

Unless policymakers are willing to engage in detailed control of markets, which seems beyond their ability as well as their intent (in spite of their current interest in mandating a few benefits, the subject of Chapter 10), they would be well advised to set the whole "hoary debate" aside. Barring the elimination of the minimum-wage law, policymakers should allow the effects of the law to continue to pass gradually out of existence through the eroding effects of inflation.

Policymakers interested in the welfare of low-income workers in the United States should set aside, once and for all, the rhetoric of worker exploitation. They must begin to accept the fact that low-income workers usually neither earn a larger income nor receive more benefits because they are not sufficiently skilled to earn more. The fundamental problem in need of correction is their skill level, not their wages. Just as market competition determines that low-skilled workers will earn low wages, market competition pushes worker wages up when workers improve their skills. The central point of this chapter is that to mandate wages is to worsen the economic positions of the very workers who are the intended object of government help.

No amount of political chest-pounding about dismally low wages and benefits for some American workers will substitute for hard thinking about how the skills and employment opportunities of low-income workers can be improved. Unfortunately, politicians demand simple solutions to complex economic problems, and they are all too frequently pressed to find solutions for which they, not the workers, can take credit. Accordingly, politicians all too frequently seek to mandate wages, thinking that they, as mighty politicians, can overpower market forces—a long-run impossibility without detailed market controls. Correcting that mistaken mode of thinking is the first order of policy. The *New York Times,* however, has shown that it can be done; the country's political leaders should surely follow suit.

Notes

1. "The Right Minimum Wage: $0.00" (editorial), *New York Times,* January 14, 1987, p. 18.

2. Ibid. The *Times* reinforced its opposition in a subsequent editorial ("Don't Raise the Minimum Wage," *New York Times,* April 15, 1987, p. 20).

3. With equal force, in earlier years, the *Times* supported increases in the minimum wage. For example, the *New York Times* editorialized in 1961, "We support President Kennedy's appeal to Congress for prompt action to raise the level of the federal minimum wage to $1.25 an hour within a three-year period. We believe also that the coverage of the existing law should be widened to include far more people than now" ("Minimum Wage Law Revision," editorial, *New York Times,* February 9, 1961, p. 30). That editorial argued that predicted adverse employment effects of the minimum wage had been grossly exaggerated. In a following editorial, the newspaper even argued that "surveys have shown that a higher minimum in low-wage communities has actually stimulated, rather than depressed, employment, and has stimulated it not only far beyond the national average but to a greater degree in specific industries affected by the new minimum wage than in industries not so affected" ("Minimum Wage: 1961" [editorial], *New York Times,* March 21, 1961, p. 36). The *Times* made raising the minimum wage something of a crusade in 1961, editorializing on the subject at least six more times before a compromise bill was approved in Congress.

In 1962, the newspaper supported a minimum wage for New York City that would supersede the federal minimum wage ("A Municipal Wage Floor" [editorial], *New York Times,* January 22, 1961, p. 22). However, by August of 1962, the paper had begun to shift its support, reminding its readers that "New York is not an economic island" and maintaining that a municipal minimum higher than the federal minimum would put the city at a competitive disadvantage for jobs ("A Municipal Wage Floor" [editorial], *New York Times,* August 13, 1962, p. 24).

4. U.S. Congress, Senate, 100th Cong., 1st Sess., "Minimum Wage Restoration Act of 1987" (S. 837), to amend the Fair Labor Standards Act of 1938. See also Keith Schneider, "Democrats Offer Bill to Raise Hourly Wage

Level to $4.65," *New York Times,* March 26, 1987, p. Y11. The current minimum wage in 1987 was less than 38% of the average hourly wage. While he later supported the Kennedy bill, Representative Mario Biaggi initially proposed (in H.R. 79) that the minimum wage be raised to $5.05 an hour by 1990 and tying the minimum wage to 50% of the average private wage thereafter ["Unfreezing the Minimum," *National Journal,* March 14, 1987, p. 648; and Mario Biaggi, "Up the Minimum Wage!" *Congressman Biaggi Reports to the People,* May 1987, p. 1]. Representative Biaggi's proposal, however, is not the highest proposed legislative minimum wage. The Amalgamated Clothing and Textile Workers Union, for example, supported a minimum wage equal to 60% of average hourly earnings, equal in 1987 to $5.29 an hour (Jack Sheinkman, "Why the Minimum Wage Should be Raised" [letter to the editor] *New York Times,* February 9, 1987, p. 18).

5. "Reagan Undecided on Wage Stand," *Greenville* (S.C.) *News,* January 14, 1987, p. 10D.

6. "Minimum Wage Raise Proposed," *Greenville* (S.C.) *News,* March 26, 1987, p. 10D.

7. Actually, the last time before 1987 that a minimum-wage bill was considered by Congress was in 1977, when several scheduled annual increases in the minimum were passed.

8. Just how much real hourly wages have fallen since 1973 is under considerable dispute. See Chapter 5.

9. The minimum wage was also equal to 56% of average hourly earnings in 1950.

10. As estimated by Sar Levitan, director of George Washington University Center for Social Policy Studies, and reported in Cathy Trost, "Hill Democrats Plan Effort to Increase Minimum Wage Amid Employer Protests," *Wall Street Journal,* March 25, 1987, p. 68.

11. Sheinkman, "Why the Minimum Wage Should be Raised."

12. Edward M. Kennedy, statement upon introduction of the Minimum Wage Act of 1987, press release, March 25, 1987, p. 1.

13. Sheinkman, "Why the Minimum Wage Should be Raised." Levitan added, in another interview, "I think the recognition is widespread that if they don't raise the earnings of the working poor, then it puts a very strong disincentive for welfare people to move on to economic self-sufficiency. . . In most states, there's very little inducement for minimum wage workers to continue working" (Kenneth B. Noble, "Now, Maximum Interest in the Minimum Wage," *New York Times,* January 7, 1987, p. 28).

Senator Kennedy argued in his press release that the current minimum wage "violates the work ethic by condemning to lives of hardship and deprivation millions of citizens who are ready, willing, and able to work. A full-time job in the workplace should never mean a lifetime of poverty or welfare dependency" (Kennedy, press release, pp. 1–2).

14. Ibid. Levitan briefly but more fully develops his position on minimum wages in Sar Levitan and Isaac Shapiro, "The Minimum Wage: A Sinking Floor," *New York Times,* January 16, 1986, p. 19.

15. Kennedy, press release, p. 2. Contrary to the arguments that minimum-wage increases provide incentives for people to move off welfare, Leffler makes the argument that the poor have a demand for minimum-wage increases because these increases restrict employment opportunities and increase legislated welfare benefits (Keith B. Leffler, "Minimum Wages, Welfare, and Wealth Transfers," *Journal of Law and Economics,* October 1978, pp. 345–58).

16. As quoted in Keith Schneider, "Democrats Offer Bill to Raise Hourly Wage Level to $4.65," *New York Times,* March 26, 1987, p. 11.

17. The best available review of the empirical impact of a minimum-wage increase indicates that for each 10% increase in the real minimum wage, teenage employment will fall by 1% to 3%. The adverse employment effect is, of course, much lower for older workers, primarily because most older workers earn substantially more than the minimum wage (Charles Brown, Curtis Gilroy, and Andrew Kohen, "The Effect of the Minimum Wage on Employment and Unemployment," *Journal of Economic Literature,* June 1982, pp. 487–528).

18. A position attributed to Sar Levitan in Noble, "Now, Maximum Increase in the Minimum Wage."

19. When the *New York Times* was supporting increases in the minimum wage, it was willing to conclude that "*no serious* unemployment effects are to be anticipated from the rise," presumably meaning that at least some adverse employment effects were in fact expected (emphasis added, "Minimum Wage Compromise," *New York Times,* May 2, 1961, p. 36).

The particulars of the economic case against minimum-wage laws are covered in almost all principles of economics and microeconomic-theory textbooks. The quantitative impact of minimum-wage laws has also been studied extensively. While the empirical studies generally agree that an increase in the minimum wage reduces employment, they disagree on the exact magnitude of the impact. However, there is general agreement that the adverse employment effects represent a relatively small percentage of the entire labor force and are concentrated on teenagers (Brown, *et al.,* "The Effect of the Minimum Wage on Employment and Unemployment").

For reviews of the conventional arguments and empirical assessments of the impact of minimum-wage laws, see a series of monographs published in the late 1970s and early 1980s by the American Enterprise Institute in Washington: Finis Welch, *Minimum Wages: Issues and Evidence* (1978); Walter Wessels, *Minimum Wages, Fringe Benefits and Working Conditions* (1980); Donald O. Parsons, *Poverty and the Minimum Wage* (1980); Ronald J. Kruman, *The Impact of the Minimum Wage on Regional Labor Markets* (1981); Masanori Hashimoto, *Minimum Wages and On-the-Job Training* (1980); David Metcalf, *Low Pay, Occupational Mobility, and Minimum Wage in Britain* (1981); and Belton M. Fleisher, *Minimum Wage Regulation in Retail Trade* (1981). See also Yale Brozen, "The Effect of Statutory Minimum Wage Increases on Teenage Unemployment," *Journal of Law and Economics,* April 1969; T. G. Moore, "The Effect of Minimum Wages on Teenage Unemployment Rates," *Journal of Political Economy,* July/August 1971; and Jacob Mincer, "Unemployment Effects of

Minimum Wages," *Journal of Political Economy,* August 1976, pp. 87–105.

20. For very brief reviews of a large number of minimum-wage studies, see Bob Mottice and Bob Potts, "The Minimum Wage: A Case for Special Interest Politics Versus *Jobs!*" (Washington: Republican Policy Committee, U.S. Senate, March 26, 1987).

21. One very recent study estimated that a 10% increase in the minimum wage would lead to a loss of between 124,000 and 619,000 jobs. The 37.6% increase in minimum wages proposed in 1987 might decrease employment by over half a million (calculated by Mottice and Potts, "The Minimum Wage," p. 1, based on estimates provided by the U.S. General Accounting Office, Report PAD-83-7, January 28, 1983, p. i).

22. "Don't Raise the Minimum Wage" (editorial), *New York Times,* April 15, 1987, p. 20.

23. James Ragan estimates that the minimum wage affects teenagers more than older workers. In fact, he estimates that the minimum wage in existence in 1972 reduced teenage employment by 320,000 and raised the teenage-unemployment rate by 3.8 percentage points (James F. Ragan, Jr., "Minimum Wage Legislation and the Youth Labor Market" [St. Louis: Center for the Study of American Business, Washington University, 1976]). Walter Williams reviews the impact of minimum-wage laws on black youth in *State Against Blacks* (New York: McGraw-Hill Book Company, 1982), Chap. 3.

24. The politics of minimum wages is developed in F. G. Stendle, "The Appeal of Minimum Wage Laws and the Invisible Hand in Government," *Public Choice,* Spring 1973, pp. 133–36; and William R. Keech, "More on the Vote Winning and Vote Losing Qualities of Minimum Wage Laws," *Public Choice,* Spring 1977, pp. 133–37.

25. Most empirical studies have found that a 10% increase in the minimum wage generally results in a decrease in teenage employment (the hardest-hit group of workers) by 1% to 3% (Brown, Gilroy, and Kohen, "The Effect of the Minimum Wage on Employment and Unemployment, p. 505).

26. It should be noted, of course, that conventional economic analysis has not explained the observed long-term decline in the *real* minimum wage since 1968.

27. See footnote 3. The shift in the *New York Times*'s editorial position is the subject of a paper that is currently being developed.

28. The phrase "practically all" is used in recognition of the fact that a small number of workers, those paid totally in terms of cash, may actually receive a pay increase with the enactment of a higher minimum wage. By definition, the money-wage increase cannot be more than offset by a nonmoney-wage decrease in such cases (very likely, a limited number).

29. This line of analysis is developed in more technical terms, using supply-and-demand models of competitive markets, in Richard B. McKenzie, *The Fairness of Markets: A Search for Justice in a Free Society* (Lexington, Mass.: Lexington Books, 1987), Chap. 7.

30. In response to the higher-minimum money wage, employers may initially reduce employment, only to add additional workers later after non-

money payments have been reduced and work demands have been increased. Consequently, the unemployment effects of minimum laws may be dissipated somewhat over time.

31. The impact of minimum-wage laws on nonmoney benefits of employment has not been studied nearly as extensively as their impact on total employment or the composition of employment. The nonmoney benefits are difficult, if not impossible, to assess with any reasonable accuracy. See, however, Masanori Hashimoto, "Minimum Wage Effect on Training on the Job," *American Economic Review,* 70 (December 1982); Jacob Mincer and Linda Leighton, "The Effects of Minimum Wages on Human Capital Formation," Working Paper No. 441 (Washington: National Bureau of Economic Research, 1980); and Walter J. Wessels, *Minimum Wages: Fringe Benefits and Working Conditions* (Washington: American Enterprise Institute, 1980). More will be said on this topic later.

32. This line of argument helps explain why many minimum-wage jobs remain unfilled in spite of the prevalence of, say, "unemployed" youth in the area.

33. Again, the value of the payment bundle must decrease because of the reduced number of jobs and the need for the value of the payment bundle to fall until the market is cleared, or practically cleared.

34. Masanori Hashimota, "Minimum Wage Effect on Training on the Job," *American Economic Review,* 70 (December 1982), pp. 1070–87.

35. Linda Leighton and Jacob Mincer, "Effects of Minimum Wages on Human Capital Formation," *The Economics of Legal Minimum Wages,* edited by Simon Rothenberg (Washington: American Enterprise Institute, 1981).

36. Walter J. Wessels, "Minimum Wages: Are Workers Really Better Off?", a paper prepared for presentation at a conference on minimum wages (Washington: National Chamber Foundation, July 29, 1987).

37. Belton M. Fleisher, *Minimum Wage Regulation in Retail Trade* (Washington: American Enterprise Institute, 1981); William T. Alpert, "The Effects of the Minimum Wage on the Fringe Benefits of Restaurant Workers" (unpublished paper, Lehigh University, Bethlehem, Pa., 1983).; and L. F. Dunn, "Nonpecuniary Job Preferences and Welfare Losses Among Migrant Agriculture Workers," *American Journal of Agriculture Economics,* 67 (May 1985), pp. 257–65.

38. Wessels, "Minimum Wages: Are Workers Really Better Off?"

39. Ibid., p. 13.

40. Ibid., p. 15.

41. Ironically, if a worker did pay an employer for the right to learn on the job, the worker would, in effect, be an employer also. Given the minimum-wage law, it is conceivable that the worker would be required to pay the employer no less than $3.35 an hour for the right to learn on the job.

CHAPTER 10

Mandated Benefits:
The Firm as the Social Agent
of the State

Although not fully recognized by policymakers, the Washington-based national labor-policy movement is being directed by a fundamental shift in the social philosophy underpinning government welfare. Proponents of welfare programs have begun to look upon firms as potential service agents of the welfare state. For many proponents, the long-term goal is ambitious, to do nothing less than democratize the country's workplaces. Workers will be given managerial rights through votes on their firms' investment, divestment, and disinvestment decisions (as well as practically any other workplace issue that affects worker interests).[1]

The proponents' intermediate goal is, however, significantly more modest. They seek to charge firms with the responsibility of providing their employees with employment and social-welfare benefits. As mentioned in earlier chapters, the proposed employment benefits include health insurance, retraining, job placement, and severance pay—now provided voluntarily by many, but not all, firms. Social-welfare benefits include health care, day care, Social Security, and unemployment compensation—now delivered by state welfare agencies. In the future, we are told, "Government bureaucracies that now administer these [welfare] programs to individuals will be supplanted, to a large extent, by companies that administer them to their employees."[2]

The legislative drive to replace government welfare bureaus with private firms was introduced to public-policy debates in the 1980s under the relatively innocuous banner of "mandated benefits." Political leaders have proposed that firms should be required to provide a range of employment and welfare benefits. Proponents say that the cost incurred should be construed as a necessary payment for the privilege of doing business in American markets.[3]

In 1987, mandated health insurance, parental leave, and plant-closing benefits appeared high on the proponents' legislative lists.

• The Reagan administration's Secretary of Health and Human Services Otis Bowen recommended that employers who provide health insurance be required to include catastrophic health expenditures in company policies.[4]

• Senator Edward Kennedy proposed that employers be required to provide health insurance for all employees working at least 17½ hours a week and cover 80% of the premiums.[5]

• Representative Patricia Schroeder (D–Colorado), with 90 of her House colleagues, advocated that the federal government mandate company leave policies, 18 weeks of unpaid "family leave" (mainly for childbirth) and 26 weeks of unpaid disability leave for all employees. The firms must continue, however, payment on all fringe benefits during both types of leave and guarantee the employees jobs on their return to work.[6]

• Senator Howard Metzenbaum (D–Ohio) wants employers to be required to give between 90 and 180 days of notice of pending plant closings and mass layoffs (depending on the number of affected workers) and consult with employees on such decisions or be subject to stiff penalties.[7]

There is no particular reason to believe that many of the intellectual and political supporters of the movement would be satisfied with such a limited assortment of mandated benefits. Indeed, there is every reason to believe that the list of desired mandated benefits would expand as political successes accumulate.[8] For this reason, before such a policy shift is adopted, the consequences of the shift must be evaluated in terms of both their impact on worker welfare and the escalating dimensions of the welfare state.

The Policy Shift

The welfare movement, from its inception in the 1930s through the 1970s, sought to centralize the control of social programs in the federal government. Accordingly, federal bureaus were established with offices in Washington and throughout the country and charged with the responsibility of administering programs for food stamps, Medicare,

Medicaid, housing, school breakfasts and lunches, unemployment payments, job placement, retraining, and any number of other programs.[9] Even when the actual delivery of the programs was delegated to the states, large agencies were organized and run by the federal govenment. The reform-minded policymaker was typically imbued with a restricted mindset that accepted, without question, the principle that if welfare was government's responsibility, then government ought to be in charge of it.

Current interest in mandated employment benefits appears to emerge from three principal sources. The first source is statistical. Studies have repeatedly uncovered gross inefficiencies in government delivery systems, regardless of whether the studied service is the post office, fire department, or public housing. Surveys have also shown that many American workers receive substantial employment benefits (and thereby are presumed to have adequate job security and personal security) at the same time that many other workers receive very few employment benefits (and are therefore presumed to lack adequate jobs).

As a matter of fact, in its 1984 survey of 1,154 firms the U.S. Chamber of Commerce found that workers received, on average, $7,842 in total employment benefits of 36.6% of their average wage.[10] These benefits include those that are legally required (disability, unemployment compensation, and workers' compensation) and those that are voluntarily provided (including, but not restricted to, pensions, life insurance, dental and medical insurance, rest periods, paid sick leave, vacations, and profit sharing).[11] At the same time, many employees—perhaps as many as 35 million people in the United States, according to the Census Bureau—do not have basic medical insurance, much less guaranteed parental leave for childbirth or day care for children.[12]

Similarly, a string of reports have emerged that indicate that many employees are not provided "adequate" notice of the closing of their plants.[13] For example, one GAO report found that approximately two-thirds of the surveyed workers received less than two weeks "notice" of their plant closings and a high percentage of those workers received no notice at all.[14]

Proponents seem to think that what is not voluntarily provided to workers, as measured by surveys, should be mandated by government. They also seem to think that the mandated benefits will improve the welfare of workers, as well as the statistical reports.

The second source of interest in mandated employee benefits emerges from the contemporary fiscal restrictions. Policymakers are reluctant to raise taxes. Rising government expenditures and the string of $200-billion-plus deficits persist (the federal debt more than doubled during the first five years of the Reagan presidency). Proponents of mandated benefits are apparently confident that they can impose the costs of these benefits on the American economy. They assume that the voting public will not perceive the legislation as causing an expansion in the overall size of government and in implicit and explicit taxes. If mandated benefits involve a tax at all, the tax is implicit (obscured in higher consumer prices and lower worker wages), or so backers of mandated benefits seem to think. Furthermore, proponents seem to suggest that businesses, as a matter of social responsibility, should incur the costs of mandated benefits.

This source of interest in mandated benefits raises interesting issues about the political economy (at least from an academic perspective). One must only wonder what it is about the political process, and the operation of markets, that a tax that cannot be imposed in an explicit manner (because of political resistance) can be imposed in an implicit manner. Are the backers resting their political drive on voter stupidity and/or fiscal illusion? Or is it that the overall tax burden is distributed differently via mandated benefits than would be the case under a change in the tax code, meaning that the composition of the opposition is different? We will return to these issues later.

Somewhat ironically, the third source of interest in mandated benefits springs from the political popularity of the intellectual and practical drive to "privatize" and "decentralize" the delivery of government services. This interest has been encouraged most prominently by the conservative Reagan administration. Spurred by a rash of economic commentaries on how private firms can save taxpayer dollars, policymakers learned in the 1980s that although welfare programs might have to be established and organized by centralized government, such programs do not need to be run by government agencies. Many government services, including welfare services, can be "privatized," that is, turned over to private firms for actual delivery.[15]

Welfare goals established by Congress can be achieved more efficiently through private firms. Why? As proponents of privatization have effectively argued, federal delivery of any given federal program generally means monopolization. The creation of a single government provider, because of the absence of alternative sources of the service, has the market power to restrict the quality and quantity of its service and to inflate costs. In short, government provision all too often spells inflated production costs, rising prices, and restricted output.

Through privatization, private firms can be induced to compete with one another to deliver the welfare benefits under government contracts. Because of their private interest in retaining their government contracts and making a profit, private firms have an incentive to deliver welfare benefits in the most cost-effective manner, or at least in a more cost-effective manner than their public counterparts.[16]

In recent years, the privatization movement has been supported by partisans from all points on the political spectrum. However, it appears that their underlying assumptions have not always been compatible. The assumption of policy commentators on the political right has typically been that privatization would involve only a transfer of established government programs and services to private firms, not an extension of government activities in the name of privatization. The view of these conservative commentators has generally been that government could be induced to operate more efficiently, not more expansively. Nonetheless, when pressed about how they would prefer to operate a proposed extension of the welfare state, proponents tend to concede that private firms are to be preferred to government agencies.[17]

On the other hand, policy commentators on the political left have, in effect, seized upon privatization as an intellectual justification for extending the array, quantity, and quality of welfare services mandated by government. After all, proposing that welfare services be *delivered* by private firms, not government agencies, is a way of arguing that provision of government services be decentralized (to an extreme degree: to the firm or plant level) and that the effective cost of the programs be lowered. Hence, liberal policy proponents have reasoned that mandated/privatized government benefits can be expected to enlist more political support than benefit programs that are mandated and run by government. Hence, if welfare benefits are privatized through government mandates, an expansion of the welfare state beyond the political bounds of a government-run welfare state can be expected. *All* the state need do is mandate the minimum kinds and amounts of benefits that all firms must provide.

Mandated Benefits and Minimum Wages: The Logical Connection

Mandating worker benefits is not new, as explained in Chapter 9. Mandated money benefits, commonly called the minimum wage, appeared in the 1930s. And there is no particular reason why the legislative logic used to support increases in a goverment-mandated minimum wage cannot be applied with equal force (and with equal flaws) to a variety of employment benefits, including the kinds of benefits mentioned in the previous section (health and life insurance, severance, pay, retraining, parental and family leave, and subsidized lunches).[18] Both mandated minimum wages and employment benefits ultimately become worker income. Indeed, Senator Kennedy argued in a speech before the United Auto Workers in early 1987, "Just as workers are entitled to be paid a minimum wage by their employers, so they should be entitled to health insurance on the job."[19] In another speech, he said, "The time has come to require all businesses in America to offer health insurance to all their workers—and all their dependents, too—as a condition of doing business."[20]

Proponents of mandated benefits appear to believe that the absence of the specified benefits in the workplace for millions of American workers is all the justification needed for government mandate of them. As is often the case in discussion of minimum wage, the proponents' chief concern appears to be how much unemployment will result from imposing the cost of additional social services for workers on businesses—whether the social costs of limited, policy-induced unemployment outweigh the social benefits of mandated benefits received by the affected workers, their families, and their communities.

A part of the private benefits received by workers comes in the form of additional income during periods of hardship; yet a part, perhaps an important part, of the social benefits of mandated benefits is the amount saved by the government: savings in expenditures and taxes on welfare programs. For example, if firms insure their workers' medical or unemployment needs and do it more efficiently than government agencies, government welfare expenditures can fall at the same time worker health and unemployment benefits can rise. Seen from this perspective, mandated benefits, or the privatization of welfare programs, is a natural, expected result of an expanding welfare state. The greater the government welfare expenditures, the greater the fiscal benefits of mandated employment benefits—and the greater the political support for shifting the burden of state welfare to firms and their workers.

What backers of mandated benefits fail to see is that their proposed mandated benefits will have much the same effects, if not the identical effects, of mandated minimum wages.[21] Mandated benefits can actually lower the living standards of most, if not virtually all, covered workers.

As stressed in the previous chapter, workers are not paid simply in terms of so much money per hour of work, but in terms of "payment bundles" that include money wages but also nonmoney benefits in the form of health and life insurance, vacation time, rest periods, subsidized lunches, severance pay, working conditions, child care, and work demands—to name just a few categories of employment benefits. Workers can be expected to maximize their payment bundles, not their money income. Given worker productivity (their contributions to revenues of their firms) and bargaining positions, the payment bundles cannot exceed a specified amount.

The concept of a maximum payment bundle, explored in detail in our discussion of minimum wages, implies that new legislation requiring employers to include specific employment (wage or fringe) benefits in their employees' payment bundles effectively requires employers to withdraw other benefits that are not required (or to make their employees work harder and longer to offset the greater costs of the mandated benefits). Just as in the case of mandated minimum wages, mandated benefits can increase the net cost incurred by employers in hiring workers.

At the same time, mandated benefits can cause the value of the payment bundles as judged by employees (not by Congress) to fall. If that were not the case, the payment bundles would be voluntarily readjusted (in the absence of legislation) by employers to favor the preferences of their workers. Workers can always negotiate the inclusion of fringe benefits—for example, health insurance and family leave—in their payment bundles. All they have to do is forgo higher wages or other benefits. When such trades are not made in worker contracts, it must be presumed that a sizable percentage of the covered workers prefer not to make such trades. If Congress mandates benefits that are not voluntarily negotiated, mandated benefits necessarily included in the workers' payment bundles are worth less than those that are extracted by virtue of congressional action.

The loss to workers because of mandated benefits can also be assessed from the impact of these benefits on employment opportunities. Obviously, those workers who remain unemployed because of the added employment costs of mandated benefits are worse off because of the government action. Workers who consequently remain unemployed lose a valuable employment opportunity—presumably, the best one they have.

Not so obviously, even the workers who retain their jobs can be worse off—to the extent that the value of their payment bundles decreases. The value of their payment bundles can be expected to fall primarily because fewer jobs, due to mandated benefits, mean less demand for workers, which, in turn, means that workers' bargaining positions will be impaired. The number of jobs can be expected to decrease because the increase in the cost of hiring labor will be reflected in higher prices and lower sales. As a consequence, fewer workers are needed. Another important point should be mentioned: the costs of mandated benefits do not have to be incurred when non-covered (foreign) workers and labor-saving equipment are used.[22]

The point of this section is relatively simple, but often not recognized. If inclusion of specified mandated benefits in workers' payment bundles did not represent an increase in payment costs to employers and a reduction in the value of the overall payment bundles to workers, the benefits would not have to be mandated. Employers would gladly rearrange their payment bundles to suit the preferences of their employees, if the rearrangement were cost-effective and desired by their employees.[23] The market would tend to clear with the number of workers demanded approximately equal to the number of workers available, but the number of jobs in the economy would be reduced. The lost job opportunities would, of course, reflect a loss of value in the production of goods and services.

Mandated benefits are especially troublesome when they do not apply to all workers more or less uniformly. Minimum-wage laws do not apply to *all* workers, only to those workers who happen to be in menial (low-productivity and low-wage) labor markets. And minimum-wage laws tend to discriminate against the low-income workers who are the object of legislative concern—precisely because they make hiring the covered workers more costly relative to other groups of workers and relative to machines. A major problem Congress has in directing the country's labor markets is that its laws are rarely universally applied.

Mandated-benefit laws that are not universal tend to discriminate against the targeted groups of workers for the same reason. Such laws make employment of the covered workers relatively more expensive. Parental-leave laws will tend to discriminate against workers in their child-bearing years, especially women workers. Catastrophic-health-insurance requirements will tend to discriminate against older workers. Laws that require firms to continue the medical coverage of their workers when they are laid off or terminated will tend to discriminate against workers who may be in unstable and high-risk jobs.

In addition, it must be added that government mandates in labor policies do not apply uniformly to all firms. Those firms that have fringe benefits that exceed the proposed mandated benefits will not be directly affected by the passage of the mandates. However, they can be indirectly affected—to their benefit. Firms beset with competition from equally productive low-wage (foreign or domestic) firms often have a private stake in minimum wages, because it "levels the playing field." The minimum wage snuffs out both existing and potential competition and increases their market share and profits.

Similarly, firms that face competition from "low fringe-benefit firms" have a private interest in mandated benefits, also in the interest of leveling the competitive playing field. R. L. Crandall, chairman and president of American Airlines, revealed much about current political interest in mandated benefits when he argued before a group of commercial pilots,

> At American, we spend about $1,666 per employee per year—that's more than $80 million this year alone—on medical benefits for active employees and dependents. And we're spending $16 million a year for medical benefits for retirees—a figure that will jump to $100 million-plus in less than a decade.
>
> Yet Continental doesn't provide any medical benefits for retirees at all—and its active employees pay for most of their own health insurance. As a result, Continental's unit cost advantage vs. American's is enormous—and worse yet, is growing!
>
> . . .The long-term consequence of this is bad news for all airline employees—unless government levels the playing field. Unless everybody in our industry offers at least minimum benefit levels, the companies that do offer such benefits will have no choice but to withdraw them. We don't want to do that—which is why we're supporting Sen. Edward Kennedy's legislation mandating minimum benefit levels for all employees. Sen. Kennedy is fighting a lonely battle—he needs all the support he can get. You should be out there helping his cause along.[24]

The Special Case of Plant-Closing Restrictions

For more than a decade, members of Congress have proposed a special form of mandated benefits: plant-closing restrictions. As noted previously, Senator Metzenbaum has proposed that firms be required to give substantial notice of plant closings and mass layoffs.

Backers of plant-closing restrictions have argued that their proposals are needed because plant closings and mass layoffs create serious personal and social problems for workers and communities affected by the closing.[25] When the closings or layoffs are unexpected because they are not officially announced, workers are left without income and communities are left without a tax base. Accordingly, plant closings can lead to marital discord, health problems, suicides, and even murder. Closings can also lead to an increase in demands on community services at the same time that tax revenues for the community are declining—or so we are told. (See Chapters 4 and 8.)

Almost every two years during the 1970s and 1980s, members of Congress have introduced proposals to restrict plant closings and mass layoffs. The proponents of the plant-closing bills have (typically) argued that jobs can be saved by increasing the cost of plant closings and layoffs. These costs can be increased by requiring firms to give substantial notice and provide workers with severance pay, requiring plant owners to consult with workers before workers are discharged, and imposing penalties on firms that fail to comply with the law.

What has remained a mystery in the public debate over plant-closing bills is that backers of the bills have always assumed they were taking the high moral ground. They have argued, in effect, that fundamental moral principles drive them to support their legislative proposals. After all, their bills would save jobs, lives, and communities. Plants are all too frequently closed, they contend, in order that the firms can move elsewhere and produce on a more profitable basis. In addition, they say that workers have ownership rights to the jobs that they help develop. In effect, when plants close, jobs, lives, and communities are being traded for the "almighty dollar"; workers are raped of their legitimate property rights—or so proclaim the proponents of the plant-closing bills.

Taking the high moral ground, AFL-CIO economist Markley Roberts maintains that plants are "supported by a social, cultural and economic infrastructure—schools, services, roads. It's wrong, immoral, antisocial and uneconomic for firms to ignore the workers and local communities that help sustain them."[26]

What has remained an equal mystery is that opponents of plant-closing bills are all too often viewed as antilabor—as defenders of corporate America, or worse, hired guns for the "greedy capitalistic pigs" who are solely responsible for plant closings and mass layoffs. The country's unbridled capitalists—or so they are often labeled—are inclined to move their plants around the country and around the world in a wanton desire for profits with little or no concern for workers and their families and communities. If this characterization of businessmen

228 · The American Job Machine

and women who actually close plants and lay off workers is accurate, it is hard to see how any reasonable person could oppose plant-closing bills.

The fact of the matter is that the intellectual and academic opposition to plant-closing bills is not driven by antilabor forces.[27] Quite the opposite is the case. Plant-closing restrictions, whether in the form of prenotification, consultation, or severance-pay requirements, will tend to work against the interests of working Americans. This is the case because plant-closing restrictions, as is true of all other mandated benefits, amount to added costs for doing business in the United States, and thereby amount to added costs for opening plants. The closing restrictions may save some jobs for a time, but they can also reduce business investment and decrease the number of new jobs. Indeed, to the extent that they reduce aggregate business investment (the country's stock of jobs is directly related to capital stock), plant-closing restrictions will reduce aggregate employment opportunities for Americans. To that extent, plant-closing restrictions can be an added source of personal and community problems—the very situation that proponents say they are trying to avoid.

Why is this true? In concrete terms, U.S. plant-closing restrictions do not apply to other countries and to labor-saving machinery. Restrictions *do* apply to American workers, meaning they are something of a head tax—a cost disadvantage—artificially imposed on American firms for their use of American labor in the United States. Plant-closing restrictions can, therefore, encourage firms to open their plants in foreign countries and to substitute, where feasible, machines for workers. In the United States, the substitution of machines for workers can be expected to add marginally to the cost of production in the United States, to increase prices, and to lower sales and incomes of Americans.

Opposition to plant-closing restrictions, thereby, springs from a concern for the employment opportunities of American workers. Granted, plant-closing restrictions may also reduce profits, but even profits are of considerable interest to many workers who have life- and health-insurance policies and pension plans with benefits tied to the profitability of the firms in which their insurance and pension funds are invested.

Opposition to plant-closing restrictions also emerges because the restrictions will likely lower the living standards of American workers, even those who retain their jobs in face of the added costs of closing a plant. If the closing restrictions are valued by workers, they represent a fringe benefit that carries a cost, like health and life insurance. As is true of other mandated benefits, workers are typically paid in various money and nonmoney forms and can be expected to receive only so much, determined by their bargaining positions and skills. When Congress requires firms to make payment in terms of closing restrictions, this mandate also requires firms to take something else out of workers' payment bundles.

Over the long run, the overall value of the payment bundles received by most covered workers can be expected to fall. The demand for labor will be lowered by the plant-closing restrictions, resulting in a less powerful bargaining position for covered workers and a decrease in the overall value of the payment bundle that can be demanded by workers.

Admittedly, many firms do give notice of pending plant closings, offer severance pay, and consult with their workers concerning alternatives to avoid closing a plant.[28] However, many proponents of plant-closing restrictions presume that all firms should be required to behave in the same "socially responsible" manner. What they forget is that production circumstances differ and workers differ in what they want in payments. Many of the firms that have given substantial notice did so because of a negotiated agreement under which workers presumably gave up something in the way of wages or other fringe benefits in order to receive the notice. The fact that many firms did not give notice — and did not violate a contract in the process — indicates that many workers do not believe that notice is worth the attendant sacrifice. If workers do not believe the notice is worth the cost, then mandated notice would impose on them what can only be called a bad deal! Workers will not avoid paying the cost of closing notice — no matter how noble the intentions of the politicians who vote for the legislation.

In addition, proponents do not seem to understand that mandated notice necessarily means *standardized* notice, applicable to all production circumstances. Standardized notice takes no account of differences in the ability of firms to accommodate the required notice or mandatory consultation or specified severance pay — or even whether workers need or want such benefits. The burden of the plant-closing restrictions will not be uniform. For some firms, those that have already agreed to substantial notice, the mandated notice will add no additional costs. However, for other firms, the added costs of mandated notice can be significant; and for still other firms, the burden can, indeed, be substantial. For that reason, plant-closing restrictions can influence the extent of competition in many markets, favoring some firms (especially those that have already agreed to give notice) at the expense of other firms (those that would incur heavy costs in order to abide by the government mandates). The closing restrictions can wipe out some competitors. Because of the impact of these restrictions on the cost of doing business, other competitors can be prevented from entering some American markets. The restrictions will also impair American competitiveness.

In short, plant-closing bills are antilabor as well as antibusiness, and they are certainly anticompetitive. Finally, they are unwarranted because alternative, nonstandardized solutions to problems of plant closings and mass layoffs already exist. Workers and communities can work with management to insure that production costs, the most certain form of plant and job security, remain competitive. Workers can negotiate their own plant-closing restrictions to suit their individual circumstances and their preferences for forms of payment.[29] They can also set aside a portion of their income to ameliorate the social and economic problems that inevitably arise from plant closings and mass layoffs.

Costs are incurred in doing these things, but the whole point of this section is that the costs of plant-closing restrictions cannot be avoided. There is no free lunch even on the job, and especially when the job is being closed down. The major difference between plant-closing solutions for individuals and mandated solutions for the collection economy is that with mandated solutions almost all will have to pay the costs, regardless of whether or not the costs can be justified.[30] The country, and its workers, will be poorer, as a consequence.

Concluding Comments

No proposition is more appealing to Washington political leaders than the view that Congress can solve worker problems through the stroke of its legislative pen. No proposition is more deceptive; congressional mandating of employment benefits is another political deception in the making.

Proponents of mandated benefits apparently have great faith in their ability to create the ruse that workers can get something for nothing—if Congress tells businesses what to do. But, if mandated benefits are enacted, the piper will be paid, even for mandated benefits discussed in the holiest of terms. The implicit tax—hidden behind higher consumer prices and lower worker wages and lower company profits needed to finance the mandated benefits—will be charged. Unfortunately, American workers will be made poorer in the process through restrictions on their work-related choices and income.

A major point of this chapter has been to raise a basic question: Who is really the object of expressed policy concerns, those who will supposedly be covered by the government mandates or those who already meet the labor-policy standards set by the mandates? Washington's new interest in mandated benefits is obviously consistent with its historical interest in redistributing the nation's income. What is not so apparent is that income is not likely to go in the expected direction, from those who already have benefits to those who do not. Rather, the income redistribution is likely to be perverse, from "have-nots" to "haves."

Practically everyone engaged in the debate over mandated benefits would prefer that all workers have more benefits and more wages. This is especially true for low-income Americans. However, the main problem of low-income Americans is lack of skills and weak bargaining position, which force them to accept low wages and low benefits. Mandated benefits will do nothing to solve constructively the fundamental problems. Indeed, by wiping out employment opportunities, mandated benefits are counterproductive, especially for the most disadvantaged in labor markets. Mandated benefits will not supplant the welfare state; mandated benefits will, instead, hasten the need for an even larger welfare state—to take care of those banished from constructive employment.

Notes

1. Economic democracy is evaluated in Richard B. McKenzie, *Justice as Participation: Should Workers Be Given Managerial Rights?* (St. Louis: Center for the Study of American Business, Washington University, 1986).

2. Robert B. Reich, *The Next American Frontier* (New York: Times Books, 1983), p. 248.

3. Attributed to Senator Edward Kennedy in Robert Pear, "Congress Acts to Shift Costs of Programs to Employers," *New York Times,* April 13, 1987, p. 8.

4. Ibid.

5. As cited in "Mandated Uncompetitiveness" (editorial), *Wall Street Journal,* April 9, 1987, p. 32.

6. Pear, "Congress Acts to Shift Costs of Programs to Employers." Three bills were introduced in Congress in 1987: H.R. 925 (Representative Schroeder's bill), S. 249, and H.R. 284.

7. Firms with fewer than 50 employees would not be required to give notice of plant closings and layoffs. However, firms with 50 to 100 workers would be required to give 90-days notice; firms with 100 to 500 would be required to give 120-days notice; and firms with 500 or more workers,

180-days notice (U.S. Congress, Senate, 100th Cong., 1st Sess., Economic Dislocation and Worker Adjustment Assistance Act, S. 538, February 19, 1987, pp. 22–30). At this last writing in mid-1987, the Senate had reduced the prenotification requirement to 60 days for all firms and had included the proposal in an omnibus trade-protection bill.

8. A major faction of the academic proponents of mandated benefits also advocates the adoption of an "economic bill of rights" for workers, including the right to a decent job, solidarity wages, shorter workweek, comparable pay, public childcare, flexible work hours, democratic production incentives, good food, lifetime learning [as outlined in Samuel Bowles, David M. Gordon, and Thomas E. Weisskopf, *Beyond the Waste Land: A Democratic Alternative to Economic Decline* (Garden City, N.Y.: Anchor Press, 1983), p. 270]. The general theme of mandated benefits and economic democracy is endorsed in Reich, *The Next American Frontier* and in Barry Bluestone and Bennett Harrison, *The Deindustrialization of America* (New York: Basic Books, 1982).

9. One study identified in 1985 more than 100 federal low-income assistance programs, 59 of which were major and all of which covered more than 6,000 federal laws and regulations. More than 52 million Americans, nearly 20% of the population, received benefits from one or more low-income assistance programs (Domestic Policy Council, Executive Office of the President, *Up from Dependency* [Washington: U.S. Government Printing Office, December 1986], p. 10).

10. Richard Rahn, *Employee Benefits: 1984* (Washington: United States Chamber of Commerce, 1985), p. 11. The benefits per employee varied widely across the 1,154 firms that responded to the survey. Twenty-four firms paid less than 18% of payroll in benefits, while 11 firms paid more than 64% of payroll in benefits [Ibid., p. 6].

11. The legally required benefits amounted to 9.6% of average worker pay, meaning that voluntary employment benefits represented the overwhelming share of total benefits provided [Ibid., p. 11].

12. Pear, "Congress Acts to Shift Costs of Programs to Employers."

13. William J. Gainer, *Dislocated Workers: Extent of Business Closures, Layoffs, and the Public and Private Response* (Washington: U.S. Government Printing Office, July 1986); John H. Gibbons, Office of Technology Assessment, U.S. Congress, *Plant Closing: Advance Notice and Rapid Response* (Washington: U.S. Government Printing Office, September 1986); and Bureau of Labor Statistics, U.S. Department of Labor, *Analysis of Mass Layoff Data* (January 1987). See also note 14.

14. The figure on percentage of workers receiving various-length plant-closing notice has been carefully crafted, referring solely to amount of "specific notice" (which is the number of days an announcement is made in advance of the exact day the closing will occur). It does not include the workers who were told their plants would close down but who were not told a precise date. Compare and contrast the following survey reports: William J. Gainer, "GAO's Preliminary Analysis of U.S. Business Closures and Permanent Layoffs During 1983 and 1984," a paper presented at an OTA/GAO workshop

on plant closings (Washington; April 30–May 1, 1986); and William J. Gainer, *Plant Closings: Information on Advance Notice to Dislocated Workers,* GAO/RD-87-86BR (Washington: U.S. Government Printing Office, April 1987).

15. The case for privatizing government services is made in Stuart M. Butler, *Privatizing Federal Spending: A Strategy to Eliminate the Deficit* (New York: Universe, 1985).

16. A major reason costs are inflated in government provision of public goods and services is that government workers are not residual claimants, entitled to benefit from cost savings created through more efficient production systems.

17. Stuart Butler, director of domestic policy studies at the Heritage Foundation and privatization advocate, opposes the movement toward mandated benefits. However, he notes, "Given a choice between mandated benefits and a British-style national health system, I certainly would favor the former" [Ibid.].

18. See Chapter 9.

19. As quoted in Julie Kosterlitz, "Kennedy's New Tack," *National Journal,* March 14, 1987, p. 610.

20. Ibid., p. 608.

21. The economic consequences of minimum-wage laws are discussed in detail in Chapter 9.

22. In analyzing employers' supply and demand curves for labor, economists observe that mandated benefits effectively increase employers' overall costs of hiring, inducing employers to move up their demand curve for labor. At the same time, rearrangement of the payment bundles drives workers down the supply curve. Overall, mandated benefits tend to drive a wedge between the actual cost of labor and the payment to labor.

23. Proponents often contend that their preferred list of mandated benefits will impose little or no cost on businesses and workers. If the costs were as trivial and the benefits were as valuable as supposed, the benefits would never have to be mandated. Profit-seeking firms would jump at the chance to provide benefits costing them little or nothing but highly valued by their workers. Thus, providing the benefits would be profitable.

24. As quoted in "Notable & Quotable," *Wall Street Journal,* August 8, 1987, p. 16.

25. The case for plant-closing restrictions is fully developed in Barry Bluestone and Bennett Harrison, *The Deindustrialization of America* (New York: Basic Books, 1982).

26. As quoted in Robert England, "Labor Aims for a Warning Shot," *Insight,* May 4, 1987, p. 22.

27. The case against plant-closing bills has been developed at length in Richard B. McKenzie, *Fugitive Industry: The Economics and Politics of Deindustrialization* (San Francisco: Pacific Institute, 1984), and *Plant Closings: Public or Private Choices?*, 2nd ed. (Washington: Cato Institute, 1984).

28. According to one U.S. General Accounting Office survey, only 45%

of the blue-collar workers received "general notice" of more than 14 days of their pending plant closing (William J. Gainer, "GAO's Preliminary Analysis of U.S. Business Closures and Permanent Layoffs During 1983 and 1984," paper presented at the OTA/GAO Workshop on Plant Closings, Washington, April 30–May 1, 1986, p. 17).

29. Even workers who are not unionized can obtain closing benefits. They can indicate to management their willingness to make the necessary sacrifices in wages and other fringe benefits in order to obtain the closing restrictions.

30. This point is especially true when it is recognized that impaired economic growth will mean that a part of the cost of plant-closing restrictions will be borne by future generations.

CHAPTER 11

"Jobilism":
The New Theology of
Public Policy

In 1980, General Motors announced plans to close two outmoded Fisher Body plants in Detroit and to replace two plants with one new $630-million Cadillac plant. GM told Detroit city fathers that if a suitable site could not be found, the company would locate its new plant elsewhere. Many jobs were at stake—potential as many as 6,000.

Under the banner of preserving jobs, Detroit responded by condemning, through its powers of eminent domain, a 320-acre section of the city known as Poletown, encompassing 127 businesses, 16 churches, and 1,753 residences in the mainly Polish community, and selling the land to GM for far less than the purchase price.[1] Because several of the lifelong residents would not voluntarily sell out, the city used force to evict them.

City fathers were unmoved by objections that state powers were being used for the private gain of a large corporation—in fact, one of the largest corporations, measured by sales, in the United States. They were equally unswayed by television news reports showing city residents, some of whom were elderly, being dragged from their homes immediately before bulldozers reduced the buildings to splinters. Something much more important than moral principle or social condemnation was at issue—jobs.

Jobs have always been important to public assessment of economic activity. After all, jobs are the principal way most people earn their livelihood. But, in the 1980s, because of mounting concern over economic change, jobs have become something of a national obsession— a holy grail to be pursued for its own sake, a *prima facie* justification for new directions in public policy.

What is now remarkable about the Detroit/GM land appropriation made in the name of preserving jobs is that it is no longer unusual. It is the type of policy that has become a part of the prevailing social ethic, captured by an awkward rubric, "jobilism." And jobilism—an analytical mind set that focuses political attention on "jobs" as a meaningful measurement of national success and failure—has flourished in the 1980s. It is at the core of the public debate over what, if anything, should be done about the restructuring American economy. Implicitly, it has been at the core of the analyses of many of the foregoing chapters.

This new public policy "ism" is neither totally unexpected nor new. The late great Harvard economist Joseph Schumpeter warned that capitalism, which is the mother of economic progress, means constant change, if not turmoil.[2] He feared that change—which jeopardizes established jobs, incomes, and market shares—would not be tolerated in democracies. As a consequence, capitalism would not be allowed to flourish.

Jobilism, in many essential respects, is a throwback to mercantilism. Both isms have similar policy goals, not the least of which is the delegation of powers of international and domestic market control to the state. Both are largely guided by the social fetishes of their respective eras. The mercantilists had their gold fetish. The modern jobilists have their job fetish. Both isms are equally flawed for much the same reasons.

A major purpose of this and the last chapter is to uncover those flaws. However, an additional purpose is to argue that the terms of the labor-policy debate need very badly to be shifted from "jobs" to "employment opportunities," a subtle distinction that can be understood only by reviewing the growing dominance of jobilism in public-policy discussions.

The Emergence and Spread of Jobilism

Modern jobilism emerged abruptly in the Great Depression when the federal government took on the responsibility of creating work for the hordes of unemployed. It was fostered in the 1960s with the acceptance of Keynesian economics that promised relief of unemployment through government deficit spending and its "multiplier effect" on income and jobs. However, in more recent years jobilism has developed in varied and creative forms, no longer restricted to the Detroit/GM-style land grab.

In 1982, the depth of the most recent recession, International Harvester (now called Navistar) began to close and consolidate several of its heavy-equipment plants. In one plant closing, Harvester informed Fort Wayne, Indiana, and Springfield, Ohio, that one of their plants would be closed. At the same time, Harvester asked each city to consider buying its plant and leasing it back to Harvester. By September 1982, each city had reciprocated and offered to pay Harvester $30 million or more.[3]

Harvester needed an infusion of capital; Fort Wayne and Springfield needed to protect their declining job bases. The Fort Wayne plant was closed; its job losses were understandably reported in the media with almost the same gloom as combat casualties were reported during the Vietnam Era. The city had been in a municipal economic battle of sorts and had lost.

The mounting job losses in the 1982 recession could not, of course, escape the attention of Congress, which responded in the only way it knew how, through the passage of a "jobs bill." The $9 billion in additional funding mainly for highway and bridge construction passed that year was advertised as the annual economic salvation for 350,000 unemployed American workers. Through the stroke of its legislative pen, Congress was confident that its construction program would create that many jobs. The program, however, was pronounced a failure in 1987 when the General Accounting Office reported that the 1983 jobs bill had actually added no more than 35,000 jobs during any given year.[4]

Now, in the late 1980s (as should be evident from so much of the discussion in previous chapters), all levels of government have joined the foray for jobs, jobs, and more jobs. To no small degree, jobilism has become the new political and economic theology. The central purpose of economic activity under this new theology is to produce jobs, not necessarily goods and services that people need and want.

The number of jobs saved and created by this or that public or private action has become the modern-day body count of economic development. The nation is "restructuring"— much worse, the United States is "deindustrializing" or is becoming a "service economy" or is broaching the "informational age." This is measured not so much by relative production of goods and services consumers want, but by changes in the measured distribution of employment across industries.

Never mind that the industrial production index is at an all-time high. Never mind that production of "goods" has remained more or less constant, as a percentage of real gross national output, over the past three or more decades. Never mind that the productivity of the manufacturing sector continues to rise relative to other sectors of the economy.[5]

As noted in the opening paragraph of Chapter 3, policy pundits still warn that the U.S. economy may enter the 21st century as a "productionless society," a nation of "short-order cooks and saleswomen, Xerox-machine operators and messenger boys. . . . To let other countries make things while we concentrate on services is debilitating both in its substance and in its symbolism."[6] The widely publicized decline of the "goods economy" is largely founded on the drop, not in production, but in "production jobs," measured in absolute numbers and, more dramtically, as a percentage of total employment.[7]

National pride is supposed to ride on those official counts of jobs. President Reagan talks with great pride about the 11 million jobs created during the first six years of his administration and tells the nation that the country's economic goal should be 8 million more jobs created during the remainder of the decade and 20 million during the rest of the century.[8] The president's supporters parrot his claims;[9] his detractors admonish the public to look behind the job totals and realize that the holders of a majority of those newly created jobs can barely earn a subsistence living.[10]

Regardless of how the debate over the "quality" of the nation's stock of jobs is settled, one thing is sure: modern policy debates have implicitly endowed the president with responsibility for job creation and destruction—power no one mortal *could* have, much less *should* have.

Understandably, the responsibility for the job structure has begun to be shared by many other government officials. On practically any day of the wcek, some state governor, accompanied by economic development officials, is trekking the world on what has come to be known as the "Great Industrial Job Hunt." Jobs have become the political "bacon" of this decade.

Many Americans are troubled by the importation of foreign goods because imported goods supposedly destroy domestic jobs. Americans are not bothered by the importation of capital because money supposedly creates jobs. They see the country entangled in an international competitive struggle over a more or less fixed stock of jobs—a struggle that gives rise to the beggar-thy-neighbor mentality. Importing goods is the mirror image of exporting jobs; exporting goods reflects the importing of jobs. (See Chapter 6.)

Almost without fail hometown newspapers report the closing or opening of local plants, measured most prominently not by changes in community production of valued goods and services but by the expected number of jobs—lost or gained. In the spring of 1987, Congress, unrepentant of its past errors in calculating the social benefits of its legislative efforts to increase employment for American workers, passed a "budget-busting" $88-billion highway bill.

Claiming that he had not seen so much lard since he gave out blue ribbons at an Iowa state fair, President Reagan vetoed the legislation.[11] Undeterred, the Democrat-controlled Congress overrode the veto because, by the time the final vote was taken, the legislation was no longer a highway bill. It was a "jobs bill." As many as 800,000 construction jobs were on the line, or so claimed those members of Congress who were backing the bill.

Jobs have become the newfound political currency in Washington politics. Legislative deals are closed—based on how the proposed funding distributes jobs across congressional districts.

Practically every economic bill before Congress is now touted as a "jobs bill." Protectionism is a boon to jobs, a claim that supposedly neutralizes the baneful connotation of the policy. Protectionists calculate the number of jobs saved by tariffs and quotas.[12] "Competitiveness," a much-abused buzzword, has become a code word for encouraging job creation and easing the pains of job destruction. Expenditures for proposed federal training and retraining are pushed as efficient methods of job creation, and plant-closing restrictions are recommended for their capacity to stave off job destruction.[13] (See Chapter 8.)

Historically, firms have sold "goods" and "services." Now, they sell "jobs" to willing federal, state, and local government buyers. Since the days of the WPA (ridiculed as standing for "We Piddle Along") in the Great Depression, federal politicians have bought jobs with federal programs. States and communities have conventionally disguised their purchases of jobs through industrial subsidies for plants, roads, water lines, and a variety of other enticements. Now they disguise their purchases of questionable plants, roads, and water projects with "job-creation" bills.

Almost all states are in the business of bidding for jobs with financing, tax abatements, and subsidies. For example, with little apparent thought, the South Carolina legislature gave Mack Truck the keys to the state treasury, handing over more than $16 million in state-financed benefits, all for the sake of 850 jobs.[14] Few in the state legislature were willing to stop and ask if Mack Truck, which at the time was a financially troubled company, would be able to pull itself out of the red or if the 4,200 Mack workers in Pennsylvania would have first claim on the South Carolina jobs (which the courts ruled in mid-1987 they did have).[15] Unfortunately for South Carolina taxpayers, because of 1987 court rulings regarding the job rights of Mack workers at closed plants in Pennsylvania, probably only half of the Mack jobs in South Carolina will go to South Carolinians.

South Carolina has more recently agreed to drop partially the subsidy veil by providing firms with a "jobs creation tax credit" for five years, ranging from $300 to $1,000 per year per new job "created."[16]

Iowa has removed the subsidy facade altogether, offering identified firms $3,000 in cash from its lottery revenue for each job that the firm brings to the state and maintaining that direct cash payments are a much more efficient means of job recruitment than in-kind payments for roads and retraining programs. No wonder employers now regularly pit communities and states against one another in a competitive struggle for the jobs they have to sell.

The Gold Fetish of Mercantilism

In many important respects, jobilism has become, in the latter part of the 20th century, what mercantilism was to an earlier epoch: a half-baked, simplistic, and fundamentally flawed rationalization for extended government control of the economy.[17] Mercantilism, a governing policy vision prominent from the 16th century through the first half of the 18th century, was premised extensively (but not exclusively) on the simple-minded view that the wealth and international power of a country could be assessed by its hoard of gold. The larger the stock of gold, the larger the country's wealth and national power.

While scholars argue over why gold was held in such high esteem and how successful mercantilism was in achieving its objectives, there is little debate over the fact that mercantilists sought to enlarge their country's gold reserves through governmental controls on trade.[18] In the absence of gold mines, a country's gold reserve could be increased principally through an excess of exports over imports, or a balance-of-trade surplus.

If payments for internationally traded goods were made in gold coins or bullion, then a trade surplus necessarily meant more gold flowing in than flowing out, and a buildup of the domestic hoard. A trade deficit meant the opposite, a loss of gold. A growing domestic hoard of gold implied increasing wealth, since gold was intrinsically valuable. More gold also implied greater national power, because the accumulated gold hoard could, in times of war or other national emergencies, be drawn upon to buy military equipment and hire mercenary forces.

The mercantilists' gold fetish justified governmental efforts to reduce imports and expand exports. Accordingly, policies that increased the prices of imports—for example, tariffs and quotas—and decreased the prices of exports—for example, subsidies and favorable government treatment—were perceived to be constructive, not destructive. So what if trade was impaired by mercantilist policies—the nation's gold hoard was enhanced. The stature of the state was also magnified.

Of course, for many mercantilists, noble talk about the enlargement of the nation's gold hoard was hardly more than a convenient intellectual smokescreen. It was intended to obfuscate their true, and far more base, purpose—the suppression of domestic and foreign competition via government controls and the increase of their personal profits.

From this perspective, mercantilism amounted to an economic regime propelled, in part, by what economists now call "rent seeking," the manipulation of public powers for private gain, under the guise of attaining wholly nationalistic objectives.[19] Mercantilist controls increased the rents of nationalists by increasing the demand for government services, of domestic import-competing industries by reducing the demand for foreign goods, and of gold owners by increasing the demand for gold they had to sell. In effect, supporters of mercantilism comprised a coalition of "bootleggers and Baptists," otherwise odd-policy bedfellows—nationalists, rent seekers, and gold bugs—whose varied personal objectives could be achieved by the same sets of market controls and, at the same time, could be obscured behind the veil of gold.[20]

Adam Smith was one of the first prominent critics to pierce the veil of gold, pointing out in *The Wealth of Nations* that a country's wealth could best be identified by its productive capacity and ability to trade with others across the globe.[21] By suppressing mutually beneficial trades, mercantilist controls obstructed production and development of wealth.

Smith spent much of his seminal treatise making a simple point: hoarded gold represents foregone production opportunities, foregone trades, and foregone wealth and social improvement, because gold held in storage could be used to buy more productive assets. Economic improvement as the end of economic activity could not be, as the mercantilists maintained, congruent with the accumulaton of idle gold. Rather, gold hoards were the antithesis of economic improvement, especially when generated by artificial, government-inspired market controls.

The Hoarding of Jobs

Jobilism, as a guiding economic and social philosophy, advances policy discussions hardly beyond the dictates of mercantilism, now intellectually defunct for two centuries. It simply substitutes production jobs for gold on the implied assumption that gold is not "all that glitters."

Jobilism holds that the stock of the nation's jobs is its hoard of gold, to be augmented by various public controls on markets. Imports are to be discouraged because they cause the exportation of jobs; exports, encouraged because they give rise to the importation of jobs—or so it is thought.

The country's economic strength and competitiveness are thereby assessed in terms of its balance of trade, which supposedly mirrors, with only minor distortions, the balance of international job flows and which supposedly records changes in the nation's hoard of jobs. Under jobilism, job creation is to be subsidized; job destruction, penalized. The world power and prestige of a nation are determined by its accumulation of jobs—not gold, just jobs, preferably the types of jobs that have been around for some time. Taken to its logical extreme, which has been done by many modern jobilists, jobilism is nothing less than a euphemism for socialism with an updated rhetorical twist.

As was the case under mercantilism, much of the political attention given to job creation and destruction is fostered by strong and persuasive rent-seeking forces. The country's fascination with jobs becomes a convenient smokescreen, and the private interests of rent seekers are promoted at public costs. For example, the steel, motorcycle, and textile industries push their protectionist measures on the grounds that congressional action will save and expand jobs in their industries. These industries rarely acknowledge that—through policy-induced shifts in consumer purchases—their profits or rents are raised while the welfare of those who consume these products is lowered. Similarly, in the name of more jobs, the construction industry lobbies hard for highway bills, never mentioning the rents embedded in its favored legislation.

Much like the mercantilists, most jobilists downplay the proposal's costs, measured in terms of lost production and alternative employment opportunities. Jobilists prefer to insist that the relevant stock of jobs that should be hoarded includes their jobs because their jobs (like gold) are "good jobs": intrinsically valuable and a part of the country's "basic (established) industries."

Modern jobilists also have much in common with the physiocrats, who followed the mercantilists and who believed that industrial growth should be thwarted because agriculture was the ultimate source of national wealth and power.[22] Similarly, modern jobilists tell us that the shift toward service employment should be thwarted via special policy concessions for manufacturing. After all, we are now told, "Manufacturing matters mightily to the wealth and power of the United States and to our ability to sustain the kind of open society we have come to take for granted. If we want to stay on top—or even high up—we can't just shift out of manufacturing and up into services, as some would have it."[23] Jobilists are neo-physiocrats who see the nation's wealth and power in plants, not acres of land.

Like the physiocrats, modern jobilists obscure the extraordinary complexity of centralizing the design of the nation's employment structure—encompassing literally hundreds of millions of existing and potential jobs—by dividing the economy into halves, "manufacturing" and "services." However, they actually know precious little about which and how many manufacturing and service jobs should be allowed to thrive—or die.

If Smith could return today, he would probably once again remind policymakers that the hoarding of any given, identified stock of jobs, as in the case of gold, amounts to lost economic opportunities. The country must be poorer and its existing jobs actually worth less—the same condition that existed when gold was hoarded in the mercantilist era—even though plant and equipment, which could have been bought with the gold, were more productive. Smith would probably say, just as with the mercantilists' gold fetish, that the jobilists' job fetish can be expected to lead to exactly the reverse of what was intended. He would say that jobilism can lead only to myopic, counterproductive policies, the sapping of the nation's long-run economic vitality—loss of its competitiveness!

The absurdity of jobilism's fundamental premise—that nations should be judged by the count and security of their jobs—is fully apparent when it is realized that China, Poland, and the Soviet Union fit the jobilist's model of world-class economies. Those countries have managed to create and insure jobs for practically everyone—at the expense of considerable economic progress. They have avoided the turmoil of capitalism to the point that sleeping on the job has become a major management problem. The jobilists in the Soviet Union have dominated public-policy forums for so long that the country has far more jobs than work.

The United States could easily match that kind of "success." All it would have to do is set a policy course of returning to the efficiency of the industrial and service sectors like those of the Soviet Union or Poland or China. Of course, there are jobilists who want to do just that, albeit indirectly, by guaranteeing "workers' rights to their jobs" and by imposing additional taxes on capital to finance jobs bills.[24]

The Inherent Political Bias of Jobilism

Half a century ago, Joseph Schumpeter warned the policymakers of his day that the fatal flaw of capitalism was likely to be its creativeness and energy, not its failures to achieve greater income, wealth, and opportunity.[25] With unusual insight, Schumpeter saw destruction in the successes of capitalism.

However, Schumpeter called the capitalistic process of perennial renewal "creative destruction," seeking to emphasize that economic improvement always involves replacing of lower-quality products with better-quality products—the less productive capital and workers with the more productive. He saw in the history of progress a saga of job destruction, but he also saw its destructiveness as the foundation of most economic success, measured by more valuable jobs that are created.

Unfortunately, Professor Schumpeter correctly feared that democracies might not allow capitalism to flourish because they cannot politically tolerate its destructiveness. Undue policy concern with avoiding the destructive power of capitalism—by preserving the status quo in, for example, jobs—would inevitably cap progress. The process of economic renewal would necessarily be slowed by an array of governmental taxes, expenditures, and obstructions to trade. Professor Schumpeter could not have been more prophetic.

The contemporary contention of policymakers that "jobs" are a meaningful measure of the success or failure of the U.S. economy is fraught with three principal problems, all of which have political origins. The first problem relates to the fact that the main concern of politics is distributing and redistributing people's "rights." Politicians are all too inclined to look upon jobs as "things," much like gold, that can be owned and stored, whereas it may be more accurate to say that jobs represent the intersection of the private interests of workers and employers. Jobs represent exchanges of rights that must be made by the parties involved to suit their interests. Under jobilism, the government has the power to force exchanges of rights in employment situations. These exchanges will be made, in spite of the fact that government officials may have little appreciation of the individual circumstances of the people affected.

The second political problem inherent in jobilism is that widespread political fascination with producing jobs will in many instances inadvertently hand over to firms significant powers that exploit the public treasury. This was true in the cases of GM and International Harvester discussed earlier in this chapter. GM and Harvester would not have had the economic power to extract the municipal concessions they did if the cities had not had the economic wherewithal to bargain for the jobs.[26]

The third and most important problem is that the public debate, conducted (as it must be) in a political arena, is necessarily unbalanced and unrepresented. People with existing jobs, who may want protection from the creative destruction of capitalism, can be fully represented in the political debate because the politicians know who they are and the nature of the jobs they have.

Nonetheless, people who may take the new jobs of the future (who represent the "creative" dimension of "creative destruction") are not nearly so well defined politically. Many of the people who will take the future jobs do not now exist (they are unborn) or are not yet a part of an established, "basic" industry with established grips on Washington-based controls.[27]

Unfortunately, at the expense of the politically unrepresented, policy debates are all too frequently settled with mischief; political concessions are typically made to the established and well-represented interest groups. Because jobilism involves an unbalanced political debate, it represents a serious threat to the vitality of American capitalism—its "competitiveness."

The expected imbalance in the political debate was never more clearly demonstrated than in the office of Senator Terry Sanford (D–North Carolina) on April Fool's Day 1987. Torn between siding with his party or with President Reagan over the 1987 $88-billion highway bill, Senator Sanford voted "present" on the first roll-call vote. Later he changed his vote to uphold the president's veto.[28]

Because Senator Sanford's change of heart was crucial, the final vote was held up by parliamentary procedure. Subsequently, steel and construction workers crowded into Sanford's office and pleaded with him to acknowledge, in his decision, that their jobs were at stake.[29]

News reports on the confrontation made no mention of the North Carolina senator hearing from people who might lose their jobs because of higher gasoline or income taxes or higher deficits, because these people could not be identified. Accordingly, the freshman senator, observing the unbalanced representation in his office, was unable to hold his ground.[30] The veto was overriden in the name of jobs, but not just any jobs. The veto was overridden for the types of jobs represented by the people in Senator Sanford's office.

Concluding Comments

Contrary to what might be thought, both market and political processes destroy jobs. Certainly, jobs are destroyed through price changes caused by shifts in supply and demand forces. Just as surely, however, jobs are destroyed through votes and taxes in the political process.

The question policymakers too often overlook or choose to ignore is whether the market process or the political process is more creative in the process of being destructive. Markets definitely destroy *current* jobs, but politics just as surely destroy *future* jobs by obstructing, delaying, or redirecting the restructuring of the stock of current jobs.

The contemporary policy debate over the restructuring of the American economy is understandable. People everywhere have a natural inclination to avoid change, especially when change requires adjustment to previously unknown competitive forces. People wish to avoid change even when new and improved products, innovative production processes, and jobs emerge.

When government is endowed with powers of intervention that are checked only by democratic votes, the public should not be at all surprised that political outcomes cater to the current distribution of jobs, at the expense of new distributions of jobs. The public should also not be surprised to learn that Washington drains the creativeness of capitalism as Washington becomes embroiled in rent-seeking policy skirmishes over how the powers of government shall affect the distribution of jobs.

The concerns raised in this chapter are hardly theoretical abstractions; they are central to the empirical controversies considered in all previous chapters. Jobilism has a long and honorable history in European countries. With industrial and labor policies designed largely to save established jobs, major European countries have managed to bring job creation almost to a halt. American citizens and policymakers have that stark record to review. It is hoped they will learn from that real-world experience.

Notes

1. Detroit bought the property for about $200 million ($150 million of this amount coming from federal funding of the project) and sold the property to GM for slightly more than $8 million. For more details on the destruction of Poletown, see Sheldon Richman, "The Rape of Poletown," *Inquiry*, August 3, and 24, 1981; "Council Opposes GM Detroit Land Grab," *Competition* (Washington: Council for a Competitive Economy), May 1981.

2. Joseph A. Schumpeter, *Capitalism, Socialism, and Democracy*, 2d ed. (New York: Harper and Brothers, 1947), Chap. 7.

3. Fort Wayne initially made a sale-leaseback bid of $9 million for a 60-year-old plant, but later raised its bid to $31 million after Springfield bid $30 million for a 15-year-old plant. For more details on the bidding between Springfield and Fort Wayne, see "Springfield-Worker: We'd Just Like to Have Some Answers" and "Fort Wayne: Community Spirit Evident, But May Not Be Enough," Dayton, Ohio, *Journal Herald*, August 14, 1982, p. 1; and "Indiana City Offers Deal to Keep Harvester Plant," *Washington Post*, August 11, 1982; "Two Towns Fight to Keep Harvester Plants, Knowing that Only One Will Remain Open," *Wall Street Journal*, September 8, 1982, p. 35; and "Ohio Wins Bid for Harvester over Old Fort Wayne Plant," *New York Times*, September 28, 1982, p. D5.

4. In addition, according to the General Accounting Office, the unemployed benefited only to a limited extent from the federal expenditures covering as many as 77 programs. By September 1984, no more than 35% of the people employed in 80% of the programs were unemployed prior to their taking the newly "created job." The cost of each job "created" by the Emergency Jobs Act of 1983 was $88,000 a year. The primary reason given for the limited employment effect and the high cost per job was the slow speed with which the funds were spent (Richard L. Fogel, *Emergency Jobs Act of 1983: Funds Spent Slowly, Few Jobs Created* [Washington: U.S. General Accounting Office, December 1986]. For an historical analysis of the ability of government to create jobs, see James Bovard, "Busy Doing Nothing: The Story of Government Job Creation," *Policy Review*, Spring 1984, pp. 87–102.

5. Manufacturing real output has cycled between 20% and 22% of real GNP since the 1940s. These points are developed in John A. Tatom, "Why Has Manufacturing Employment Declined?" *Review* of the Federal Reserve Bank of St. Louis, December 1986, pp. 15–26. See also Richard B. McKenzie, "The Pace of Economic Change," *Occasional Paper* (St. Louis: Center for the Study of American Business, Washington University, March 1987), and "The Emergence of the Service Economy: Fact or Artifact?" *Policy Analysis* (Washington: Cato Institute), April 1987.

6. Felix G. Rohatyn as quoted in David M. Alpern, "Mr. Fixit for the Cities," *Newsweek,* May 4, 1981, p. 29.

7. Manufacturing employment declined from nearly 29% of the civilian labor force in 1953 to approximately 18% in 1985.

8. Ronald Reagan, remarks during a speech to business leaders on competitive initiatives (Washington: White House, February 17, 1987) p. 5.

9. See Dennis P. Doyle and Terry W. Harris, "Job Creation in the United States: An Overview" (Washington: American Enterprise Institute, 1985).

10. Barry Bluestone and Bennett Harrison, *The Great American Job Machine: The Proliferation of Low Wage Employment in the U.S. Economy* (Washington: Joint Economic Committee, U.S. Congress, December 1986). These authors report that 58% of the jobs created between 1979 and 1984 paid less than $7,000 in 1984 dollars, up from just under 20% in the 1973–79 period (Ibid., p. 19). Their central conclusion is disputed in Chapter 5.

11. The president made these remarks in defense of his veto of the highway bill on his weekly radio address, March 28, 1987.

12. Recognizing the emotional appeal of social measurements made in terms of jobs, free traders estimate cost of employment losses, due to protectionist measures, on a per-job basis.

13. See Task Force on Economic Adjustment and Worker Dislocation, *Economic Adjustment and Worker Dislocation in a Competitive Society* (Washington: Office of the Secretary, U.S. Department of Labor, December 1986).

14. The state agreed to spend $1.5 million on a training program for prospective Mack workers. The training would be done by Mack employees at state expense.

15. Tom Inman, "Mack Truck Backfires on South Carolina," *Greenville* (S.C.) *News,* July 5, 1987, p. 2E.

16. The tax credit provided depends upon the location of the newly created jobs. The more economically depressed the county, the greater the tax credit. Using per-capita income and unemployment for counties, S.C. counties are divided into "less developed," "moderately developed," and "developed" categories. The tax-credit program provides a $1,000 tax credit for each new job more than ten created in less-developed counties, a $600 tax credit for each new job more than 18 added in moderately developed counties, and a $300 tax credit for each new job more than 50 added in developed counties (S.C. House/Senate conference committee report on the General Appropriations Bill for 1987–1988, part II–042, section 70).

17. The classic studies of mercantilism include Eli F. Heckscher, *Mercantilism* (New York: Macmillan, 1955); and Gustov Schmoller, *The Mercantile System: Its Historical Significance* (New York: Augustus M. Kelley, 1967).

18. For competing assessments of the purposes and value of mercantilism, see Walter E. Minchinton, ed., *Mercantilism: System or Expediency?* (Lexington, Mass.: Heath, 1969).

19. This rent-seeking view of mercantilism is developed at length in

Robert B. Ekelund, Jr. and Robert D. Tollison, *Mercantilism as a Rent-Seeking Society: Economic Regulation in Historical Perspective* (College Station: Texas A&M University Press, 1981), especially Chap. 3.

20. The phrase "bootleggers and Baptists" was coined by Bruce Yandle, who first noted a tendency of bootleggers and Baptists to work together to restrict liquor sales. However, the two groups have dramatically different objectives. The Baptists want to discourage drinking and drunkenness, while the bootleggers want to suppress the consumption of legalized spirits in order to enhance their own sales. The phrase was first used in economic literature by Bruce Yandle, "Bootleggers and Baptists: The Education of a Regulatory Economist," *Regulation,* May/June 1982, pp. 12–16.

21. Adam Smith, *An Inquiry into the Nature and Causes of the Wealth of Nations* (New York: Modern Library, 1937), especially Book IV, Chap. 1.

22. The physiocrats, several of whom published their criticisms of mercantilism before Smith's *Wealth of Nations,* were often advocates of freer trade. After all, many of the mercantilist restrictions on trade retarded trade in agriculture. However, physiocracy, which means "rule of nature," was grounded in the belief that agriculture should be accorded special treatment in public policy. For example, physiocrats recommended shifting agriculture's tax burden to industry, because industry was clearly less important to national wealth and power than agriculture.

23. The opening statement in Stephen S. Cohen and John Zysman, *Manufacturing Matters: The Myth of the Post-Industrial Economy* (New York: Basic Books, 1987), p. 3. Unfortunately, similar statements could be made, as they have been made, by partisan reformists of other sectors of the economy. The authors continue, "Despite all the upbeat talk to the contrary, the United States cannot hope to let manufacturing go and reconstruct a strong international trade position in services. . . . [A] decisive band of high-wage service exports are linked to mastery and control of manufacturing. Services are complements—not substitutes or successors—to manufacturing" (Ibid., pp. 3–4.].

24. For advocacies of mandating workers' rights to their jobs, see Robert A. Dahl, *Preface to Economic Democracy* (Berkeley: University of California Press, 1985); Martin Carnoy, Derek Shearer, and Russell Rumberger, *A New Social Contract: The Economy and Government After Reagan* (New York: Harper and Row, 1983); and Catholic bishops, "Pastoral Letter on Social Teachings and the U.S. Economy" (first draft), *National Catholic Report,* November 23, 1984. Opposing arguments are found in Richard B. McKenzie, *Competing Visions: The Political Conflict over America's Economic Future* (Washington: Cato Institute, 1985), Chap. 6. The Tax Reform Act of 1986 indirectly but effectively shifts the U.S. tax burden to capital by reducing individual taxes by about $120 billion over the 1987–91 period and increasing corporate taxes by approximately the same amount (U.S. Congress, House, 99th Cong., 2nd Sess., 1986, *Tax Reform Act of 1986,* H.R. 3838 [Washington: U.S. Government Printing Office, September 22, 1986], p. II–865.)

25. Schumpeter, *Capitalism, Socialism, and Democracy,* pp. 83–84.

26. This line of argument is developed in Richard B. McKenzie, *Fugitive Industry: The Economics and Politics of Deindustrialization* (San Francisco: Pacific Institute, 1984), Chap. 6.

27. The very nature of innovation prevents a pressure group from effectively representing many innovators. When innovation becomes well-defined enough for a pressure group to form, it generally ceases to be an innovation.

28. Linda Greenhouse, "Senate, for Now, Upholds the Veto of Roads Measure," *New York Times,* April 2, 1987, p. 1

29. The crowded scene in Senator Sanford's office was reported on both CBS and NBC nightly news programs, April 1, 1987.

30. Actually, Sanford's main concern was apparently not with the excessive-spending level incorporated in the bill, but rather with the fact that his home state, North Carolina, would be shortchanged in the distribution of expenditures (Greenhouse, "Senate, for Now, Upholds the Veto of Roads Measure," p. 1).

CHAPTER 12

Principles of Responsible Labor Management

One of the highest goals of any society is for its people to behave responsibly. Responsible behavior is especially desirable in places of work simply because people's jobs are so important to their livelihood, social position, and self-esteem. Little or no debate exists over goals at such an abstract level. Intense conflict invariably emerges, however, when political partisans seek to define through specific legislation "responsible behavior" in worker-management relationships of the real world. All too often, through specific legislation, policy goals encroach on society's more fundamental concern: achieving a tolerably free, open, and competitive economy. Fundamentally, this book is concerned with achieving just such an economy.

Like beauty, responsible behavior may be viewed as little more than a question of personal taste and preference, relegated to "the eye of the beholder." Admittedly, given workers' and employers' diverse employment circumstances and thereby their disparate needs and wants, responsible behavior in the workplace is not always easy to define. Nevertheless, the conceptual search for guidance on determining responsible labor-management practices is not a meaningless undertaking. Not searching for guiding principles may be tantamount to denying the need for responsibility—for some constraints—in our dealings with one another. Leaving the policy process unconstrained can produce nonsensical (irresponsible) policies. Whether formal or informal, whether in workplaces or in the halls of Congress, constraints are the hallmark of a society that takes seriously its goals of personal, political, and economic freedoms.

Before tendering questions of policy, we must address a crucial, easily avoided question: What kinds of constraints should we seek? That question implies another: How do we insure that policymakers are responsible in their quest and can, therefore, make the rest of us responsible? Arguing that policymakers (who are neither better nor worse than those they seek to govern) should be left unconstrained in their search for constraints on others is a contradiction—a blatant denial of the need for constraints on anyone.

The central task of this last chapter is to address those difficult questions involving *types* of constraints. Specifically, one concern is whether responsible behavior in workplaces (or employment relationships) involves the development of constraints through detailed specifications of exactly *what* employers and employees can and must do in their dealings with one another. The other concern is whether responsible behavior emerges from detailed specifications of exactly *how* employers and employees must go about defining their mutual obligations in their dealings with one another.

The former set of constraints imposes restrictions on the exact content of the behavior of both employers and employees. For example, employers may be told they must provide workers with a given fringe benefit: severance pay. The latter set of constraints imposes rules on how employers and employees can settle what each will do for the other. For example, employers and employees may be told that questions of severance pay will be settled only with reference to contracts and that each party must uphold obligations as specified in the negotiated contracts.

The importance of the distinction in the two types of social constraints can be illustrated by considering alternative sets of "principles" for closing plants and laying off workers, a political question faced by Congress for the past two decades, if not longer.

Content Constraints

Data on the scope of displaced workers and plant closings have been widely reported and evaluated (see Chapter 5).[1] Because these reports have indicated that the official count of displaced workers is large and widespread (1 to 1.2 million workers annually in the U.S.[2]), these reports have understandably led to fundamental policy questions concerning what, if anything, should be done through government and through firms for these displaced workers. Such questions have given birth to study groups in and out of government. For example, the staff of a task-force subcommittee of the U.S. Department of Labor, when asked to prepare a preliminary set of "Principles for Responsible Management of Plant Closings and Permanent Layoffs," surveyed case studies of successful plant closings.[3] The subcommittee considered a variety of data, including the Bureau of Labor Statistics (BLS) and General Accounting Office (GAO) studies, before tendering a set of "principles." Although the statement developed by the staff was never officially adopted by the subcommittee members as a first working draft, the staff report reveals how many people (the staff, *per se,* in this particular case) assess the responsibilities of employers in instances of plant closings and permanent layoffs. Many people and interest groups, including churches and unions, would like to see similar sets of constraints carry the force of law under the banner of a "worker bill of rights."[4] For that reason, the staff proposal developed for the task-force subcommittee is worthy of examination solely as a case study.

The staff's principles are as follows:

1. Employers have a responsibility to communicate with their employees and the surrounding community on issues related to the stability of the plant.

2. Employers have a duty to show cause why they must shut down, move operations, or reduce the work force. Companies should consult with workers or their representatives on alternatives to closure. Reasonable proposals by trade unions, impacted workers, and government to avert shutdown or dismissals should be given a fair hearing.

3. Advance notice of significant layoffs and plant shutdowns should be given to affected trade unions and individual workers as soon as the employer reaches the decision. Six months prenotification period is a procedural prerequisite for constructive action.

4. Adjustment assistance for displaced workers — e.g., severance pay, mandatory transfer rights, optional early retirement benefits, guaranteed social security credits, health benefits and adequate income maintenance benefits — should be provided by the company until the individual is re-employed. Benefits should not be defined if the employee finds a new job before termination.

5. For an outplacement program to succeed, companies and unions must demonstrate a mutual commitment to, and take primary responsibility for, helping their redundant workers find good new jobs to replace those they have lost. In non-union establishments,

employers and their employees must share this responsibility and commitment. Government should play a supportive role in the out-placement process.

6. Constructive actions to mitigate the impact of plant closings might include the following services for displaced workers. They should start in the pre-layoff period and extend as long as needed after closure:

   a. establishing a joint labor-management outplacement committee
   b. providing counseling for employees and their families. . .
   c. establishing an adjustment assistance center, on premises if possible, to continue operations as long as possible and needed
   d. helping workers form job clubs
   e. evaluating and considering use of professional outplacement firms
   f. providing aggressive job development by the company, union, and state employment service
   g. providing retraining (for those who need it) in employable skills for identified jobs
   h. providing basic education helpful to reemployment
   i. staggering layoffs, if feasible, to facilitate outplacement
   j. cooperating with local, state, and federal agencies
   k. undertaking industrial development, e.g., finding a new owner, another use for the plant, or exploring possibility of worker ownership
   l. providing job-search training
   m. providing job placement
   n. providing relocation expenses

Whether or not this list of actions is ever adopted as specified (or with or without additions and deletions) is not particularly important to the purpose of this chapter or, for that matter, book.[5] The important point is that the list includes highly specific activities that *should* or *must* be followed, within limits, on moral or legal grounds. However, an important question remains: Does it make sense to even consider such a listing or to elevate whatever exact list is adopted to the status of guiding principles, irrespective of the exact listing? In other words, is the concept of the listing a worthy social objective? The list of principles may sound reasonable, but is it, in fact, reasonable on a mandated or even on a voluntary basis? Clearly, not much harm is done if the implied obligations are totally voluntary. No one has to change his or her behavior; everyone can continue to behave as in the past. The list is only suggestive. It can be adapted by individual workers and employers to their own situations, if they deem the list appropriate. However, the issue becomes more problematic if the listing implies a "moral responsibility" or "legal obligation," which suggests externally imposed changes in behavior of workers and of employers. Proponents of such lists of imposed responsibility for business fail to appreciate a much-needed distinction between social and legal obligations.

Clearly, workers, managers, and owners of firms have social obligations and responsibilities, not the least of which is to conduct their activities in effective, responsible, and reasonable ways. Social responsibilities often extend far beyond their obligations. After all, any legal system has self-imposed limitations. It would be silly to think that legal institutions would ever be so pervasive in people's dealings that all of human behavior would be guided effectively by the threat of legal penalties. How students should walk down crowded halls, for instance, could not be supervised by the agents of government — police, judges, and juries — even if the costs for such supervision were not prohibitive. There is typically no dispute over the general proposition that people must behave responsibly — must constrain themselves and live within tolerable limits.

However, there are considerable grounds for disputing any presumption that social responsibility defined in vague and ambiguous terms (for example, "Employers have a responsibility to communicate with their employees") should be converted into a legal obligation, enforceable by the powers of governmental agencies and the courts. The justly acquired human right to act as one sees fit is at stake. In addition, as already noted, the government can do only so much, and any proposal that requires government to do more in one area — for example, relief for displaced workers — can cause a drain on its ability to do as much in other areas, such as relief for the poor who do not qualify as having been "displaced" from their jobs.

Furthermore, when left unenforced, social responsibilities are highly flexible and adaptable to individual circumstances and preferences. The responsibilities can be interpreted in a variety of ways. Indeed, any agreement over social responsibilities, such as those in the itemized list, may actually reflect the mere *pretense of agreement*. This is because each person interprets the stated social responsibility differently, meaning that any vote that may be taken on the responsibility is a vote for different behavioral outcomes. The supposed agreement may then be more imagined than real. A responsibility that is legalized can be disruptive and counterproductive because it, necessarily, is selective of various interpretations and reduces the flexibility and adaptability of prior social responsibility.

Of course, legalization of social responsibilities can also be questioned on grounds of property rights and invasion of established rights of exchange. There is a legal reason for disputing the proposition that employers have, or should have, a legal "responsibility to communicate with their employees and the surrounding community" on any issue (such as the issues relating to the stability of a plant) and have a "duty to show cause why they must shut down, move operations, or reduce the work force." To say that an employer has a responsibility to communicate decisions and a duty to show cause for any action is to assume the terms of a contract. Such a statement further presumes that there are not tradeoffs between rights of communication and showing cause, or providing other forms of compensation and benefits. Imposing any responsibility or duty can be equivalent to denying employees and communities a greater economic advantage when a different bundle of benefits is negotiated. This is true because such requirements can amount to an increase in the cost of hiring workers and can lead to a reduction in the demand for labor and to a decrease in the amount of wages paid to those who have jobs, a point central to Chapters 9 and 10.[6]

As explained in Chapter 10, if termination benefits could be obtained without cost, few could object to their being provided. There would be no reason why workers would not want them and businesses would not provide them. There would be no public-policy debate over them; they would be provided without fail—even voluntarily by firms that maximize profits. The firms would incur no cost through the provision of termination benefits and would gain by giving their workers something their workers (presumably) value. However, the very fact that the specified termination benefits are often not provided suggests there are costs involved.[7]

In summary, the list of "principles" developed by the staff of the task force overlooks three critically important points emphasized at critical junctures in this book.

• First, as noted in a pamphlet published by the National Center for Occupation Readjustment, "It should be clear that there are numerous valid reasons that can contribute to a plant closing or major layoff. Because the factors can occur in infinite combinations and with varying impact, each plant closing is a unique event that simply does not lend itself to a fixed solution."[8]

• Second, compensation for work is paid in a multitude of forms, most prominently money wages and fringe benefits. However, compensation comes in many nonmoney forms, including working conditions and termination provisions, and imposed restraints force modification of the bundles of benefits received by workers to the detriment of many of the affected workers.

• Third, needs and preferences of workers for various forms of compensation vary considerably across occupations, plants, industries, and regions of the country. Furthermore, the ability of firms to provide different forms of compensation varies just as greatly.

The concept of "principle," especially when superimposed on a public-policy debate, suggests the existence of a rule that can be applied or imposed broadly—perhaps to all circumstances. But, the *uniqueness* of employment circumstances and worker preferences mitigates against the broad application of such rules, especially if they are interpreted specifically. For example, "adjustment assistance for displaced workers. . . [in specified forms] should be provided by the company until the individual is re-employed." If circumstances do not warrant the provision of such a benefit or if e ployees do not want to make the required trade-offs, it is agair hard to see how the "principle" can be applied without adversely .ffecting the welfare of many of the very workers who are the objecc of the policy concern.

Clearly, the list of benefits could be mandated, but we must wonder which list—and whose interests will be served by the specified benefits. People and circumstances are different, and the specification of the established mandated list *absolutely cannot* be adapted to fit with equal facility the circumstances of all affected workers. If the decision is made to adopt such a list of benefits, it is not unreasonable to expect that the various worker and industry groups will work to insure that the specified legalized list meets their particular needs as closely as possible. Some worker and industry groups, of course, will also work to prevent the list from worsening their competitive position in their markets.

Rule Constraints

To reconcile the competing, divergent interests of employees and employers, termination principles must inevitably rely on the principles of rights established through contract. Contracts establish the rights and responsibilities of the parties involved. The most attractive feature of these types of controls is not so much that they are enforceable by government (a nontrivial and crucial economic role for government). The most attractive feature is that they allow for adapting of worker-termination benefits to individual workers' and employers' preferences and circumstances even in a world of infinitely varied people and places. When viewed in contractual terms, the statement of the principles of employee-termination benefits would have to be radically revised, but might take the following general form:

Public policy toward plant closings and permanent layoffs should be guided by three factual and philosophical points.

First, plant closings and permanent layoffs cannot be considered separately from plant openings and job creation. Without question, plant closings and permanent layoffs often cause economic and social problems for the affected companies, workers, and communities. Public policies designed to correct the perceived problems should provide demonstrated benefits to the affected parties without harming others. Governmental restrictions on plant closings and permanent layoffs should be avoided because, in the process of retarding plant closings and layoffs in the short run, these restrictions can discourage plant openings and the creation of new and better jobs in the long run.

Second, worker compensation can be provided in a variety of forms, including wages, fringe benefits, and closing and layoff benefits. Compensation in one form — for example, closing benefits — generally comes at the expense of compensation in other forms — for example, wages and fringe benefits. This is because closing benefits must be considered as a cost of employing workers. If the affected firms are to remain competitive in a global economy, the cost must be offset.

Employees and employers differ on the types of compensation they need and prefer. Specified termination benefits and closing restrictions not only limit the rights of firms to close their plants, but also the rights of employees to choose the combination of compensations they can seek. Closing restrictions deny workers the right to trade closing benefits for higher wages and fringe benefits.

Third, the U.S. market economy is founded on the proposition that people — acting in their roles as workers, employers, investors, and consumers — should be trusted with the right and responsibility to negotiate exchanges through contracts that meet their individual and group preferences and their circumstances. By the same token, all groups must be held responsible for the contracts they negotiate. Contracts largely define their legal rights to benefits and obligations.

All parties to contractual arrangements have a fundamental legal, moral, and social obligation to abide by their contracts. However, they do not have a legal obligation to do more than their contracts and the law require. Moral and social obligations, which are not matters of law and which are not matters subject to policing by government, may or may not exceed legal obligations.

Plant closings and permanent layoffs represent an unfortunate economic and social problem that can best be remedied by contracts. In closing plants, the terms of closure — including, for example, the amount of notice, severance pay, and outplacement services — can be specified by contracts. Firms and their employees have a legal, moral, and social obligation to develop and fulfill the closing provisions of their contracts. But all parties must understand that firms and their employees do not have a legal obligation to do more than is required by their contracts.

In instances of plant closings and permanent layoffs, given the great variety of closing conditions, the moral and social responsibilities of employers and employees are exceedingly difficult to specify in the abstract. Specific closing and layoff methods employed productively in some instances may be totally unneeded and counterproductive in other circumstances. Furthermore, the financial conditions of a firm will frequently prevent it from providing more closing benefits than those required, even when it genuinely prefers to do more.

Nevertheless, firms and employees may often find that voluntarily doing more than is contractually required is compatible with the interests of all concerned. For example, even though firms are not required by contract to provide prenotification, severance pay, or outplacement services to their workers, firms may find that such actions ease the adjustment problems faced by themselves and their workers, and by affected communities. To ease the problems associated with plant closings and permanent layoffs, firms should consider:

• Asking their workers to forego some wages and fringe benefits in exchange for a specified legally binding policy on prenotification, severance pay, and extended health-insurance benefits.

• Giving as much notice as possible to their workers and officials in the affected communities.

• Establishing joint labor-management outplacement committees and providing counseling for their employees and employee families to aid with personal, financial, retraining, and re-employment problems.

Similarly, employees and communities should consider:

• Becoming better informed about their firms' closing and permanent layoff policies and the state of the law on plant closings and permanent layoffs.

• Establishing employee committees to monitor the financial health of their plants and firms and to issue warnings on pending layoffs and closings to their fellow workers and community residents.

• Making provision through savings programs for the economic hardships and retraining problems associated with extended layoffs.

• Alerting their employers to their interest in an established, legally binding closing and layoff policy and their willingness to make wage and other benefit concessions in exchange for closing and layoff rights (severance pay, advance notice, and extended health-insurance benefits).

Closing services provided by firms under contract have often proved helpful to the firms and their employees and their communities. However, it must be stressed that because of the diversity of worker groups and circumstances under which plant closings and permanent layoffs occur, specifying the terms for plant closures is untenable. As indicated, such policies would deny employers and employees the right to negotiate contracts (that include wages and fringe benefits) and closing terms that are more suitable and favorable to the people involved.

On principle, after reviewing the foregoing statement, it is all too easy to conclude that a hidden agenda lurks behind high-sounding rhetoric. Specifically, it may appear that the author is interested only in preserving the interests of employers in the policy process. Nothing could be further from the truth because the employment relationship is perceived (from the contractual perspective outlined above) as an interactive one, of mutual exchange and give-and-take. The worker gives something to the employer—his or her time and a multitude of objective and subjective skills—at the same time that the employer gives something to the employee—income and a variety of other work-related and termination benefits. The real quality of these contributions cannot be known with clarity to outside observers. In an important sense, the employer employs his employees for the tasks they can perform while the employees employ their employer for the place of work that is provided.[9] The central problem faced in the employee-employer relationship is finding the most mutually beneficial exchanges for their variety of interests. Standardization of workplace exchanges, through standardizaion of wages and benefits, can cause mismatches between the varied interests among employers and their employees and between employees and their employers.

Does this mean that there is nothing that Congress can do to improve the way in which the American job machine works? Of course not. Congress can focus its necessarily limited abilities on creating a legal environment that allows Americans the *opportunity* to create their own employment. It can stop worrying about how many *jobs* the federal government can create and start thinking in terms of creating opportunities for contracting, not specifying the content of people's contracts. This means that it must inevitably look to guiding market principles. (An agenda of labor-policy reforms that are consistent with market principles has been developed elsewhere.[10])

Concluding Comments

Economists have long argued that the distinguishing characteristic of economics, as a discipline, is its focus on the fact of *scarcity*: the pervasive conflict in all of life between our wants and our inability to fulfill all of our wants. While this perception of the core concern of the discipline is instructive, it overlooks the even more fundamental fact that we are all different in many major and minor ways. As stressed, we have different preferences and operate in different circumstances. All of us have information on our preferences and circumstances that cannot be known by outside observers, especially those far removed from us in governmental power centers.

In our political economy, which involves matters of institutional design, the crucial problem is finding creative and constructive ways to live with our differences. We must create economic systems that will allow us to tailor our own exchanges to meet our needs. We must not allow someone else's perception of our needs—a perception necessarily based on very primitive or nonexistent information—to determine our economic system. That is what reliance on markets is about.

Notes

1. Paul O. Fliam and Ellen Sehgal, *Displaced Workers of 1979–83: How Well Have They Fared?* (Washington: U.S. Bureau of Labor Statistics, U.S.

Department of Labor, July 1985); William J. Gainer, "GAO's Preliminary Analysis of U.S. Business Closures and Permanent Layoffs during 1983 and 1984," a paper presented at the OTA/GAO Workshop on Plant Closings (April 30–May 1, 1986); Task Force on Economic Adjustment and Worker Dislocation, *Economic Adjustment and Worker Dislocation in a Competitive Society* (Washington: Office of the Secretary, U.S. Department of Labor, December 1986); and Research and Policy Committee, *Work and Change: Labor Market Adjustment Policies in a Competitive World* (Washington: Committee for Economic Development, December 1986).

2. The count of "displaced workers," which depends critically upon a precise definition, is a highly contentious issue. The count reported should not be taken very seriously without additional research into the definition of displaced workers. For a discussion of the problems in using the official count, see Chapter 4.

3. The staff, composed of U.S. Department of Labor career employees and research assistants for national unions, worked for the subcommittee on the private sector's response to the problem of plant closings for the Task Force on Economic Adjustment and Worker Dislocation. The 21-member task force was composed of representatives of large businesses, unions, and public institutions and was organized by Secretary of Labor William Brock in November 1985. Its assignment was to study the worker-dislocation problem and to propose public-policy remedies. The report was released in early 1987 (Task Force on Economic Adjustment and Worker Dislocation, *Economic Adjustment and Worker Dislocation in a Competitive Society.*

4. Samuel Bowles, David M. Gordon, and Thomas E. Weisskopf, *Beyond the Waste Land: A Democratic Alternative to Economic Decline* (Garden City, N.Y.: Doubleday, Anchor Press, 1983), p. 263. See also Martin Carnoy, Derek Shearer, and Russell Rumberger, *A New Social Contract: The Economy and Government After Reagan* (New York: Harper and Row, 1983); and Catholic bishops, "Pastoral Letter on Social Teachings and the U.S. Economy" (first draft), *National Catholic Reporter,* November 23, 1984.

5. Practically every principle in the list, however, is covered by a policy recommendation for either governmental or private-company action by the task force for which the staff and its subcommittee worked. See Task Force on Economic Adjustment and Worker Dislocation, *Economic Adjustment and Worker Dislocation in a Competitive Society.*

6. As noted in Chapters 9 and 10, the demand for labor can fall because of a substitution of machinery for labor and a substitution of other labor not covered by the legal requirements. (The requirements, for example, might not apply to workers outside the United States.)

7. To the extent that workers value the termination benefits, we would expect the supply of labor to increase and their wages to fall, which would be an extra incentive for firms to provide the termination benefits voluntarily, if they could be provided without cost.

8. *Why Plants Close: Growth Through Economic Transition* (Washington: National Center for Occupational Readjustment, n.d.), p. 7. The "valid

reasons" cited in the pamphlet were classified in the following ways: product obsolescence, plant obsolescence, domestic competition, foreign competition, changing technology, changing consumer tastes, high costs, mergers/acquisitions, divestiture, government actions, and poor business judgment (Ibid., pp. 2–7).

9. This point is developed at length in Richard B. McKenzie, *Competing Visions: The Political Conflict over America's Economic Future* (Washington: Cato Institute, 1985), Chap. 6.

10. Richard B. McKenzie, *U.S. Job Creation in a Competitive World Economy: A Positive Agenda of Labor-Policy Reforms* (St. Louis: Center for the Study of American Business, Washington University, 1987).

Index

The Author

RICHARD B. MCKENZIE is professor of economics at Clemson University and an adjunct fellow at the Cato Institute. He has written widely on contemporary economic-policy issues. His latest two books are *The Fairness of Markets: A Search for Justice in a Free Society* (1987) and *Regulating Government: A Preface to Constitutional Economics* (1986, with Dwight Lee). Professor McKenzie's book with Gordon Tullock on *The New World of Economics* (1975, 1978, 1981, 1984, and 1988) has been used in most of the nation's major universities and has been translated into four languages. His research papers, mainly in public-choice economics and applied microeconomic theory, have been published in a variety of scholarly journals and have been widely reported in the media, including the *New York Times, Wall Street Journal, Los Angeles Times, Washington Post, Christian Science Monitor, National Review,* and *Forbes.*

Other books by Professor McKenzie include:

Economics (1986 and 1988)

Competing Visions: The Political Conflict over America's Economic Future (1985)

Plant Closings: Public or Private Choices? (1981 and 1984, edited)

Fugitive Industry: The Economics and Politics of Deindustrialization (1984)

Constitutional Economics: Containing the Economic Powers of Government (1984, edited)

National Industrial Policies: Commentaries in Dissent (1984)

The Limits of Economic Science: Essays in Methodology (1982)

Bound to be Free (1982)

Economics Issues in Public Policies (1980)

Restrictions on Business Mobility (1979)

The Political Economy of the Educational Process (1979)

Modern Political Economy (1978, with Gordon Tullock)

An Economic Theory of Learning (1974, with Robert Staaf)